THE COVERS ARE OFF

Civil War at Lord's

CHARLES SALE

MENSCH PUBLISHING

Mensch Publishing
51 Northchurch Road, London N1 4EE, United Kingdom

First Published in Great Britain 2021

ISBN: PB: 978-1-912914-28-9
eBook: 978-1-912914-29-6

Typeset by Van-garde Imagery, Inc., • van-garde.com

To Richard Sale (left-handed opening
batsman for Oxford University,
Warwickshire and Derbyshire), who
introduced me to
MCC and Lord's.

Contents

Foreword

IN THE NINETEENTH CENTURY, EUROPEAN diplomacy was cursed by an obscure territorial dispute known as the Schleswig-Holstein Question. 'Only three people ever understood it,' Lord Palmerston is supposed to have said. 'One's dead and one went mad. I'm the third, and I've forgotten.'

The mysterious question of the Lord's tunnels may well be the modern equivalent. I only know three journalists who have ever tried to wrap their heads around the subject. Ivo Tennant has covered the story manfully for two decades in *The Times*. I'm the second and I've tried to forget it, to avoid going mad. Now Charles Sale, a dogged digger in his years on the *Daily Mail*, has set out to tell the full bizarre story.

Essentially, it involves a collision between an unstoppable force and an immovable object. On the one side, the property developer Charles Rifkind, obsessive, implacable, annoying. On the other, Marylebone Cricket Club, traditionalist, in many ways offering magnificent stewardship of the game it practically invented, in other ways dysfunctional. Neither is above a bit of vengefulness. Beneath their feet: the railway tunnels, forlorn, disused, surprisingly spacious. In the dying days of the twentieth century they were sold off. MCC had every chance to buy them but dithered.

MCC had never heard of Rifkind, though he was a neighbour and walked by regularly, staring at the forbidding wall that stands alongside the least well-utilised part of the world's most famous cricket ground. He fantasised and when the utterly improbable opportunity came, he acted.

Of course his vision involved £ signs, but money was only part of the object. Batsmen who sense the chance of a century hate to miss out. Writers who sense a big story feel the need to get it into print. Property developers who see land they believe could be better used want to bring their ideas to fruition, but MCC's rulers did not think like that. Which is why, as owners of seventeen acres in one of London's richest suburbs during an unprecedented and unrepeatable housing boom, they blew the chance of securing the future of cricket at Lord's for ever.

'How to' books are very popular. There are some fine beginner's guides to cricket. There may well be *Property Development for Dummies*. This is a 'how not to' book.

Charles Rifkind is an unusual man. MCC is a most unusual club, trying to balance its three roles: guarding cricket's soul, operating the game's most revered venue and acting for the benefit of its members. It was founded before Britain became a proper democracy and has never quite come to terms with the concept. John Major, who as prime minister had to negotiate the Maastricht Treaty, walked out shaking his head when he got involved in Lord's politics.

The committee tolerates dissidents, knowing they will always be outvoted by the backwoodsmen, provided there is no assault on the members' pockets or privileges. Even so, one sometimes suspects that MCC would dearly like to dump all its critics in a deep dungeon. In fact they have the perfect place for this, very close by. Alas, it belongs to Charles Rifkind.

Matthew Engel
Herefordshire, February 2021

CHAPTER 1

'Slit Up a Treat'

Doug and Dinsdale Piranha now formed a gang, which they called 'The Gang'. They used terror to take over night-clubs, billiard halls, gaming casinos and race tracks. When they tried to take over MCC they were, for the only time in their lives, slit up a treat.

THIS IS AN EXTRACT FROM the script of 'The Tale of the Piranha Brothers', a sketch from 'Monty Python's Flying Circus' that parodied documentaries about the East End gangsters Reggie and Ronnie Kray. It might seem an unusual way to begin an examination of a 20-year battle over the future of the world's most famous cricket ground. The average age of an MCC member at Lord's hovers around 60; many of the 18,000 membership will remember *Monty Python's Flying Circus* and possibly Doug and Dinsdale Piranha, who were brought to justice by Harry 'Snapper' Organs of Q Division.

The story told in this book boils down to whether the successful property developer Charles Rifkind, who has been trying to build flats at the Nursery End at Lord's for two decades, was 'slit up a treat' by MCC. Robert Griffiths QC, who led the MCC development committee that was unceremoniously disbanded at the height of the conflict, related to Monty Python's take on MCC. He said: 'I remember the tale of the Piranha brothers and its MCC reference. I thought it was an amusing summary of what happened at Lord's. The Python scriptwriters must have looked around and thought "What's the most conservative and ruthless institution?" and come up with MCC.'

Rifkind's challenge against the 200-year institution that is often described as the most powerful old boy network in the world turned into a marathon conflict; he had to build up his own support network to put his case to MCC, who were never prepared to engage with him fully. At the very least, he wanted a fair hearing for his ambitious plans for a residential development on the Wellington Road boundary of Lord's, in return for a windfall of over £100 million for MCC. His vision included Lord's having more community engagement, but it was never going to be a level playing field. MCC is a private members' club, despite its public face, and they make up their own rules.

Rifkind, whose office is close to Lord's in St John's Wood, introduced himself to his neighbours when he outbid a shocked and embarrassed MCC at an auction for the head lease for that strip of land at the Nursery End in December 1999. It was being sold by Railtrack, who had been in negotiations with MCC for months ahead of the auction. The club believed they would be the only party interested in buying a leasehold within the confines of Lord's. They had debts of £9 million at the time, following a considerable overspend on the newly built Media Centre; pre-auction, their best offer of £1.25 million was significantly less than Railtrack were prepared to accept.

Having failed to receive an acceptable offer from MCC, Railtrack took their asset to auction, where Rifkind's bid of £2.35 million proved successful. MCC offered £1 million more than they had done in the talks beforehand, but were the underbidders at £2.325 million. Allowing part of the Lord's estate to fall into the hands of a third party is now regarded as one of the biggest mistakes in the 234-year history of MCC.

Rifkind's business partner Johnny Sandelson had been first to see the potential of a residential development along the Lord's boundary of the Wellington Road, but the two of them went their separate ways after the auction. Rifkind also bought the development rights for the two Victorian railways tunnels underneath the Nursery End strip after further negotiations with Railtrack.

There then followed a 20-year stand-off. Rifkind needed the agreement of MCC to develop the land, with the club having a rock solid tenancy until 2137. He returned time and again with development proposals, but was knocked back on every occasion. The major problem early on – when collaboration should have been easier before acrimony had festered – was that MCC felt aggrieved about losing out at the auction and refused to deal with Rifkind under any circumstances.

Rifkind won some highly influential backers for his 'Vision for Lord's', including former prime minister Sir John Major, leading QC Lord Grabiner, City grandee Sir Simon Robertson and his fellow Old Etonian Simon Elliot, and the former MCC chief executive Keith Bradshaw. But he never gained the support of the two people who mattered most within Lord's at the time – MCC committee chairman Oliver Stocken and treasurer Justin Dowley. The pair were not going to put Lord's future at risk, however tempting the offers to MCC.

Stocken: 'I invited Sir Stuart Lipton, who is a visionary around property, to the chairman's box at Lord's. He stood there, looking out on the ground, and told me: "Just remember, as chairman, you are responsible for one of the most iconic sights in London, maybe in the UK. Don't do anything to damage it." I was very influenced by that.'

Rifkind was just as determined to change that Lord's landscape. One associate said about him: 'You have to understand about Charles. He doesn't need the money. This has become a mission for him. And he's never ever going to give up.'

The impasse was summed up by Robert Leigh, who has held MCC committee positions for over 40 years. He said: 'MCC didn't understand Charles and Charles didn't understand MCC.'

'The Club', as they like to call themselves, have had their own way of doing things throughout their long history. A Lord's Test is a special occasion. As the broadcaster and MCC president Christopher Martin-Jenkins commented: 'The whole place is presented on Test match days like a bride on her wedding day.'

The Lord's ceremonial approach would not be easily altered just for one property developer, however dynamic and visionary he might be or however much money he might be offering. Despite its global public face, MCC is only accountable to its 18,000 members, most of whom are only bothered about coming to St John's Wood to watch the cricket a few times every summer. Nothing much has changed since *The Cricket Quarterly* magazine, which ran between 1963 and 1971, quoted an MCC member as saying: 'The people at Lord's think of themselves as the officers and the members as the troops. There to receive the officers' orders without explanation and to provide unquestioning loyalty. Of course, the troops should have mutinied long ago.'

There are some perennial dissenters amongst the troops. Christopher Martin-Jenkins wrote: 'Every year the president approaches the AGM in May with some trepidation because of a small, articulate but somewhat obsessive band of MCC members who seem to have a permanent mission to embarrass and criticise the committee.'

Certainly, the tunnel saga has provided plenty of ammunition for the MCC activists. However, the members are not generally interested in the politics of the club. They put a tick in the box to back committee recommendations every time, some of them without even reading the resolutions they are supporting. Sir Ian Magee, MCC reformist turned chairman of the membership and general purposes committee, said: 'The lack of transparency in most of the club's decision-making processes is astonishing, especially one which is, or should be, answerable to its membership.'

The MCC committee structure is self-perpetuated by a revolving door of like-minded people staying in positions of influence for years on end. The same old faces crop up as chairman, treasurer, trustee, president or running one of the principal committees. The culture was personified by Gubby Allen, the former England captain and cricket administrator whose word was law inside MCC for 30 years. He reputedly decreed that the first Compton and Edrich stands, completed in 1991, two years after his death, should be low enough for him to see the tree line in the St John's Wood Church Gardens from his favourite chair by the window in the pavilion's committee room.

Fast forward 30 years, and that same MCC culture ensured that the new Compton and Edrich stands were designed in such a way that they severely hamper opportunities for residential development at the

Nursery End. The footprint of the two stands intrudes onto the previously 'sacrosanct' Nursery Ground. It means that when cricket matches are held on that pitch, the boundary rope will need to be placed right up against the Wellington Road wall to provide a big enough playing area.

That same MCC culture that passes the baton to like-minded people will see the investment banker Bruce Carnegie-Brown succeed Gerald Corbett as MCC chairman in October 2021, just as Carnegie-Brown took over from Corbett as chairman of price comparison site Moneysupermarket.com in 2014. The world inside the Grace Gates is one of set-piece tradition, annual dinners, AGMs, resolutions, reports and committees. There are minutes of meetings that go back to 1826 , a fire on 29 July 1825 having destroyed the club's early records dating back to 1787, as well as one of the finest wine cellars in London. Who said what in fractious committee debates over the redevelopment of Lord's is laid bare for the first time in this book.

The MCC committee is the high table and its decision is final, with all the other principal and sub-committees making recommendations for their approval or rejection. Robert Griffiths and other heavy-hitters on the development committee couldn't accept the main committee being all-powerful in 2011, when they had more expert knowledge and experience of the issue under debate.

Comparisons can be made with Wimbledon's All England Club and the Augusta National as to the way MCC runs its affairs. But although both those private members' clubs also host great sporting events that attract global attention, they have far fewer members and as a result can conduct their business without the scrutiny MCC face.

MCC trustee Andrew Beeson: 'I think the All England Club keeps its counsel very much within the club. There is a huge difference between having 500 members and 18,000.' Structures, be it a media centre at Augusta or roofs over Centre and Number One Court at Wimbledon, are built without much fuss and most problems are kept in-house. The same cannot be said for MCC, who would love to have the privacy surrounding their decision-making process that Augusta and the All England Club take for granted.

MCC chief executive Keith Bradshaw was so concerned about leaks in 2010 that he had the committee room and his office swept for bugs. There was also a plan formed to give false information to one particular committee man and see if it made it into the press.

Before sitting down for his first meeting, MCC committee newcomer John Fingleton was told by chairman Oliver Stocken: 'Remember, Fingleton – new members are expected to keep their mouths shut for their first two years on the committee.' The same John Fingleton, who only lasted on the main committee for four months, once referred to spectators allowed into the Lord's pavilion for a Twenty20 match as 'the great unwashed'. As Bradshaw said: 'It just reinforced the perception and image that a lot of people outside MCC had of the club.'

The redevelopment saga has largely been played out behind closed doors, making this a story that is unknown to the bulk of the 18,000 MCC membership. Keith Hague, a former chief executive at the Wellington Hospital next door to Lord's, said: 'I go and watch the cricket at Lord's and look around the MCC members. They hardly know what's happened behind the scenes, such has been the secrecy, the politics and the division.'

In November 2020, MCC published a list of 206 milestones in the club's 233-year history and asked members to choose their favourite moments, which are to be commemorated on the Lord's Father Time Wall behind the Grand Stand and the new Compton Stand. The landmarks include the first lawnmower being used at Lord's in 1864, but there is no mention of the tunnels or the two-decade-long development saga – it is as if MCC want to forget it ever happened.

An artist's impression of the wall ahead of its installation in 2021 includes a picture of Pakistani batsman Misbah-ul-Haq celebrating his maiden Lord's Test hundred in 2016 by doing ten press-ups. It was for that Test match that Rifkind received his only invitation from MCC to watch the cricket at Lord's since he became the club's landlord at the Nursery End in 1999.

MCC's civil war over the Nursery End development has been a dominant issue inside Lord's ever since Rifkind's audacious auction purchase. Derek Brewer, MCC chief executive between 2012 and 2017, mentioned the deep scars that remain when he turned down an interview request for this book. He said, 'It is now two years since I left MCC and I always vowed to stay away and not interfere. I have some great memories of the privilege of leading a fantastic team of people, but much less happy recollections of the leasehold land saga which was, throughout my time, deeply unpleasant, divisive and, quite frankly, horrible. I have no desire to reopen the issues which I have put to the back of my mind.'

Fortunately, over 60 people involved in the saga gave me their time, including most of the major players on both sides. Much can also be learnt from those who preferred not to talk, including a trio of famous England and Middlesex cricketers. Mike Brearley, Mike Gatting and Angus Fraser have all been MCC committee members. Brearley and Gatting have also served as president, and Fraser will no doubt follow them into that role. Fraser told me he didn't want to jeopardise his committee position by contributing to the book. Gatting said his views about flats at Lord's are already well known. And Brearley sent the following charmless email.

'Dear Charlie Sale, Thank you for your email. My answer though is no. I don't want to be involved. I suggest that you contact Lauren Best, the publicity person at MCC. Best Mike Brearley.'

The similar stance of the MCC secretariat is coupled with a strong desire to move on from the tunnel years, under Brewer's successor Guy Lavender. It is summed up by Robert Ebdon, MCC assistant secretary (estates and ground development), who was previously an enthusiastic project manager for the proposed £400 million redevelopment, the Vision for Lord's.

Ebdon wrote: 'Having reflected and discussed with Guy, it would be inappropriate for any employee to have any involvement with a publication about Lord's that is not one that is being commissioned or otherwise endorsed by the club. In any event, following the emphatic vote by members at the club's SGM in September 2017, the club is focused on the redevelopment of the Compton and Edrich stands.'

Lavender told me: 'I haven't told people who have asked my opinion not to contribute, but I have told them my view. Derek Brewer told me how deeply divisive and deeply personal the issue became during his time.'

David Batts, MCC deputy chief executive and project director for the Vision for Lord's, and past president Anthony Wreford were two other people who toed the MCC party line. Batts wrote: 'I have decided not to become involved as I really can't see the point of it. In any event I am bound by a confidentially agreement which I was asked by MCC to sign at the outset of the project, and which I would not be prepared to break.' And Wreford replied: 'I have decided that there's little point in meeting, as I don't want to be part of the book or any historic account of the discussions on ground development. I know you have been in touch with other MCC representatives, but I think you will find there's little appetite for this initiative following the very conclusive vote at the SGM two years ago.'

Nevertheless, I have been given access through a number of sources to the minutes and summaries of many crucial meetings, as well as to important letters and email exchanges. Contemporaneous notes are the most valuable of all documents, especially when supported by first-person accounts of what happened during those super-charged exchanges, both inside and outside Lord's.

MCC president Wreford gushed in an MCC newsletter in October 2019 that England's thrilling Super Over win against New Zealand in the World Cup Final seemed made for a Hollywood production, yet it is the battle over the tunnels at Lord's that has attracted the interest of filmmakers. Paul Brooks, producer of the 'Pitch Perfect' film trilogy that grossed £480 million at the worldwide box office, has agreed an option to look into making a stage or TV production. He sees it as a David versus Goliath struggle between one man and an institution. But whether Charles Rifkind was, in Monty Python vernacular, 'slit up a treat' by MCC, is for the reader to decide.

CHAPTER 2

Moses to Marsden

OF THE 3,000 PAINTINGS IN the MCC collection, none could have been more fittingly positioned than the one on the left-hand wall in the Lord's pavilion, beside the entrance to the committee room. It served to remind MCC decision-makers of the massive mistakes made in the nineteenth century and repeated 140 years later, every time they entered their meeting place.

The oil portrait from 1884 is of Isaac Moses, a successful retailer who provided large shop windows and glass atriums for department stores. Moses had bought the freehold for Lord's for £5,910 at an auction on 8 February 1858. MCC didn't attend, despite being told in advance that the Eyre Estate were selling. It proved to be the costliest error in MCC's history until another auction over a century later, when the club were outbid by Charles Rifkind for the leasehold of the strip of land owned by Railtrack at the Nursery End.

Not bidding in 1858 resulted in MCC having to pay Moses three times more than he had paid for the freehold in 1866. The failure to acquire the head lease for the tunnels in 1999 has been a running sore for over 20 years. The 124-foot-wide strip running the length of the Nursery End and bought by Charles Rifkind for £2.35 million has since been valued – with planning permission – at over £300 million.

The portrait of Moses has been moved to the Long Room, and in its place are less evocative portraits of three MCC secretary and chief executives: Roger Knight, Keith Bradshaw and Derek Brewer, all of whose tenures were affected by the Nursery End conflict. Moses can now be found next to one of Lord's great benefactors, William Nicholson. He had loaned MCC the £18,333 6s 8d needed to buy the freehold from Moses in 1866, who by then had changed his name to Robert Marsden.

The rich history of the Marylebone Cricket Club dates back to 1787, when the first Lord's ground opened on the site of Marylebone Field (now Dorset Square). It was the inspiration of Thomas Lord, a merchant from Thirsk who had worked at an even earlier cricket club, the White Conduit Club in Islington, as a ground bowler and general factotum for the rich and privileged.

George Finch and Charles Lennox the ninth Earl of Winchilsea indemnified Lord against any loses in setting up a new ground. Lord obtained a lease on Dorset Fields, halfway between Baker Street and Marylebone, and the Marylebone Cricket Club opened for business on 31 May 1787. When the rent increased, Lord looked for a more cost-effective site on the Eyre Estate. On 15 October 1808, he agreed terms with the same landlord for the hire of the Brick and Great Fields in St John's Wood for 80 years, at an annual rent of £54.

However, when five years later the new Regent's Canal was due to cut through the second MCC ground, the Eyre family provided Lord with another nearby plot on a new 80-year lease. The turf used at Dorset and Brick Fields was transferred to the third and current Lord's ground for the start of the 1814 season.

Despite all the time and dedication that Lord had put into cricket, he was keen to make money from the ground that bore his name. In 1825 he shocked the cricket establishment by announcing that the Eyre Estate had given him permission to build 16 houses on the outfield, leaving only a small portion left for cricket. William Ward, a member of parliament and a director of the Bank of England, who in 1820 had recorded the highest score at Lord's – 278 for MCC against Norfolk – came to cricket's rescue. He wrote a cheque for £5,400 to buy the remaining 69-year lease from Lord and save the ground.

The name of Lord's remains synonymous with cricket and the ground bears his name, yet he had attempted to profit from the site through a major property development. As if that would ever happen again?

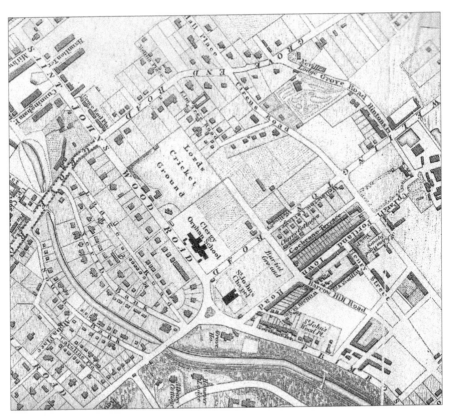

A map of St John's Wood in 1827

The Lord's lease changed hands once more a decade later, when Ward sold on the remaining 58-year agreement to the businessman James Dark for a £450 annuity and annual rent of £150. Dark had cricket in his blood, having begun his association with Lord's at the age of ten when he earned pocket money as a fielder at MCC's ground in Dorset Fields. He planted 400 trees around the estate, but didn't find it easy to make money from cricket. Between 1830 and 1863, there were as few as nine matches a year at Lord's.

This lack of revenue meant that in 1864 Dark decided to relinquish his head lease. He had been approached by Moses, who wanted to own the lease as well as the freehold he had acquired five years earlier. This would have enabled Moses to build houses on the site, as Lord had been planning to do nearly four decades earlier. Fortunately for MCC, Dark offered the club first refusal on his lease, for £15,000. Railtrack would do the same when they were selling their Nursery End leasehold in 1999.

But whereas MCC didn't come up with an acceptable bid at the turn of the twenty-first century, 135 years earlier they had the fore-sight to do so. This was mainly due to the vision of the MCC secretary Robert Fitzgerald. At a meeting on 8 April 1864, it was agreed that they would buy Dark's interest for £11,000 plus £1,500 for fixtures and fittings. Fitzgerald also negotiated a new 99-year lease at an annual rent of £550, without the need for costly arbitration that has become a feature of the five-yearly rent reviews between the Rifkind and MCC at the Nursery End. The good relationship between Fitzgerald and Moses allowed MCC to acquire the freehold from Moses two years later. Isaac Marsden, as he was called by then, trebled his auction purchase in seven years, making a £12,000 profit.

The money was raised thanks to William Nicholson, owner of Nicholson Gin, who also loaned the club enough money to rebuild the pavilion and buy Henderson's Nursery – from where the Nursery End gets its name – from the Clergy Orphan Corporation. As a result of his support, MCC adopted the yellow and red branding of Nicholson Original London Dry Gin – the colours that have since become in-stantly recognisable around the cricketing globe.

Nicholson had to wait a further 150 years for a proper accolade, when MCC put on an exhibition to mark the anniversary of the club buying its ground and recognised Nicholson as the man who saved Lord's. And when Nicholson Gin was revived in 2017 by direct descen-dants of the Lord's benefactor, the first place it went on sale was Lord's.

The start of the tunnel saga came in 1891 and is still being played out 130 years later, so it's no wonder some of the MCC committee felt there was no great rush to conclude a deal with Rifkind. The Manchester, Sheffield and Lincolnshire Railway Company – soon to be part of the Great Central Railway – had been granted compulsory purchase powers to extend the railway line into the newly opened Marylebone Station, which meant building railway tunnels under the Nursery End. Moving grounds, as MCC had done when Regent's Canal cut through their

Brick Fields ground in 1813, was not an option. The club had only just opened their magnificent pavilion – still the most famous building in cricket and completed at a cost of £21,000 a year earlier.

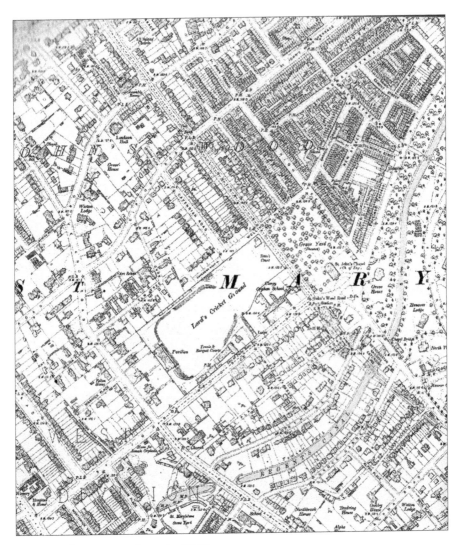

The Lord's surroundings in 1890

The railway company found MCC unwilling sellers, but eventually a compromise was reached. The southern half of the Nursery End ground – where the indoor cricket school, England and Wales Cricket

Board (ECB) offices and MCC shop are now situated – was occupied at the time by the Clergy Female Orphan School. The railway company bought the school in a deal that saw it rehoused outside London, offering MCC the orphanage site freehold in return for the 124-foot-wide strip running the length of the ground parallel to the Wellington Road. As a sweetener, the railways agreed to restore the land above the tunnels after they had been built and to lease the top 18 inches back to MCC.

At a special general meeting on 6 April 1891, members agreed a 99-year lease with tunnelling that began in 1896 and was completed two years later. The lease remained in place until the first hint of a new negotiation came in January 1969, at which point MCC were looking to either extend the lease for another 125 years or acquire the freehold.

MCC were also aware by then that two of the tunnels were no longer in use. They had become redundant in 1966, as part of the nationwide Beeching cuts to the railway system. A third tunnel is still used by Chiltern Railways for commuter trains into Marylebone.

MCC asked British Rail whether they had any objections to the defunct tunnels being used for car parking, but British Rail had the vision of a potential residential development along the Nursery End strip. Discussions about a possible joint venture continued during 1969. It was provisionally agreed that if MCC wanted to pursue such a development, British Rail would take 66.67 per cent of any profits.

The talks stopped when one of the negotiators fell seriously ill, but that percentage split, though it was never officially signed, is why MCC pay only 66.67 per cent of the market rental value of the leasehold land, and it has remained a matter of contention to this day. Rifkind will not budge from a 50/50 division of any development spoils, while MCC believe it should be between 70/30 and 80/20 in their favour.

It was 17 years later, in 1986, when MCC started negotiating to extend the lease for which they were still paying only £200 per year. MCC property agents Gardiner & Theobald negotiated terms with British Rail for a new 150-year agreement until 2137, with an annual rent of £20,0000 subject to 'upward-only' five-yearly renewals. A further clause stated that the leasehold land could only be used for cricket-related activities, storage and car parking purposes.

Gardiner & Theobald wrote to British Rail saying: 'Every cricket lover will feel reassured that the future of the Nursery Ground and its amenities have now been preserved for the foreseeable future. MCC, in particular, is appreciative of the co-operation and goodwill of the British Rail property board.' If only the MCC agents knew about the turmoil ahead.

Just as British Rail were selling off their property interests, MCC had seriously overspent on the construction of the futuristic-looking media centre, completed for the 1999 World Cup that was held in England. The finance committee had agreed a budget of £1.7 million, but the cost escalated and the final bill was £5.8 million.

This meant there was little in the MCC coffers when the opportunity to purchase the British Rail lease at the Nursery End arose in the spring of 1999. However, a few months earlier an ambitious local property developer called Johnny Sandelson had put a development proposal for the Nursery End to MCC. He had an ambitious vision of what could be done on the Wellington Road. He also had the advantage of being the son-in-law of MCC grandee Lord Alexander, chairman of NatWest Bank.

Sandelson: 'I had picked up a salt beef sandwich on St John's Wood High Street. I crossed the road to Lord's, looked up and saw the development possibilities along the Wellington Road, from the Wellington Hospital to the Danubius Hotel. I was a young guy in property in my thirties. I couldn't understand why Lord's hadn't built behind that wall. I thought it was incongruous when the rest of the Wellington Road had been built on. There would have been no encroachment on the Main Ground. I know what institutions are like – I thought they just couldn't be bothered. Just in passing, I mentioned it to my father-in-law. He said he didn't know either and suggested I go and speak about it to the MCC secretary, Roger Knight. He set up a meeting.

'It wasn't about personal gain. I suppose there was a bit of vanity. If I made a good presentation to MCC, I might end up on the estates committee one day. To a young cricket fan obsessed with property, that would be about as good as it gets. I went to see Roger Knight, who was incredibly friendly and courteous. He didn't know why it had never been built on either. It was agreed I would come back in a couple of months with a scheme. I went away quite excited. I spent what seemed a lot of money at the time, around £50,000 to £70,000. I got the engineers to see if it could be done and the quantity surveyors to see what it would cost.'

Sandelson worked with the architect Tchaik Chassay from Chassay & Last on his blueprint.

Chassay: 'Johnny came to see me. We had done work together. He had some good very innovative ideas, and sometimes they came off. He was often in our office. I did some drawings for a development, which we took to Lord's. It was for a hotel with residential above. We worked out the scheme between us. It was good fun, but we were flying a kite at the time.'

Sandelson: 'Our focus was on a hotel with rooms for visiting players, back-up staff, dignitaries and umpires, with hospitality areas, bars and restaurants. There were to be residential units on the top floors. It wasn't about the maximum amount of money we could generate. We tried to put together a plan that worked for Lord's. It would also have been a biosecure option during the coronavirus pandemic, although that part of it would have been a complete fluke.'

'We went to see Roger again. He said it was fascinating and that he was very grateful for the time I had spent on it. He organised a meeting a month or so later. It was really exciting. It was held in the committee room in the pavilion. We had a rehearsal that morning – it was a big thing to make a pitch inside the pavilion. We had no idea how it would go – we were just following dreams at this stage.

'I remember feeling really nervous. We walked into the room. It was like walking into the Foreign Office in the nineteenth century as a young adventurer wanting a parcel of Asia, that's how it felt.

'We had a team of people. They didn't even offer us a biscuit. I started my spiel. After about 15 minutes, two or three of them looked at each other and just walked out of the room. Maurice de Rohan was one of them. A couple of MCC people remained to hear the rest of the presentation, but it petered out a bit because it was such a shock to see them just up and leave. Something that we thought was heroic and ambitious had suddenly become the most damp squib meeting of all time.

'I wrote to Roger afterwards, enclosing a copy of the plans. I said if he wanted more information, I was here to help and looked forward to hearing his thoughts. We heard absolutely nothing – we received no acknowledgement whatsoever.'

Chassay: 'It was a bewildering meeting, pretty horrendous really. The walk-outs amounted to a flat rejection of the whole scheme. Johnny being married to Mary, daughter of Lord Alexander, was supposed to help us, but I don't think it did. They thought we were wide boys.'

MCC might not have wanted to explore the development possibilities on the Wellington Road, but the meeting had provided them with information about what could be done along that strip of land. And this makes MCC's stance all the more bewildering when they were given the opportunity shortly afterwards to buy the Wellington Road lease from Railtrack.

The details of Lot 11 from the auction in 1999

CHAPTER 3

Lot 11

SANDWICHED BETWEEN RENTAL OPPORTUNITIES ON Royal Wootton Bassett's High Street and a shopping precinct at Liverpool Central railway station, lot 11 in the Jones Lang LaSalle auction at 2 p.m. on 9 December 1999 at the Four Seasons Hotel off Park Lane wasn't billed as anything out of the ordinary.

There were 35 lots up for sale, comprising a mixture of freehold and leasehold opportunities. Lot 11 was described in the brochure as 'a rectangular-shaped parcel of land, having a frontage to Wellington Road of 179 metres totalling 1.66 acres. It is currently used as a car park and corporate hospitality accommodation. Part of the land also forms part of the Nursery Cricket Ground. Ground rent is £37,333 per year.'

The decision to put the land up for auction had followed eight months of negotiations, during which Railtrack had failed to reach an agreement with MCC for the head lease. They were selling off assets nationwide, including the land on which The Shard now stands. MCC seemed the obvious buyers for the Wellington Road tunnels that bordered Lord's at the Nursery End, but after the overspend on the new media centre, they had bank loans of £15 million and further borrowing was considered unwise.

MCC had no intention of paying over the odds for a head lease on which they had a secure tenancy for the next 138 years. Their question was whether it was worth the capital expense when they were content paying £37,333 a year in rent, although they should have known from the recent presentation by Johnny Sandelson that there was genuine development interest along the Wellington Road.

Negotiations began in March 1999. Railtrack's team took MCC's representatives into the tunnels through a door in the basement of the

Wellington Hospital, and in return the railway men were given a tour of Lord's. But the talks between Railtrack and MCC's property agents Knight Frank got nowhere.

How Lord's looked in 1999

Knight Frank had the tunnels valued and went back to Railtrack with a paltry offer of less than £1 million. It was later increased to £1.25 million, which was still well below Railtrack's target of around £1.75 million. MCC were playing hardball, believing they were the only interested party.

Railtrack's Steve England: 'If they had offered a fair price, we would have done a deal. We told them we were looking for £1.75 million. They offered around £900,000 and then came back with £1.25 million, but never more than that.'

There was no chance Railtrack would sell on the cheap – they had to justify the price to their shareholders. They decided to go to a public auction, in the hope of galvanising MCC to improve their offer. On 9 November 1999, Railtrack advised MCC that the lease would be sold at auction a month later. MCC were again invited to make a pre-auction offer, but they declined.

A further complication was that MCC and Railtrack had an ongoing arbitration case over the five-yearly rent review for the leasehold. Railtrack had put in for a major increase, from £37,333 a year to £133,000. When MCC's finance and estates committees met to discuss how much MCC should bid at the auction, they recommended a maximum £2.3 million, over £1 million more than MCC had previously offered. Upping their bid by half that extra amount would have secured a deal ahead of the auction. The main committee accepted the recommendation and made arrangements for a £2 million bank loan to have the cash readily available.

Oliver Stocken, who was shortly to become MCC treasurer and later chairman, said: 'I was totally unaware of any negotiations with Railtrack before the auction. All I knew was that the treasurer David Hudd told me about the chance of buying the strip of land and the bank loan. As I was taking over from him, he wanted to make sure I was OK with that. At the time I would have only paid £800,000 for the lease – anything more than that didn't make financial sense just for the rental yield.'

The decision to only offer £1.25 million ahead of the auction was, in hindsight, the worst call in the history of Marylebone Cricket Club.

The club wanted the freehold, but Railtrack needed control of the third tunnel under the Wellington Road that was still in use.

Consultant dentist Nigel Knott, who has spent a lifetime calling the MCC hierarchy to account, realised the club was making a seismic error and alerted them to his fears. He said: 'Michael Blow, the club's assistant secretary finance, told me a little about the background to the negotiations with Railtrack. I contacted the president, Tony Lewis, to advise him that we had to buy the lease, whatever the cost. I warned him that if anybody else bought it there would be nothing but trouble. A third party could hold us to ransom. Lewis sent back a very cursory email saying: "Talk to Michael Blow."'

Ironically, the Railtrack chief executive at the time was Gerald Corbett, who became MCC chairman 16 years later, when the fall-out from the auction was still being felt. He said: 'Railtrack was a huge company and I was unbelievably busy. I was just a humble backbencher at MCC. I used to watch a day's cricket in the summer, that was all, but I knew what was going on and kept in touch. I supported approaching MCC because they were the obvious buyer. I was supportive of putting it out to auction because MCC's offer wasn't good enough. And I was supportive of going back to MCC to see if they would up their offer.

'We had to get a price that the shareholders would accept, and £1.25 million wasn't the right price. I was surprised when MCC didn't come back before the auction. We went back to their agent and said we would take it out of the auction if they made us a proper offer, but nothing happened. MCC were seeing it purely as a comparison between how much it would cost to acquire the head lease compared to the rent they were paying.'

There was also little or no protest amongst MCC committee members about the club's risk-averse approach.

Julian Vallance: 'The view of the treasurer was that we didn't have the money. We agreed to bid up to a certain point – it was what we could afford. In hindsight, it was a bit weak. It was a big mistake. It wasn't a big issue before the auction. People were relaxed about the length of lease.'

Phillip Hodson: 'There was a lack of understanding about the tunnels and the development potential. There was no debate in committee.'

When the main committee met on 2 December, they at least agreed to be represented at the auction – not something they had done when the Lord's freehold was bought by Isaac Moses in 1858.

Railtrack sales manager Chris Atkinson: 'MCC's strategy was to pressure Railtrack into selling at a good price for MCC. It didn't work out for them, but I would not use hindsight to criticise MCC. Had Charles Rifkind not appeared on the scene, it might well have been a winning strategy.'

Rifkind had been alerted about the auction the day before, by the architect Malcolm Last.

He said: 'My partner, Jill, had seen the auction advertisement in the *Estates Gazette* and mentioned the Lord's lot. I first contacted a Singaporean client of mine, Mei Hsien Yong, but she wasn't interested. I then thought of Charles, whom I knew as he was very busy doing property deals in the St John's Wood area. He expressed interest, so I sent him the details.'

This was Rifkind's introduction to the Wellington Road frontage that would play a big part in his life for the next 20 years. It had been Last's business partner, Tchaik Chassay, who had worked with Johnny Sandelson on his presentation to MCC the previous year, and Jill Facer asked Chassay to tell Sandelson about the Lord's opportunity, too.

Sandelson's first cousin Simone had married Rifkind and the two property developers had done a number of deals together in the years before the auction. However, his position was complicated by his relationship with the MCC grandee Lord Alexander.

Sandelson: 'I took a back-seat role. I had been working with Charles Rifkind and his partner Johnny Levy. They were my seniors by 10 or 15 years. They were in the prime of their careers and naturally would take the lead going into those negotiations. There was a sense also that Bob's son-in-law having a connection to any sense of commercial gain was uncomfortable. I was putting at risk a family relationship. Bob said to my ex-wife Mary: "I hope Johnny's not going to get involved in this," the "this" being the auction. He wouldn't want to be a father-in-law curtailing or frustrating ambition, but on this particular occasion he hoped I wouldn't do it.

'It transpired that they didn't own the land. This seemed crazy to me. How could they not own the land? Perhaps I should have thought "that's interesting" and done absolutely nothing, but I was slightly piqued that I had done all this work and spent all that money and they hadn't even acknowledged it. Charles had been my mentor and so it was logical I would fall into line behind him, but there is no doubting that it was my vision, my baby.'

Andrew Donn, Railtrack's senior sales surveyor, takes up the story: 'We get to the day before the auction and I received a phone call from Sir Philip Beck, the Railtrack chairman. He rang me out of the blue at 4 p.m. when I was just about to go home. I thought he just wanted an update. I had never spoken to him before. He says: "I want you to meet a friend of mine, Charles Rifkind. He's coming to see you."

'Charles arrives at our office. He is very theatrical. He gets out the auction catalogue and puts it on the table. Then he lays an auctioneer's gavel on top of the catalogue and starts explaining what he wants to do – buy the strip of land and build a six-floor residential development along the Wellington Road, of which the lower two floors would be leased back to Lord's to do with them what they wanted. The tunnels would be utilised for underground parking. It was a spectacular plan. My boss Chris Atkinson and I just looked at each other wondering what to do.'

Atkinson: 'We would very much like to sell to you, Charles, but we can't. We're a public body and we need to be seen to be selling on the open market.'

Rifkind: 'What's the indication of the price?'

Atkinson: 'The starting price is going to be in excess of £1 million.'

Rifkind: 'What I'm buying is the lease for a £37,000-per-year rental income, and for that it's a bit over-valued.'

Atkinson: 'We're in for a review on the lease rental and we've put in for a much higher claim.'

Rifkind: 'Unfortunately, it's for a lease above the ground, not below the ground.'

Atkinson: 'It's very unusual circumstances as we have the tunnels underneath. One live tunnel and two disused tunnels.'

Rifkind: 'I've seen them. They are magnificent Victorian tunnels, but they don't look like they've been used for decades.'

Atkinson: 'They haven't, but we have to keep responsibility for them because we're a railway company.'

Rifkind: 'I would still like to buy them prior to auction, and I'm prepared to pay more than £1 million.'

Atkinson: 'I really can't sell and as you haven't come with your lawyer, I can't take you seriously.'

Rifkind: 'That's not a problem. I'll phone him. Can you stay a bit longer?'

Atkinson: 'We can give you until 6.15 p.m.'

Rifkind: 'That's fine. Let me phone the lawyer.'

So Rifkind made a phone call to Graham White at Slaughter & May, who was acting for him at that time. He told him that he was at Railtrack trying to buy the tunnels and asked him if he could he act for him.

White: 'No, I can't act for you, Charles.'

Rifkind: 'Why not? I'm in the offices of Railtrack.'

White: 'It's a bit difficult. I'm acting for MCC.'

Rifkind: 'That's interesting. How has that happened?'

White: 'I picked it up recently because Simmons & Simmons, who historically act for MCC, are acting for Railtrack.'

Rifkind: 'Good lord, this is a small world – we haven't even started! Fine, Graham, are you going to the auction tomorrow?'

White: 'Yes.'

Rifkind: 'I'll see you there.'

Following that conversation, Rifkind said to the Railtrack representatives: 'If Graham White is going to the auction to represent MCC, I don't need a lawyer. I'm happy. I might have saved some fees.'

Rifkind produced his chequebook, wrote out a cheque to Railtrack for £1 million, and passed it over the table.

'It's yours,' said Rifkind. 'I'll tap the gavel, sign the contract and it's a done deal.'

Donn: 'I'm not touching it.'

Atkinson blew the cheque back to Rifkind.

'You can't do that,' said Rifkind and blew it back again.

Atkinson: 'We can't take it, Charles, we can't. There's the auction tomorrow – we'll see you there.'

Rifkind: 'How do I know I'm going to get it?'

Atkinson: 'If you want it, you'll get it. But you might have to pay more than £1 million.'

Rifkind: 'I don't want to go to the auction room.'

Atkinson: 'That's up to you.'

Atkinson rang Sir Philip Beck and told him what happened. Beck was satisfied they had given Rifkind a fair hearing and asked to be informed what happened the following day.

Rifkind recalled: 'I must have phoned Philip Beck at 11 o'clock-ish. I get a call back from Chris Atkinson at 2-ish. He said, "Don't bother coming – we're too busy." I said, "I would like to come and see you." He said "We close at 5.30 p.m." I would have called Johnny Sandelson at that point and told him, "I'm having a meeting about Lord's. I don't know much about Lord's. I know you like cricket – why don't you come along?" I don't think Johnny said anything at the meeting. He certainly didn't say anything about his previous talks.'

The auction at the Four Seasons Hotel took place in three adjoining rooms in which the partition doors opened up. There was a buffet lunch for the auctioneers and the key clients in a side room before the 2 p.m. start.

Rifkind walked into the room at 2.10 p.m. It was already quite full. Standing at the back were Donn and Atkinson, who exchanged smiles with him.

Rifkind: 'It was a feeling of support. Almost like "Go for it." I got a warm environment. It seemed I had their support to go for the development rights. I was playing for high stakes. Everything was for sale. I do feel those smiles gave me the cue.'

About 11 rows from the front, Rifkind spotted three grey-suited men, one of whom he recognised as his erstwhile lawyer Graham White, now acting for MCC.

Rifkind: 'They looked like civil servants from HMRC.'

Lot 11 came up at 2.40 p.m. The auctioneer Richard Auterac opened the bidding at £1 million and MCC came straight in. Auterac gave the impression that there was another initial bidder in the room, although it wasn't clear whom it might be.

Rifkind: 'I don't believe there were any other bidders in the room – I think it was just MCC at the start. The auctioneer was pushing the price up to the reserve of £1.5 million.'

Steve England: 'MCC were blindsided by Charles at the auction. They didn't see him coming. We didn't know if Charles was going to bid. He might not have turned up. There were only two bidders. The auctioneer fired "off the wall", up to the reserve price. They usually pick someone they know. They're very good at it, but they're never going to "take it off the wall" above the reserve price. I only saw two bidders, Charles and MCC.'

When the price reached £1.5 million, Rifkind's hand went up for the first time. He bid an extra £50,000 and the bidding moved swiftly in £50,000 increments, up to £2 million. The other bidders, if there were any, had disappeared at this stage. There was only Rifkind and MCC left to fight it out. When the price reached £2.1 million, the auctioneer switched to upping the bidding in £25,000 additions. At £2.2 million, the MCC team started to slow in their decision-making. They only had the authority from the committee to go to £2.3 million.

Rifkind: 'I sensed that when they made the first increment of £25,000, their budget was starting to shrink.'

MCC did go above their £2.3 million budget to £2.325 million, because Knight Frank put their £25,000 fee into the mix. But when Charles went up a further £25,000 to £2.35 million, there was no counter offer from MCC. Auterac brought down the gavel and Lot 11 was Rifkind's.

Rifkind: 'There were three very unhappy men from MCC walking out of the room. They did not want to acknowledge me. They must have seen me. I could feel their annoyance.

'I went downstairs to have a coffee and instructed my lawyer – my Uncle Maurice. He was a first-class lawyer in Birmingham. I had decided to give him the job because he was based outside London. I wanted to keep things confidential, with not many people knowing what was going on. Maurice told me: "Charles, you have bought something that is not straightforward."

'I replied, "I think this is a 20-year problem." I said it slightly in jest, but I knew I was in for the long haul. I had seen three very angry gentlemen leave the auction. The night before I didn't sleep. I knew I was going to be taking on an unreal challenge. But once I had received an indication from Railtrack that the tunnels were for sale for development purposes, my price would have been very much higher.'

Railtrack's negotiators were astonished at MCC allowing a third party to outbid them for a leasehold inside Lord's.

Andrew Donn: 'I couldn't believe what MCC had done. They had bid far beyond the figure we would have accepted pre-auction, as I told them afterwards. They were ashen-faced. They hadn't seen Charles coming. They thought no one else would be there. They thought they would get a good deal.'

The repercussions began with a fall-out between Alexander and his son-in-law Sandelson, who said: 'For a few months following the auction it caused a strain in my relationship with Bob. I think he offered his resignation, which MCC didn't accept. He had done nothing wrong.'

MCC secretary Roger Knight: 'I don't remember any resignation talk by Lord Alexander, but he was certainly very embarrassed about what had happened.'

Rifkind: 'Soon after buying the lease, Johnny called me and said that I need to talk to Bob Alexander. The auction is on a Thursday and on the Friday night I see Bob. I told him that if there was any embarrassment or difficulty, I was very happy to step to one side. He told me: "You don't have a problem, Charles." "Are you sure about that?", I replied. "Yes," he confirmed. I don't think I was there for more than half an hour.'

Charles Fry, who was to become MCC chairman in 2004, says the club didn't see further than the yield to be gained from the lease, nor was there much joined-up thinking between the various committees.

He said: 'We didn't have much money at the time. We had a discussion about how much to bid and set a limit of £2.3 million.

'Any negotiation before the auction was news to me. I have only heard rumours about this. We left it to David Hudd, the chairman of finance, and the estates chairman Maurice de Rohan to deal with. We only saw the lease potential and a 2 per cent return was not good value for a £2.3 million spend. Knight Frank advised us, but only on the right price to pay. None of us saw the development potential of the tunnels – it was only Charles who visualised what could be done. He's a clever bloke, good luck to him. We weren't that bright. It's easy in hindsight, but there was no one to blame. MCC were not very commercial at the time.'

Nigel Knott, who had warned MCC about the perils ahead if they lost control of the Nursery End, wrote to MCC president Tony Lewis: 'Just mark my words – nothing but trouble lies ahead, now that an outsider has a significant interest within our walls. I think the committee have made yet another blunder of titanic proportions. Whoever has bought this land must be rubbing their hands with glee.' Lewis did not respond.

MCC secretary Knight wrote to members and tried to put a brave face on the auction defeat: 'Although it is disappointing that the club was unable to purchase the overriding lease interest, the committee believes it would not have been in members' interests to have attempted further to overbid the actual purchasers. Additionally, the committee is advised that there is no legal reason why the club should not continue to enjoy the tenure of the land for the next 137 years and beyond. Negotiations proved unsuccessful and at the auction the land was sold to RLS Ltd for £2,350,000, in excess of the upper limit agreed for the club's bid. RLS subsequently transferred the asset to RLP.'

Rifkind: 'I pulled away very fast from RLS. The presumption was that it stood for "Rifkind, Levy, Sandelson". There wasn't a legal entity – it was just a name we put to the association. I realised the conflict of interests and it didn't look good. But my business changed at that time and RLP – Rifkind Levy Partnership – reflected those changes. Johnny Sandelson went off to do his own thing.

'It's fair for Johnny to claim it was his idea. He opened the door. He also had the initial contact with Investec. Johnny has a very definite style. He's a larger-than-life character, very different to me. In 20 years I did not involve him in a single meeting with MCC. We are in a very different place.

'I didn't want Johnny anywhere near it – it would have just added to the difficulty. Four or five years before the auction, Johnny's father asked me in the nicest possible way to look after Johnny. I partly bankrolled him and taught him about the property business. Unfortunately, our views changed in the way you manage things. It couldn't have been wider. I cut the umbilical cord. I don't operate in the same way. I can't relate to the way he works.'

However, Sandelson's family connection to Lord Alexander meant that Rifkind was viewed with suspicion from the moment he acquired the head lease for the Nursery End strip of land, and the MCC chairman of estates Maurice de Rohan would never properly engage with him. De Rohan believed that Alexander had told Sandelson the maximum price that MCC would bid at the auction – false news that has festered for two decades. He told the MCC senior figures Blake Gorst and Robert Leigh of his suspicions.

Gorst: 'Maurice thought Lord Alexander had tipped off his son-in-law and he remained absolutely appalled about it. Johnny Sandelson had a difficult reputation. Maurice flatly refused to speak to Charles in any circumstances.'

Charles Rifkind: 'It's just a myth that has grown out of spite over the years. Lord Alexander couldn't have been more highly respected. It's ludicrous to assume he would do such a thing. He was above reproach in all his dealings.'

Having secured the leasehold, Rifkind wanted to follow up as quickly as possible with a development deal to maximise the potential of the tunnels. He knew Railtrack would sell him the rights – but at a price. He hoped to close the negotiations with Railtrack in the three-week period before going to Cape Town to watch England play South Africa in the New Year's Test. He knew there would be an opportunity at Newlands to meet with the MCC party, which would include the incoming president Lord Alexander.

He went to Railtrack on the first working day after the auction, intent on acquiring the development rights before his trip to South Africa. Railtrack wanted to bring MCC into the conversation and agree a tripartite deal, but Rifkind was close to agreeing a 999-year lease for the tunnels with development rights, for £250,000. The documentation was being prepared, but while Railtrack were waiting for the necessary board approval, they decided to bring in a third party to advise them on whether they were getting commercial value. The consultant they hired was surveyor Jeremy Fooks, who knew Rifkind from previous property development projects. Fooks sensed the extent of Rifkind's ambitions at Lord's and negotiated a far more lucrative deal for Railtrack. Instead of receiving an upfront payment, it entitled them to a multi-million-pound windfall when planning permission is achieved. The base price was £5.25 million but the contract was index-linked and now worth around £12 million to Railtrack.

The deal was eventually signed in December 2000, with MCC having no knowledge of or involvement in any of the talks. The extent of MCC's misjudgement was that within nine months of acquiring the development rights, a formal valuation of Rifkind's asset by Savills valued it at £27 million. With that valuation, Rifkind was able to secure a £9 million investment from Investec, who have remained in partnership with him ever since. The idea of approaching them had come from Johnny Sandelson, though it was Rifkind who did the deal with the bank.

Rifkind: 'They came in quickly at the number I suggest. The land was valued at £27 million and a third of £27 million is £9 million. When I told Lord's, they didn't believe me. I got £4 million on day one and £500,000 a year for ten years. I had my £9 million by 2009.'

Steve England: 'We thought that within five years of doing a deal with Charles, a development would be in place. Now we're 20 years on. You could argue that we should have put a longstop date in there, so if Charles hadn't delivered in ten years, we get the 999-year lease back. But it's not going anywhere because of the way MCC have reacted to losing the auction. Attitudes need to be changed.'

But changes in attitudes at MCC take a long, long time.

CHAPTER 4

Hitting the Brick Wall

ARMED WITH THE CONTRACT FOR the head lease of the Wellington Road strip, Rifkind travelled to South Africa for England's New Year's Test in Cape Town – and to meet MCC. South Africa won the match comfortably by an innings and 37 runs, with Jacques Kallis and Daryll Cullinan making hundreds, but Rifkind would have been more disappointed with the reception he received from MCC secretary Roger Knight than England's poor showing.

He had travelled there with the express purpose of talking to the MCC high command, who were now his tenants at the Nursery End. Despite Lord Alexander's embarrassment over the auction result, he was still happy to introduce Rifkind to Knight in the hospitality box at Newlands, where the MCC dignitaries were being hosted by the South Africans.

Rifkind met Knight for the first time on the third day of the Test. Knight admitted MCC's disappointment at not securing the lease but quickly passed the buck in dealing with the tunnels and Rifkind to Maurice de Rohan, the chairman of estates.

Rifkind: 'They are very charming to me, but unfortunately Roger Knight tells me it is not his role to discuss it, although he understood where I was coming from over the potential development. Knight told me: "You need to discuss it with a man called Maurice de Rohan. He's not here, but I will introduce you when you're back in London." Knight was anxious because I had suddenly walked through the door and he didn't know who I was.'

Knight: 'I was on the fringes of any development discussions. Maurice de Rohan was in charge of the estates side, and I referred people to deal with him on these issues.'

MCC further frustrated Rifkind by refusing to have any dialogue until the arbitration process over the rent for the Nursery End tenancy, ongoing since before the auction, had been settled. The previous lease-holders Railtrack had put in for a sizeable increase on the rental figure that is negotiated every five years, and MCC were disputing the figure.

During this silent stand-off with Rifkind, MCC had also been using the Nursery Pavilion for Law Society exams, bar mitzvah celebrations, car auctions and wine tastings, breaching the terms of the lease that limited its use to cricket-related events.

Over a year after their Cape Town meeting, Rifkind used the issue as a way to resume talks with Knight. On 30 March 2001, he wrote: 'It is good news to see the England cricket team have enjoyed a winning run since Cape Town. At your suggestion some 15 months ago, it was agreed that no direct contact should take place until the outstanding Railtrack rent review from 1 January 1997 had been determined.

'We are only nine months away from the next review, which I am hoping will not be so torturous. There is cause for concern in relation to the uses of the Nursery Pavilion. I would prefer rather than formally dealing with this matter, as encouraged by our advisers, to have an informal dialogue with you. It has always been our intention to maintain a friendly working relationship, I am therefore writing to you to as to whether it would be possible for you and me to have an informal chat.'

Knight wrote back on 19 April 2001, almost three weeks later: 'It is indeed good news the England cricket team has recently had success. I hope that it continues. I understand the arbitration process will come to an end in the next four to six weeks. As and when the decision is available, I would be happy to meet you for an informal chat. I shall contact you as soon as that arbitration is finalised in order to arrange a mutually convenient time to meet.'

Rifkind and Knight eventually met on 19 November 2001. Also present were estates chairman Maurice de Rohan and David Batts, the deputy chief executive. Earlier that year, Westminster City Council had informed Lord's that they wanted to see a Masterplan design for the whole of the estate rather than piecemeal planning applications, so this could have been a timely opportunity for Rifkind to engage with MCC.

Rifkind brought to the meeting the model of the Munkenbeck & Marshall design he had commissioned a year earlier. It portrayed six blocks of flats at the Nursery End, plus new offices for MCC, ECB and International Cricket Council (ICC) on the St John's Wood Road freehold land. Munkenbeck & Marshall would later utilise the same design for their distinctive residential apartments with curved balconies in Paddington.

An impatient Rifkind phoned Knight later the same day to discuss how the talks had gone. Knight told him the meeting had gone well and that both de Rohan and Batts were interested in the plans. He followed this up with a letter on 29 November, which illustrates the differing approaches of a fast-moving property developer, who wants answers immediately, and the leisurely way of working at Lord's.

Knight wrote: 'Maurice de Rohan, David Batts and I were pleased to meet you the other day in the committee room. Thank you for coming to put forward some suggestions regarding a potential development at the Wellington Road end of Lord's.

'Your telephone call to follow up the meeting came before I had had time to write on behalf of MCC. In our conversation, you mentioned that you had other thoughts which you would like to bring to us. I have discussed your comments with Maurice and with David, and all three of us would be prepared to meet for a second time to hear any further thoughts that you might wish to put to us. May I suggest you make contact with my assistant Stephanie Lawrence, who will try to arrange a mutually convenient date for us all.'

The mutually convenient date was two months later on 9 January 2002, when Rifkind met with the same MCC trio, Batts, Knight and de Rohan.

Rifkind: 'There is no urgency with anything. When a letter comes in, it sits on somebody's desk until it suits them to respond.'

When MCC did respond again to Rifkind, they put in writing that any money spent by Rifkind on presenting his development plan was his responsibility. They also wanted to make clear that any decision about redevelopment would be made by MCC as and when they were ready to do so.

Knight wrote to Rifkind on 16 January: 'Thank you for spending time on 9 January 2002 with Maurice de Rohan, David Batts and myself to discuss your proposals for possible developments at Lord's. Of your own volition, you have obviously committed considerable time and expenditure in developing your ideas and proposals, and we appreciate you now sharing them with us.

'As we indicated at the meeting, MCC needs some time to digest and consider all the implications of any developments at Lord's and you should not expect an early response, particularly given that we are a members' club. It is appropriate for me to record the fact that the work you have undertaken has been entirely at your initiative and cost and was undertaken by you without the prior knowledge of MCC.'

There was little correspondence between the two parties for the rest of the year. This was due to MCC's inability to make any quick decision and because another rent review on the leasehold land was under discussion. Unlike the protracted negotiations for previous reviews, the 2002 rent talks went smoothly enough for a settlement in February 2003. And, for a change, MCC moved swiftly and the Lord's accounts office paid the money owed to Rifkind – £294,183.51 – just eight days after receiving the invoice. Not long afterwards, Rifkind received a letter from de Rohan that was surprisingly positive.

Rifkind: 'When I first engaged with Maurice de Rohan via letter following the introduction from Roger Knight, he didn't want to meet. The power in the whole place was Maurice de Rohan. It became very clear that the MCC secretary and chief executive had no power. He was just a secretary. De Rohan was in charge over estates matters – there was no doubt about that.'

The formal letter from de Rohan in April 2003 invited a number of parties, including RLP, to tender for a development partnership with MCC. It advised that applications should be sent to MCC's property adviser Alistair Parker of Cushman & Wakefield, to whom Rifkind had shown his Lord's models the previous October.

Parker: 'My first dealings with MCC were with Maurice de Rohan, who was a very strong character. When he first came to see me, he said he had a problem with "a ghastly man" – or words to that effect – who had outbid them at the auction. It was clear MCC felt that this should not have happened. But it had, and now it was a case of what must be done.

'The MCC view was that Rifkind would take a bit of extra money and go away. I said he wouldn't, as he effectively owned the freehold. They would have to come to an agreement. Maurice de Rohan was more against RLP than a development. I suggested a partnership, which is why we decided on a tender process.'

Rifkind employed architects, surveyors and engineers in order to show the seriousness of his ambitions, despite requests from Knight and de Rohan not to involve third parties at this stage. His blueprint incorporated his Munkenbeck & Marshall model from 2000 with another design prepared by Richard Rogers and the Tchaik Chassay and Malcolm Last partnership, the architects who had first alerted Rifkind and his erstwhile business colleague Johnny Sandelson about the possibility of buying the tunnels in 1999.

Rifkind: 'It's the same footprint. It comes down to 300,000 square feet and what you want to do on it. How do you want to cut it? The Chassay & Last design had two residential blocks. It was a starting point. "What do you want to do, guys?" was the message to MCC.'

The presentation took place on 27 May 2003 in the Writing Room in the Lord's pavilion. RLP were competing with heavyweight rivals British Land, Development Securities and the Grosvenor Estate. All four companies were allocated an hour and a half to present.

Rifkind: 'I walk in to face David Batts, Roger Knight and Maurice de Rohan. There's an extraordinarily cold atmosphere in that room. I did not feel comfortable. I didn't even get offered a cup of tea or a glass of water. It was as if I shouldn't have been in that room – it was very unwelcoming. They were never going to do business with me. I went furthest in terms of design. I prepared models of what I saw as the look of the development. The others didn't go into the same detail.'

The next day, the relentless Rifkind emailed Batts: 'I am very conscious there was a lot of information to absorb in a relatively short period of time. If you or any other members of the committee have any questions, we would welcome the opportunity to discuss these in more detail with you.'

Batts replies immediately: 'I think that everyone had a fairly clear idea of the proposals that you set out for us to consider.'

A week later, Batts was back in touch with Rifkind – not to seek more information about his Lord's presentation, but to give the property developer a severe reprimand for using outside help in preparing his pitch. He wrote: 'It has come to the notice of MCC that you have engaged in discussion with at least one third party about the development proposals that you have made to MCC on a strictly confidential basis.

'Throughout our dealings on this matter, we have made it clear that any discussions or meeting between us would be conducted on a strictly confidential basis. So we are very concerned that this agreement has been broken by you. I must advise you that the MCC committee might take the view that your action may well have prejudiced your potential to be considered as a development partner to the club.'

Rifkind: 'That letter sets the tone for the difficulties we were facing. Who writes a letter like that? We had spent £100,000 plus putting the plans together and you get a letter like that.'

However, Rifkind had broken confidentiality agreements laid out by Knight and de Rohan in advance of the tender. He wrote back to Batts, defending his actions:

'I write further to your letter of 5 June 2003, which I was rather disturbed and concerned to receive. We specifically asked your advisers Cushman & Wakefield whether it was necessary to identify all parties to whom we would be speaking. It was confirmed that provided confidentiality was respected, there would be no problems. We were also informed that we could even bring such parties to the actual presentation. It was only at the last moment that we were informed by Cushman & Wakefield that MCC required only the principals to be present.

'It is difficult for me to deal specifically with your letter without MCC being more precise about whom we are supposed to be having discussions with and the nature of these discussions.'

It wasn't a surprise when, after five months of deliberation, MCC chose the Grosvenor Estate as their development partner. Rifkind received official confirmation in a letter from Batts on 25 November.

'We have decided to continue discussions with Grosvenor Ltd to look at a possible framework for working together on a potential project to improve the facilities at Lord's and secure its future. We appreciate our joint interest in the piece of land at the Nursery End. As our ideas progress, we would expect to have further discussions with you on our plans and how they affect our mutual interests.'

MCC development adviser Alistair Parker: 'Grosvenor knew what they were doing. They were much bigger than RLP. It was also reassuring for the MCC committee to have experienced property development professionals Stephen Musgrave and Jeremy Titchen leading the work.'

Rifkind, who would never give up the struggle, arranged an appointment with Grosvenor to see if he can form an alliance, but the meeting was cancelled at the last minute when Rifkind had already arrived at their offices. It transpired that Grosvenor had been instructed by MCC not to see Rifkind or allow him to explain his landlord interests in the Nursery End. Maurice de Rohan was not entertaining Rifkind at any price, and was telling others involved with MCC not to do so either.

The Grosvenor partnership with MCC was short-lived. In October 2004 their proposals were rejected by the main committee, who decided they didn't want any substantial non-cricket related development within Lord's. Grosvenor had planned a mixture of retail and residential, including a supermarket next to the Grace Gates.

Stephen Musgrave, who six years later was be hired by MCC as a consultant, was chief executive of Grosvenor UK and Ireland at the time. He believes MCC were half-hearted about the development from the start.

Musgrave: 'It just fizzled out. There was no great impetus to take it forward. For it to happen, it needed everyone at MCC to be fully behind the project, and that was never the case.'

The estates committee, under the all-powerful de Rohan, spent the next 18 months working up another development plan with HOK architects, excluding Rifkind's leasehold strip.

Rifkind, having been frozen out of any development talks by de Rohan, looks to counter that by trying to build up support for his ambitions elsewhere within MCC. Anthony Wreford, an MCC committee member, was one of those with whom Rifkind made contact. But after showing initial interest, Wreford referred Rifkind back to de Rohan.

Wreford's email read: 'I have discussed the appropriate course of action on this within MCC and the conclusion is that any communication of your ideas should continue through the estates committee. Maurice de Rohan, chairman of estates, is the appropriate person to contact.'

Rifkind also reached out to Keith Hague, chief executive of Wellington Hospital, across the road from Lord's at the Nursery End.

Hague: 'Charles asked me to come and have a look at the tunnels. It seemed a bit crazy to me, but I said I'd have a look. I thought the tunnels would be a rabbit run, but it was an absolutely huge space. The thick walls underground were perfect for radiotherapy cancer treatment.

'The tunnels ran from the Wellington Hospital to the side of the Danubius Hotel at the other end of Lord's. It would have been dead easy to connect both ends. We were going to clad the whole hotel, make it posh. Half of it would have been hospital facilities. It would have been seamless. Here was an opportunity to build an enormous new facility. We went through the whole paraphernalia for years, but there was always very polite resistance from Lord's.'

Rifkind's next move was to form an alliance with Development Securities, as a way of getting back into a negotiating position with MCC. Under the Development Securities banner, his proposal was for a Wellington Road residential development. MCC would receive £30 million and the use of the new building's ground floor for a peppercorn rent. But again, the proposal received short shrift from de Rohan.

An exasperated Rifkind, having had no official dialogue with MCC for nearly three years, wrote to Knight on 7 March 2006 making clear his deep frustrations.

'David Batts, in his letter of 25 November 2003, said: "We would expect to have further partner discussions with you on our plans and how they affect our mutual interests." To date, we have not been further updated.

Development Securities believed it was an appropriate time to put to MCC an alternative proposal. It would have provided MCC with a large amount of additional funding and a substantial increase in permanent floor space. Maurice de Rohan's response was: 'The committee is not interested in surrendering the lease on this land and is presently not looking to undertake any non-cricket-related development at the Nursery End of the ground."

'We are writing to you because our original contact was with your-self and in the confident expectation that this matter will now be prop-erly considered by the club and its committee.

The unequivocal reply came from Knight over a month later on 27 April, backing de Rohan and criticising Rifkind for trying to engage anyone else, including the MCC chief executive.

'The MCC committee has now had the opportunity to discuss the contents of your letter to me of 7 March 2006. All development pro-posals should be directed through the chairman of estates, Maurice de Rohan. The committee believes any other approaches to members of the MCC committee or club officers are counter-productive. I appreci-ate that this response may not be as positive as you might have hoped.'

It was Knight's last correspondence with Rifkind before he retired from MCC. As he had consistently done from January 2000 in Cape Town through to St John's Wood in April 2006, he referred Rifkind to Maurice de Rohan.

Rifkind: 'MCC were doing everything possible to avoid a relation-ship. It forced me to start acquiring those properties on Grove End Road.'

And those properties are a chapter in themselves.

CHAPTER 5

Hot Properties

WHEN THE FIFTH EARL LUCAN, president of MCC, stood up to speak at a special general meeting on 4 March 1929, he was looking for membership backing to take MCC to the zenith of their property ownership. He explained the strategic importance of paying £66,500 for a number of houses in Elm Tree Road. It would mean that MCC would own every house backing onto Lord's from the corner of St John's Wood Road and Grove End Road to 22 Elm Tree Road behind the Grand Stand.

Earl Lucan said the purchases 'would considerably enhance the value of the freehold already owned by the club. It would free the club from the risk of an adverse owner erecting flats … which would overlook and spoil the amenities of the ground.'

He added: 'It is difficult to say how the properties might be utilised other than as dwelling houses, from which only a comparatively small return will be received. Higher rentals should be obtained when the leases expire in three years' time. It is impossible to forecast the growth of the club. But I am quite certain that if the opportunity were lost, it would probably never occur again except at a considerably increased figure.'

The members agreed unanimously with their president. He wouldn't have imagined when he referred to increased house prices that in 2014 the club would pay £8.5 million for a single property on Grove End Road.

After buying the freehold of Lord's in 1866, MCC had pursued a long-term policy of acquiring houses around the edge of the estate. The first purchase in 1880 was a house in St John's Wood Road belonging to James Dark, landlord of Lord's for over 30 years. The freeholds to 1 and 3 Grove End Road were bought in 1889, with 43 and 45 St John's Wood Road following in 1894. By 1914, only seven houses around the Lord's perimeter did not belong to MCC.

Throughout the 1920s, all the remaining houses on Grove End Road that backed onto Lord's were snapped up. And MCC's ambition of owning all the properties on their perimeter was realised in 1929, with the purchase of those Elm Tree Road houses as recommended by Earl Lucan. It meant that an urban estate of 14 houses came under the control of the MCC Secretary. By the end of the 1930s some of the properties were getting old and MCC received advice that they should be demolished and new houses built.

The Second World War came at a cost to the club. Air raids in 1940 virtually demolished 6 Grove End Road, while numbers 4, 10, 12, and 14 were damaged and 8 and 16 rendered inhabitable. 6 Elm Tree Road was one of the older properties on the Lord's list. So went it suffered a direct hit from a bomb in March 1945, the destruction achieved what the club had been advised to do back in 1939. In 1951 the house was rebuilt as a residence for the MCC assistant secretary. Another bomb site, 6 Grove End Road became a car park in 1951.

In July 1954, MCC decided to proceed with the building of seven new houses on the sites of 4, 8, 10, 12 and 16 Grove End Road. Then, during the late 1950s, the club lost their way on the property front, and those seven new houses and others on Elm Tree Road were sold on 60-year leases. The club had been warned not to sell any property on leases of that length, as control of the land was effectively lost.

There remained the MCC-owned plot on the corner of Grove End Road, which had been retained for flats, and by 1965 there was some urgency to get started on a development tender. It was agreed to accept W. T. Chown's offer of £150,000 for the right to build a 12-storey block of 57 flats on a 99-year lease.

Two years later came the Leasehold Reform Act, which allowed owners of leases longer than 21 years to buy the freehold, bringing home the warnings MCC had received about selling property on long leases. The leaseholders of six MCC houses – 2, 2a, 6, 8, 10 and 14 Grove End Road – all took advantage, as did those who had bought flats in Century Court. The seventies and eighties saw more short-term decisions that were seriously flawed. In 1978, six houses – 2, 4, 6, 8, 10 and 12 Elm Tree Road – were sold to a development company for just £170,000. Then, in 1982, the rest of the Elm Tree houses were sold off for £400,000.

MCC ringmaster Gubby Allen, whose word was law inside the Grace Gates at that time, shoulders most of the blame. Colin Maynard, who had joined MCC straight from school in 1975, remembers: 'Gubby Allen sold houses rather than put up the membership fee when the annual subscription was around £20. When Gubby was treasurer, nobody questioned him. The finance committee just supported his view.'

St John's Wood estate agent Paul Bennett: 'MCC sold the freeholds. It was madness. Why get rid of a perfect arrangement? They controlled the whole of their perimeter, road to road. Nobody could build over them. They had all this land.'

Oliver Stocken: 'The great Gubby Allen never liked putting up the membership fees. So he sold another house instead. Imagine if we had kept all those houses.'

At least MCC kept 4 Grove End Road, Gubby Allen's house until his death in 1989, when it became the MCC secretary's accommodation. It was in February 2006 that Rifkind, angered that MCC were totally ignoring his leasehold land in their development thoughts, came to Grove End Road on a mission.

Aware that MCC were considering developing at the Pavilion End of the ground, where the club still owned two properties – 4 and 12 Grove End Road – Rifkind was determined to match or better them. No one knew the property market in St John's Wood better than him. He had built up his considerable fortune over the previous 20 years doing deals in the surrounding roads.

Rifkind: 'In 1983 I bought three terraced houses and converted them into 20 apartments, which was very significant at that time. The apartments were unusual – there was no wood chip, no green bathrooms. They were very smart properties selling at £250,000. They are now worth around £2.25 million.

The houses on Grove End Road that back onto Lord's

'During construction, the whole of the rear elevation collapsed. I was 27 and a young guy. We managed to complete the process. I kept hold of the properties until they were completely finished. It was a huge risk, but we sold the whole lot in one day.

'I realised I was in a market that I could wake up. Out of that, I probably did around 300 apartments around here. I moved from street to street. In the mid-eighties I became known as the man who sold properties in this area. There were little teams bidding for properties. Some you win, some you lose. At that time of my life, I was coming first.

'My biggest move was to acquire Carlton Gate in 1993. It was a very big acquisition which has paid off magnificently – we sold 430 apartments. So when I came to buying on Grove End Road in 2006, I knew how to do it. I understood the process.'

Rifkind's house-buying spree started with 2a Grove End Road, located directly behind the Harris Garden at Lord's. He exchanges contracts on 6 February, having only approached the owners – Gerry and Shirley Hart – earlier that day.

Rifkind said: '2a Grove End Road was not on the market and a local estate agent approached Mr and Mrs Hart to see if they would consider selling. The house is very well presented, the lights are on. It is smelling of coffee and giving me the atmosphere of a house for sale. I go in about 10.30 to 11 a.m. and walk around the house fairly quickly. I come down the stairs with the estate agent and the husband and wife are waiting on the ground floor.

I say: 'Are you happy to sell your house?'

Gerry Hart: 'We're thinking about it, and the answer is probably yes.'

Rifkind: 'How much do you want?'

Hart: 'I'll probably be prepared to accept £3 million.'

Rifkind: 'If I was to offer you £3 million, when could I have vacant possession?'

Hart: 'We would probably need six months.'

Rifkind: 'If I was to give you the six months and £3 million, when could we exchange contracts?'

Hart: 'I haven't spoken to my lawyer yet, but not too far in the distant future.'

Rifkind: 'Your house looks very nice. It suits my needs absolutely perfectly, but there are three conditions to my offer. I'm happy to give you £3 million, happy to give you 1 September as the completion, especially it being my wife's birthday. The third condition is that I want to exchange by 2.30 p.m. this afternoon. Is that acceptable?

Hart: 'I need to speak to my lawyer.'

Rifkind: 'Why don't we get your lawyer on the phone and see if we can do it?'

Hart phoned his lawyer, who told him that it is very unusual to sell within four hours, but can be done if the purchaser has the money available. Rifkind puts in motion £300,000 being sent to the lawyer, to show he has the necessary finances.

Rifkind tells Hart: 'My lawyer will be at your lawyer's at 12.30 p.m. and we will exchange by 2.30 p.m. I will turn up at 3 p.m. because I have a lunch that I have to go to, but I will see you at 3 p.m.'

Rifkind puts his hand out. 'Is it done?'

Hart: 'Yes, it's done.' They shake hands.

Rifkind: 'Mr Hart goes with the estate agent to his lawyers and I go off to my lunch at the Grosvenor House Hotel. At 2.20 p.m. I get a phone call from my lawyer to tell me: "The Eagle has landed." The deal has been done.'

Rifkind had bought a house in less than four hours, from first viewing to completion. He continued his property spree two days later, acquiring 8 Grove End Road on a short lease and later the freehold. Next on the list was 10 Grove End Road, where he persuaded the existing owner to enfranchise the 60-year lease from MCC, which had about 40 years to run. He then bought the freehold. Again, MCC were unaware of the transaction. He had, in quick succession, acquired three of the Grove End Road properties backing onto Lord's, one more than MCC owned.

Rifkind: 'I let MCC know formally by letter. They had upset me so much with their behaviour – they left me with no choice but to control the other end of the ground, too.'

It cost him £9.275 million, but all three of the houses have each since been rented out for around £170,000 a year.

MCC's property manoeuvres on Grove End Road had run rather less smoothly than Rifkind's. The club had been looking to open up the land next to Century Court occupied by 2 Grove End Road. The house was owned by the former MCC president Colin Ingleby-Mackenzie, who had bought the freehold from MCC in 1996, for £302,000. He strongly objected to the development plans that would have meant him having to move out of his house. He died in 2006 and his widow Susan occupied the house until her death on 12 November 2020.

Fry was also keen to lease out 4 Grove End Road, the MCC secretary's house that had been bought from Gubby Allen's estate for £450,000 in 1990. Fry wanted the new secretary Keith Bradshaw to live elsewhere.

Bradshaw: 'The use of the house on Grove End Road wasn't included in my contract. Charles Fry told me they were going to lease it out. He even drove me around some potential properties one day. Eventually, a group of esteemed former presidents, Lord Bramall, Tony Lewis, Lord Griffiths and Tom Graveney, got together and summoned Fry to a meeting in one of the Tavern boxes to tell him in no uncertain terms that the secretary should live in the secretary's house.

'I enjoyed living at 4 Grove End Road, but there was uncalled interference in my private life.

I felt sometimes I was in a goldfish bowl, as everyone could see who was coming and going. I remember being particularly annoyed when the chairman Oliver Stocken said to me: "I just need to say that I'm hearing stories about young women leaving your house." I angrily replied: "That's because I have an 18-year-old daughter who lives in the house and her two friends have been coming and going."'

Bradshaw's arrival at Lord's had also opened the door to a potential development partnership with the Rifkind Levy Partnership. To that accord in April 2007, Rifkind wrote to MCC deputy secretary David Batts detailing his £9.275 million property portfolio on Grove End Road. He also gave an estimate of how much it would cost to acquire the two houses on Grove End Road bordering Lord's – 2 and 6 – that were not owned by MCC or RLP:

2 Grove End Road (Storms Ingleby-Mackenzie)

'This property equates in size to 2a Grove End, although I understand it is in need of updating in order to secure a suitable tenant. To take into account the increase in property values since the acquisition of 2a, the advice that has been received is that in the current market, the price for this property would be in the region of £3.25 million.

6 Grove End Road (Lionel Frumkin)

'I understand that this property to be in fairly good condition and slightly bigger than 2a. Therefore we have been advised that the market value for the property to be in the region of £3.5 million.

'Both houses have a restrictive covenant to being retained as single dwelling houses and furthermore there is a proposal for Westminster to have them included in the conservation area. I hope the above assists you.'

It certainly assisted Batts's briefing paper for the MCC committee meeting in May 2007 that was deciding whether to start a joint venture with Rifkind.

Batts wrote: 'RLP now own 2a, 8 and 10 Grove End Road, although building covenants held by MCC currently restrict any development potential other than the replacement of one house with another. Two properties which would be crucial to any Grove End Road residential development are at present owned by Mrs Ingleby Mackenzie (number 2) and Mr Frumkin (number 6). It could well be in the interests of the club to acquire the freeholds of these properties in order to enable the development of Grove End Road in any future scheme.

'RLP have offered to finance the purchase of these properties. But the working party feel that it would be in the best interest of the club to own the properties and finance them from the club's present cash facilities.

'The working party has agreed that discussions be engaged with Mrs Ingleby Mackenzie and Mr Frumkin in order to establish their willing-ness to sell as well as establish a price range, since in the absence of any sale, any Grove End Road scheme would be substantially less viable.'

Mrs Ingleby Mackenzie was approached by MCC to see if she was a willing seller, but she wasn't. 'And that was the end of that,' said chairman Charles Fry. Concern had been expressed by MCC committee members about undue pressure being put on a woman whose husband had died 14 months previously.

MCC also contacted the owner of 6 Grove End Road, the wine merchant and Lord's tour guide Lionel Frumkin, trying to buy his house without Rifkind's involvement. The letter from MCC's estate agents Knight Frank was sent just five days after Rifkind had confirmed his agreement in principle of a heads of terms joint venture between RLP and MCC. Knight Frank partner Robert Orr-Ewing's letter even included the information about the house, including its estimated value, that had been supplied to MCC by Rifkind.

> Dear Mr Frumkin,
>
> We are writing to you on behalf of our clients MCC in respect of the above property which we understand has been the subject of discussions between yourselves.
>
> Having inspected the house we can confirm that the property is a non-basement family home set behind a high brick wall that backs onto Lord's. The property is in generally good decorative order. For the purpose of this opinion, we have not inspected any title documents and are therefore basing all figures on information supplied in this connection.
>
> We understand that there is a restrictive covenant in respect of this property in that it must be retained as a single family dwelling house. In addition, it has been brought to our attention that there is an intention to incorporate the houses along Grove End Road within a conservation area.
>
> Taking all factors into consideration, including evidence gained from recent sales within this immediate location, we are of the opinion that the property could be sold for a price in the order of £3.6 million.

Our clients MCC have advised us that they would be interested in acquiring your property at this particular time, as it may be considered for incorporation into their medium-term Masterplan for Lord's. As such, they have instructed us to submit an offer of £4.45 million.

The offer is based on a £700,000 premium being offered over and above the price obtainable in the market to take into account the enhanced value. That may be attributable to MCC being considered a special purchaser.

MCC have a committee meeting early next month, 8 August 2007, and we would be grateful if you could respond to the terms offered prior to 27 July.

In the event you consider the offer acceptable, and subject to the MCC committee sanctioning the proposed purchase, then we envisage MCC could exchange contracts immediately and provide you with a completion date for your convenience. We confirm that we act for MCC, who will be paying our fees.

MCC were trying to do the same as Rifkind had done the previous year and exchange contracts as soon as possible to stop any interference with the sale process. But Frumkin didn't want to sell at that stage and ten days later Rifkind wrote to Bradshaw, having got wind of what MCC were trying to do.

Rifkind wrote: 'We have previously discussed that it was in neither party's interest to compete against each other in trying to acquire numbers 2 and 6. Following discussions between us, you agreed that we should work together in acquiring these properties and upon acquisition they should be held jointly either by acquiring them in joint names or one of us holding the legal title with a "declaration of trust" holding a half of the beneficial interest in trust for the other. I trust that this accords with your understanding in respect to the above properties and I would be grateful if you could confirm your agreement.'

In October 2008, a heads of terms drawn up by MCC lawyers Slaughter & May included a plan agreed by both parties for a potential development on Grove End Road. It proposed that MCC and RLP would co-operate in a strategy for the combined ownership of 2 and 6 Grove End Road. Both sides were to agree that following the acquisition of the properties, they would be held in their joint names. However, MCC had long forgotten any joint agreement when the club eventually bought Frumkin's house in 2014, for a staggering £8.5 million including stamp duty.

Frumkin, who had received a number of approaches to sell from both MCC and Rifkind in the intervening years, says he eventually agreed a deal because he couldn't face the upheaval from the building of the new Warner Stand. He didn't want a repeat of the disruption he had suffered when the Grand Stand had been rebuilt in 1997 and 1998, though a cheque for over £8 million might also have something to do with his change of mind. He happily took the money and bought a flat in a mansion block across the road from Lord's. MCC had conducted the purchase in great secrecy, in order that Rifkind didn't put in a counter bid.

Oliver Stocken: 'Charles was working on Lionel, we knew that, and the MCC trustees had to agree on any expense over £2 million. I couldn't take it to the MCC committee because it would get back to Charles within five minutes. So what we did was get all the documents ready to go and then the moment the committee agreed, the head of legal would leave the meeting and ring the other lawyers to exchange immediately.

'We knew we would have to pay a premium, but it was a critical acquisition. It wasn't as much as Lionel wanted, which was £10 million – we split down the middle. We didn't want Charles to know, otherwise he would have come back to Lionel with a higher offer. You've got to plan these things through.'

Rifkind: 'The day MCC bought 6 Grove End Road from Lionel Frumkin, I had a phone call from Derek Brewer saying could I come and see him or could he come round. I went round to his offices, where Brewer announced proudly that they had acquired Mr Frumkin's house for £8 million and were about to inform the members by email.

'I gave him a smile and said: "There's no third party owning it and I'm glad it's your money not mine – I'm just a little bit disappointed that you have paid £2 million more than you should have done. When I was talking to Mr Frumkin, we could have bought it for under £6 million, so I assume you paid a premium to avoid doing a deal with me."'

MCC treasurer Robert Leigh: 'We had to buy 6 Grove End Road for strategic reasons. It gave us number 4 and number 6, the houses either side of our car park on Grove End Road. It meant we could develop a new entrance to the ground, with or without Charles.

St John's Wood estate agent Paul Bennett: 'Frumkin had a relationship with Lord's. He loved cricket. But he played his own game around the sale of his house. He invested money to find out the worth of his house if a development took place. He's an intelligent guy. He didn't get what he wanted, which was £10 million – he got £8 million. Good luck to the fellow. The prospect of paying £6 or £7 million in that market was feasible, but £8 million was ludicrous. MCC were desperate. Why couldn't they have worked together with Charles and saved themselves over £4 million?

'We only found out that MCC had bought it while we were negotiating on Charles's behalf with Lionel. I admire Lionel – he was loyal to MCC up to a point. He was very clever and they were not thinking straight. MCC have always lacked a strategic plan, despite their expensive advisers. They are always reactive.'

MCC member David Dodd wrote on the online forum: 'Can the club afford something similar when Colin Ingleby-Mackenzie's widow Storms decides to sell? Thwarting Charles Rifkind, just for the hell of it, is becoming an expensive business.'

Rifkind's ambitions for Lord's became even more ambitious after his Grove End Road acquisitions in 2007. He employed architects including Munkenbeck & Marshall, Chassay & Last and the Richard Rogers Partnership, who came up with various schemes for a Grove End Road development, including a new grand entrance to Lord's.

The land value at the Nursery End, with planning permission, was reckoned to be around £300 million. The Grove End Road development would add another £150 million – a total of £450 million.

Rifkind: 'It would have been so easy to finance. The land is worth several hundreds of millions of pounds with planning permission, but MCC never got it. They never sat down to discuss it. They never wanted to engage. They never understood the mechanics of it.'

There had also been a long-running battle between RLP and MCC over 12 Grove End Road, the residence of the Cuban Ambassador on a leasehold from MCC. Rifkind was aware that the lease was running out. He also knew after the Frumkin house purchase that any joint venture with MCC was not going to happen, so he made contact with the Cubans.

The Cubans were critically short of money during Fidel Castro's Communist regime. They also faced having to spend £300,000 to restore 12 Grove End Road to its original pre-let state at the end of their contract. Rifkind offered to pay for those repairs and write a cheque for £1 million as a down payment, in return for the Cubans buying the lease from MCC. The plan then was for RLP to buy the freehold from the Cubans, having found a cheaper home for the ambassador in Queen's Park.

MCC's legal team countered, informing the Cubans that they were not able to enfranchise the property, as UK embassies are not allowed to take advantage of the Leasehold Reform Act.

Rifkind responded by telling the Cubans that they were entitled to do so, as 12 Grove End Road was the residential home of the Ambassador, with the business part of the Cuban Embassy based in Holborn.

MCC's next move was to consider a Grove End Road house exchange between the Cubans at number 12 and MCC Chief Executive Derek Brewer at number 4 to protect their ownerships of both properties. In a pointless letter to Rifkind, Brewer informed him that MCC were no longer examining a joint approach for 12 Grove End Road, which was already obvious. The Cubans were now in a position to play both sides off against each other. The house swap never materialised, so MCC would have to offer the Cubans attractive terms to see off Rifkind's proposals.

Surprisingly, Rifkind withdrew from the fight for 12 Grove End Road in March 2017. He announced at the end of an acrimonious meeting ahead of MCC's development review report that he was no longer supporting an enfranchisement claim, saying 'It is MCC's house if MCC want it.'

Rifkind: 'It was a very sensitive time and I didn't want to provoke MCC, so I pulled back. In any case, I already had ownership of three houses on the road.'

It took until August 2018 for MCC to complete a new deal with the Cubans on a 15-year lease. Lord's waived the legal need for the tenants to spend around £400,000 restoring the property to its condition at the start of their occupancy. The Cubans also have seven years paying no rent, followed by a further seven years on favourable terms until the end of the lease. The only advantage to MCC is that the new lease arrangement ends any enfranchisement opportunities.

To add to the lack of any income from 12 Grove End Road, MCC's annual accounts in March 2019 showed a remarkable drop in value of the club's most expensive property purchase. When they arranged mortgages for their three houses on Grove End Road to raise £15 million as a contingency fund during the building of the new Compton and Edrich stands, 6 Grove End Road, which had cost £8.5 million five years previously, was valued at £4 million. It was an extraordinary devaluation of 50 per cent, at a time when almost every other comparable residential property in St John's Wood would have risen by a double digit percentage over the same five-year period.

Oliver Stocken: I can't understand why they put it down in the accounts at £4 million. They should see it as part of a property portfolio. It was completely ridiculous, all you do is expose yourself to criticism.'

CHAPTER 6

The Tea House and No Sympathy

Two events in 2006, six years after the tunnels had been purchased, finally opened the door to Rifkind. One was the retirement of MCC chief executive Roger Knight and his successor Keith Bradshaw being far more predisposed to listen to Rifkind. But there was no way into the Lord's inner sanctum for Rifkind whilst Maurice de Rohan led the estates committee. But in August de Rohan and former MCC chairman Bob Alexander both died. According to some of his MCC colleagues, de Rohan went to his grave believing Lord Alexander had tipped off his son-in-law Johnny Sandelson over the maximum amount MCC were prepared to bid at the tunnels' auction.

The latest development proposals that MCC were considering – from HOK – were put in cold storage by Knight's departure and de Rohan's death, which allowed for a fresh start on the redevelopment front.

Bradshaw: 'When I first arrived at Lord's, Maurice de Rohan was emphatic that I should not meet Rifkind, who in his estimation would eventually sell his land back to MCC. He would be smoked out – of that there was no doubt, according to de Rohan. I put the case that I thought there was no harm in my having lunch with Charles, to meet him socially and get to know the man I'd heard so much about. But continually I was told that I was not allowed to meet him. They had such feelings of disdain towards Charles. But following Maurice' passing away, the chairman Charles Fry said I could reach out to him.'

In October, Rifkind and Bradshaw went to lunch at Oslo Court, an old-fashioned restaurant on the ground floor of a mansion block in St John's Wood. Rifkind found the personable Bradshaw a 'breath of fresh air'. He listened with enthusiasm to Rifkind's vision and was apologetic about his previous interaction with MCC. After lunch, Rifkind took Bradshaw back to his office in St John's Wood, a Japanese-style tea house hidden in the trees on a plot of land behind Rifkind's garden.

Bradshaw: 'I saw the most amazing models. I was quite awestruck as we envisaged the potential of this grandiose project. That started a process that was to continue for five years until the end of my time as secretary and chief executive. Charles mentioned that some committee members, notably Anthony Wreford and Peter Leaver, had been to view the models. Wreford had attempted to put this matter up for discussion on the committee agenda, but was prevented from doing so by de Rohan.'

Oliver Stocken: 'Keith Bradshaw arrived, and his relationship with Charles was very close. They were lunching once or twice a week. When he submitted his expenses, it was always "Lunch with Rifkind". Keith is a very, very nice guy, but very chaotic. He always said yes to the last person he spoke to, which is hopeless. He came across at the interview stage as the most presentable character, but he probably wasn't the best choice. When we appointed Derek Brewer, we had a couple of panels and he had to do psychometric tests.'

Rifkind: 'I almost invariably pick up the bill. The few times I didn't with Keith was to show MCC that at least their chief executive was prepared to look at the club broadening their horizons.'

The first letter from Bradshaw to Rifkind on 27 October 2006 following their long lunch was very different in tone from Knight's correspondence:

'Thank you for making the time to meet with me, which was greatly appreciated. I look forward to further productive discussions during the coming week with yourself and Jonathan Levy.'

Rifkind: 'The one thing I have in my life is if I say something to somebody, I stand by it. I completely stand by it. When I met Keith Bradshaw, I believed I was dealing with an honourable man. After he heard my story and saw the models, he was horrified the club had not engaged in a dialogue. He said, "We have to enter a dialogue."'

That dialogue went well enough for a meeting to be arranged with members of the MCC committee in Rifkind's Tea House two months later. Around the oak table on 16 December were the MCC high command, including president Doug Insole, chairman Charles Fry, chairman designate Oliver Stocken, chief executive Keith Bradshaw, treasurer Justin Dowley, assistant secretary (cricket) John Stephenson, chairman of estates Blake Gorst, former president Tony Lewis and former chairman Sir Michael Jenkins. Most of them had been reluctant to make the short walk from Lord's to Hamilton Terrace.

It was the first time the MCC decision-makers had seen the designs since Rifkind presented them to de Rohan, Batts and Knight three years previously. The plans for both ends of the ground included new Tavern and Allen stands, a 100-bedroom hotel and residential accommodation, floodlights and a sports clinic and health centre. Rifkind had also gone a step further in his presentation this time, including a plan for tennis matches to be staged on a grass court in front of the pavilion.

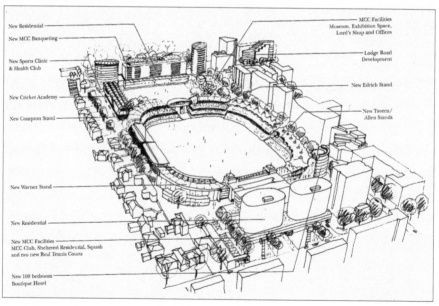

RLP's redevelopment proposal for MCC

The meeting started at 11 a.m. and at 11.30 a.m., just when the discussion had turned to a tennis tournament at cricket's headquarters, tennis legend Boris Becker made a dramatic entrance. He introduced himself to everyone, adding 'three-time Wimbledon champion' after his name. The plan was for him to front a two-day charity exhibition after the England vs India Lord's Test in 2007.

Rifkind had had detailed plans drawn up by Munkenbeck & Marshall, which included an undercroft at the Nursery End that would house a number of permanent tennis courts.

Bradshaw: 'I was keen on the idea but the committee, alas, took the view that there was sufficient to occupy them already without taking this on as well.'

Dowley: 'Charles can be quite a showman, and Becker's arrival at the Tea House was evidence of that. Most of us were not convinced, but Charles had a lot of good ideas.'

Rifkind: 'It was stupid, in hindsight. It looked stage-managed, although I didn't tell Boris what to say. I was suggesting what could happen, but it looked like I was in charge. It was a mistake.

'They were probably a bit bamboozled – they hadn't wanted to come to the Tea House. They wanted to be on their own territory, but after my uncomfortable feeling in the Writing Room in 2003, I wanted them here. But it was clear they didn't want to be here or to be told how they could improve Lord's. Stocken and Dowley were the last to arrive, and I knew at that point that the chairman and treasurer were not on board.'

The negativity of the top two men set the tone for the relationship between Rifkind and the MCC committee. Rifkind offered numerous invitations to committee members for a variety of events, but these were turned down and he received next to nothing in return. Individual alliances with MCC figures proved difficult for him to build. He reached out to certain people, who engaged and then backed off, usually under instruction.

Rifkind: 'The power base is such that they never wanted to be associated with me. They never wanted a relationship. When people got close, they were told they were getting too close. It happened with Charles Fry. Initially he was supportive and then he pulled back. The same with Sir Michael Jenkins, who unfortunately died. The same with

Anthony Wreford – he was supportive, then unsupportive. The same with David Batts. It goes back to no one wishing to upset MCC hierarchy – it's all about that.

'Charles Fry came to the Tea House on his own, to discuss his debenture scheme. I said I would buy 20, which delighted him. In the end they were oversubscribed and they sold me eight. When it got back to MCC, he was told not to get too close to me.

'Anthony Wreford also came to the Tea House to see the models, but he wouldn't come on his own – he brought along Peter Leaver and

Phillip Hodson. Then Wreford pulled back, saying I should speak to Maurice de Rohan.

'I had asked Gerald Corbett to many events, but he felt that it wasn't appropriate for him to be seen publicly with me. I invited him to Queenwood to play golf, Queen's Club to watch tennis, to lunch. He declined everything.'

Rifkind received a rare invitation to a dinner organised by Sir John Major in the pavilion's Writing Room to promote the proposed Vision for Lord's to politicians and Westminster councillors. Despite The Vision being a joint venture, with Rifkind paying 50 per cent of the running costs, his invitation to the dinner arrived a week before the event.

Rifkind: 'It became very clear that I was a spare part. I was not classified as a partner. Prior to the dinner, John Major and I took a walk on the cricket ground. Major put his arm around me and said: "I understand that things are not straightforward here. It will take time, but I'm sure one day it will happen, Charles."'

To get into Lord's, Rifkind had to pay his own way by either hosting dinners in the Long Room or by renting the hospitality boxes on either end of the media centre. The building had a new sponsor in Investec, after Rifkind introduced Bradshaw to his banking partners.

Rifkind: 'Bradshaw tells me the NatWest sponsorship of the media centre is coming to an end and would I be interested in the opportunity. I introduce Bradshaw to the chief executive of Investec, and out of that encounter Investec end up sponsoring the media centre for £500,000 a year.'

'As a thank you from Investec, I ask them if I can use the hospitality boxes for the big games, but there's no atmosphere behind the glass. The only way to use the box is like a cocktail party. So instead of having 14 in there, I had about 28 to 34 and it was buzzy and noisy. The cricket was sort of ancillary to what was going on in the box. Quite a few committee members came in to say hello.

'On one occasion, David Batts saw or heard that my box was quite noisy. He got his binoculars out in the pavilion and texted me to say "Charles, I'm looking from the pavilion and I can count 28 in your box. I text back: "What do you want me to do?"

Batts: 'Get rid of them.'

Rifkind: 'I can't – they're my guests.'

Batts: 'You're in breach of health and safety.'

Rifkind: 'Hold on a second. The other box is empty, and that takes 14. And 14 and 14 makes 28.'

Batts: 'Get them out, Charles.'

Rifkind: 'You can ask them to leave, because some of them are your committee members.'

There was no further riposte from Batts, but the following year MCC restricted the amount of usage by bringing in security passes. So Rifkind no longer used the boxes to entertain guests.

The text exchange illustrates Rifkind's fractured relationship with MCC – even when they were working together on the Vision for Lord's. Nevertheless, in the Ashes summer of 2009, Rifkind and Batts decided to host a box together to promote The Vision. Rifkind auctioned off his media centre hospitality boxes and raised £150,000 for charity.

Rifkind: 'When it came to the guest list for our joint initiative, some members of the development committee felt it would be appropriate to invite the likes of Sir Philip Green and Sir Richard Branson, those kind of personalities. I couldn't understand why they wanted to do that – I only wanted cricketers and people who would help promote The Vision. Eventually I was asked to fill the box.

'There was a very good atmosphere on the day. When it came to the cost, MCC sent me a bill for £30,000, half the food and drink and half the hire fee, even though I had donated the proceeds from using my boxes to good causes. It was a double whammy. This was a time when we were supposed to be having a joint venture. It was an unbelievable mentality, yet I ended up paying it. We were doing the Vision for Lord's, and it was right we were seen doing something in terms of The Vision.'

'Bradshaw was trying to bring us together and Batts was in the way. He tried to be nice to me, but behind the scenes, whatever someone at MCC said, Batts followed. Every time we went down one path, he went down another path. Bradshaw was powerless – he was a secretary, not a chief executive. He always promised something but couldn't deliver it. He started with good intentions but could never deliver.'

Rifkind was still trying to build relationships with MCC committee members. There was a dinner in the Long Room to raise money for the Duke of Edinburgh's Award that was attended by Boris Becker and Prince Philip.

Rifkind: 'I put Keith Bradshaw next to the Duke of Edinburgh, but Keith thought it more appropriate that the chairman Oliver Stocken should sit there. But I regarded it as my invitation, and I did not want Stocken at the top table.

'I'd invited the MCC committee to share a table of ten, which they declined. The answer came back that they couldn't take anything that benefited Charles Rifkind. I then worked a way around that situation whereby the invitation came from Prince Philip, which MCC accepted. Keith again turned down a top table position, deciding to sit with the committee. It became embarrassing at that point.'

On the night, Rifkind's wife Simone and Lord Grabiner sat either side of Prince Philip. Other invitations to MCC didn't even reach the dining stage, despite Rifkind working with Lord's towards a heads of terms for the Vision for Lord's.

Rifkind: 'The Tate Gallery gave me a party for my involvement in their summer exhibition in 2008. I extended an invitation to all members of the MCC committee, but the invites were never sent out. David Batts put them in the bin, calling them "inappropriate". I also suggested that we should have a dinner to celebrate the Vision agreement. Zero response from MCC. For whatever reason, it never took place.'

Rifkind and Stocken, the two chief protagonists in the development saga, finally sat down for lunch in April 2017, at the Beaumont Hotel in Mayfair.

Rifkind: 'Oliver Stocken sends me a text to invite me for lunch, five years, eleven months and one week into his six-year chairmanship. Knowing there is roughly only three weeks to go of his tenure and probably embarrassed by the relationship, I think he wanted to depart on better terms. It was a generous gesture. But I felt, rather than take up the lunch opportunity whilst he was chairman, it would be better to do it later to retain a civilised relationship.'

Gerald Corbett took over as MCC chairman in October 2015 and Rifkind encountered Stocken at Twickenham during an England Six Nations match in early 2016.

Rifkind: 'I put an arm on his shoulder and say: "Remember that lunch we were going to have? Would you like to do it now?" At the lunch we talked for about two hours on lots of topics. We didn't talk about MCC – we talked about life generally, and departed as if we were dear old friends.

'Stocken wrote me a very charming handwritten thank-you note, in which he says he will watch with interest from afar with his glass of whisky. Then, over the forthcoming weeks and months, it is very clear that Oliver Stocken's hand is very much still in play at MCC.'

Yet despite Rifkind and MCC's dysfunctional relationship, a potential joint venture emerges. A Masterplan working party chaired by past MCC chairman Sir Michel Jenkins, was set up in February 2007 to examine the options for ground development at Lord's. And Rifkind's futuristic models were still fresh in the mind from the Tea House gathering two months earlier.

CHAPTER 7

Vision 2021

So it's the start of the 2021 Ashes summer and the ever-green Phil Hughes is leading the Aussies on what will be his last tour, with Ricky Ponting's batting record firmly in his sights. The head groundsman has a busy schedule. Working out of his energy efficient workshops, he is preparing the Wellington Ground for an England women's under-21 match. The women's side has been world number one for six years and the success, going back to winning the World Cup in 2009, has seen a massive increase in women's cricket.

Meanwhile Middlesex, the County Champions in 2020, start the defence of their title with a four-day match against Surrey on the Wellington Ground. This takes place the day after Middlesex play their first floodlit Twenty20 match of the season on the Main Ground. So that is the overall Vision for Lord's in 2021. A ground with not one but two first-class squares; a permeable, welcoming centre for cricket, attracting people of all ages and abilities to play, watch and train; a very successful commercial enterprise, generating jobs and income for the Westminster and London economies; all delivered through high-quality architecture, which retains Lord's great history whilst looking to the future.

Meanwhile, in the new cricket museum, which opened in 2016 and features the Ashes Urn in pride of place (England retained the Ashes in Australia in 2019), MCC announced it has welcomed the one millionth visitor to the new facility, who is given a bat signed by the England team, including the captain Stuart Broad.

THIS LOOK INTO THE FUTURE was written in April 2009 for a proposed Lord's development brochure by the PR consultant Robert Gordon Clark, whose London Communications Agency was co-ordinating the PR campaign for The Vision. Clark wasn't to know that Phil Hughes would be tragically killed during a Sheffield Shield match in November 2014, struck on the neck by a ball after missing an attempted hook shot. Nor has the Nursery Ground been renamed the Wellington Ground, and nor were Middlesex County Champions in 2020 when the coronavirus pandemic severely affected the season. However, Stuart Broad is still playing for the England Test team – not as captain, though that was a good prediction in 2009.

Gordon Clark said: 'We helped MCC work up The Vision. Westminster Council wanted to see a masterplan for the whole ground rather than piecemeal developments.'

Rifkind: 'It was a lot of fluff, but for whatever reason Robert Gordon Clark had influence over David Batts – and I was asked to pick up half the bill.'

Robert Gordon Clark's predictions give a snapshot of the breadth of ambition for the Vision for Lord's, as Sir Michael Jenkins's Masterplan working party looked into future development possibilities. The group considered the two different proposals that had emerged since 2005: Rifkind's plans and the HOK blueprint – put on hold after Maurice de Rohan's death – that excluded development on the leasehold land.

The four key factors for MCC were that Lord's remained a cricket club, a desire to increase seating capacity and modernise the older stands, the belief that it would be a wasted opportunity to confine a major development to the stands alone and a clear preference from Westminster City Council's planning department for an overall masterplan rather than frequent one-off applications for new buildings.

The HOK scheme, at an estimated cost of £170 million, achieved most of the club's objectives and included a hotel on the site. The RLP alternative proposed residential development at both ends of the ground, which would generate the funding for the improvements.

Robert Griffiths QC, who sat on Jenkins's working party, wrote in a briefing paper for the main committee: 'RLP put forward a coherent and imaginative approach to a major masterplan for the redevelopment of Lord's. My own view is that the club should regard these proposals as realistically achievable.' The briefing concluded: 'On balance, the members of the working party believe it would be in the club's best interest to proceed with the RLP proposal.'

A special meeting of the MCC committee was held in the committee dining room at Lord's on 22 May 2007. The minutes reveal a scattergun debate from an oversize committee that was not suited for reaching any coherent decision, a problem that hindered progress throughout the saga.

Sir Michael Jenkins (chair, as Charles Fry was absent): 'We need to establish a consensus about our choices for the Masterplan. How ambitious do we want to be? A core requirement is modernising various stands, which we could finance ourselves. But the committee could decide to go further and appoint a development partner, and this partner as things stand would be RLP.

'The second option would produce a financial dividend for the club, secure the future of Lord's for many decades and provide funds for a substantially increased contribution to cricket from MCC. If we take that option, we need to decide whether to engage RLP in the planning stage only or to enter into a full development partnership.'

Wreford: 'There is no plan about the retention and recycling of rainwater needed to retain the quality of the grassed area.'

Gatting: 'Special attention needs to be paid to the grassed areas. There have been various problems with the Nursery Ground nets since the media centre was built.'

Heyhoe Flint: 'The cricket facilities should be increased, improved and enhanced. The RLP proposals include underground cricket facilities. The cricket committee feel the RLP plan would be more realistic and provide funding that would provide substantially increased financial resources that could benefit the game in general.'

Faber: 'I'm concerned that the RLP proposals do not provide extra grassed areas at Lord's.'

O'Gorman: 'Car parking spaces are an important factor.'

Batts: 'The RLP plan involves the railway tunnels, which will provide extra car parking.'

Gorst: 'The HOK schemes have been costed by quantity surveyors.'

Griffiths: 'In my view, the HOK schemes do not amount to strategic proposals befitting Lord's. The prospects of obtaining planning consent is significantly greater with RLP. Lord's would be transformed.'

Dowley: 'The HOK plans leave a funding gap of £32 million out of the £170 million needed, although the figures are hypothetical.'

Faber: 'It had been indicated that residential property would not be built on the club's land, yet the RLP plans show that floors two to twelve of the proposed Grove End Road building would be on land currently used by the club.'

Batts: 'Under the RLP proposal, the MCC secretary's house would be demolished and the club would lose Number 6 Car Park.'

Faber: 'The new residential development will be on the club's land, then, approximately in the position of the existing tennis court.'

Batts: 'It will be necessary to establish how far into the ground these residential developments would be positioned.'

Faber: 'The new residential development at the Nursery End is technically not on the club's land, but the majority of members would consider it part of Lord's Cricket Ground.'

Griffiths: 'RLP would prefer a scheme including Grove End Road. The houses there are covered by a covenant under the control of the MCC committee restricting new developments to single-dwelling properties.'

Jenkins: 'The building of residential properties and the ownership of the land on which they will be built will be a key element of the proposals.'

Fleming: 'We should walk through the plans outside and see exactly where these proposed developments will take place.'

Batts: 'Those who haven't seen the models produced by RLP should visit Mr Rifkind in order to do so. There are two options if the club want to enter into a partnership with RLP.

In option A, the club would share the land value for residential development after the deduction of each party's contribution and costs. It is possible that MCC's share could be greater than 50 per cent in this arrangement. In option B, the club could become a full development partner with RLP and take an appropriate share of development costs and the potential development profit.'

Dowley: 'Option B would potentially produce very large sums of money, but there are concerns over the risks involved.'

Sturt: 'The value of the land per square foot has been overstated. It has been calculated at £1,900 per square foot and I've been told by an estate agent that a lower value is more likely. And the square foot valuation makes a massive difference to the financial projections – RLP might be trying to seduce the committee by overstating these values.'

The minutes record that Sturt later revises his view that the figures in the discussion paper had been overstated – they were, if anything, conservative.

Griffiths: 'The square foot calculation is one reason why it is too early to evaluate the respective benefits of options A and B.'

Jenkins: 'It will be crucial to have the best possible advisers. I propose that we ask Sir John Ritblat what is required. His views on strategy with third parties such as RLP will be extremely valuable. So, are the committee ready to consider a full development partnership with RLP if planning permission were to be granted?'

Fellowes: 'The committee should make progress with RLP but not become too close in the early stages of the negotiation.'

Heyhoe Flint: 'I agree.'

Dowley: 'My predecessor Oliver Stocken would prefer a full partnership with RLP, provided the deal was acceptable.'

Griffiths: 'The club must not be an obstacle in any planning consent required by RLP.'

Griffith: 'I'm wary about the club becoming a property developer. It is essential for the club to bear in mind exactly what is best for the club. The playing of cricket is a far greater priority than the provision of a swimming pool.'

Sturt: 'I'm opposed in principle to any proposal that blocks of flats be built within Lord's.'

Jenkins: 'If the club agree to an expenditure of £500,000 and then turn our back on the next stage of the proposal, the committee would be open to wide criticism.'

Gatting: 'There is huge potential to develop the Pavilion End of the ground.'

Jenkins: 'The club could reserve the right to develop only those parts of the ground it wishes to include. It might be necessary to apply for planning permission for the maximum scheme, yet agree with RLP over MCC's right to limit development to one end of the ground. All this would need to be set out in the heads of terms.'

Batts: 'There is a need for clarity in negotiations with RLP. It is essential there are no misunderstandings.'

Rice: 'Are there any other reasons, other than cash, which has prompted RLP to produce the plans?'

Batts: 'Mr Rifkind has a mission and he views the Masterplan for Lord's as a world-beating project. RLP had been developing plans over the last six years.'

O'Gorman: 'I had not originally been in favour of working with RLP, but the development behind the pavilion is a good idea. I would like to see revised figures based on different square foot values. I am now in favour of exploring terms with RLP.

Jenkins: 'Work on the drafting of a suitable paper should begin.'

Wreford: 'I'm worried at the prospect of RLP's publicity machine overshadowing the club's requirements. I'm hesitant about a full-scale development partnership.'

Griffiths: 'The club will have to create publicity at an appropriate time. It is important to agree a timetable with RLP – any adverse publicity would not be in RLP's interests, nor the club's.'

Faber: 'The documents which the committee received are slanted heavily in favour of entering into an agreement with RLP. I'm suspicious of RLP's plans – there's an attempt to seduce the committee. I'm also concerned about the committee demolishing houses on Grove End

Road and undertaking underground developments. The special atmosphere at Lord's, particularly behind the pavilion, might be destroyed by a full-scale development. I don't accept the schemes could be interpreted as being of national significance.'

Sturt: 'I favour an increase in the capacity of the ground, but the committee should retain control over all parts of Lord's. I'm in favour of the HOK plan.'

Jenkins: 'In the light of these discussions, the Masterplan working party will try to present proposals for a team to deal with negotiations between the club and RLP to the committee at its meeting on 13 June.'

The briefing papers prepared by David Batts for that meeting on 13 June reported that the majority of the May meeting chaired by Sir Michael Jenkins had supported entering into negotiations with RLP. It was agreed to appoint a negotiating team including a top-level property consultant and legal firm to negotiate heads of terms.

MCC committee member Michael Sturt had been vocal in his opposition to Rifkind's residential ambitions, yet his views expressed in the committee room were rather different to those given in his personal property dealings. Sturt had sold two flats in Pavilion Apartments, across the road from Lord's, to Rifkind, who saw one of them as a potential home for MCC secretary Keith Bradshaw if the Grove End Road development saw his MCC grace-and-favour house demolished. The other was to be the office for the Vision project.

Rifkind also bought two more apartments on the floor below. One was earmarked for Lionel Frumkin, if he could be persuaded to sell 6 Grove End Road. The second was seen as a possible home for Sir Bernard Schreier, who owned and lived in the Danubius Hotel. The grand blueprint was for operating theatres in the tunnels linking the Wellington Hospital with floors of private patient rooms in the Danubius.

Sturt had described Rifkind as 'overstating' a near £2,000-per-square-foot value for his planned Nursery End apartments. He thought £1,200 was a much more realistic figure, yet he wanted Rifkind to pay £2,000 per square foot for his two flats on St John's Wood Road.

Rifkind paid the asking price, and an embarrassed Sturt revealed his predicament at the start of the next main committee meeting on 13 June. Sturt and David Faber remained strongly opposed to any residential at Lord's.

Sturt: 'I have a potential conflict of interest, which I want to put on the record. I sold property to Charles Rifkind in November 2006. It was purely a business transaction and I have never met Mr Rifkind.'

Fry: 'Following the informal committee meeting on 22 May, David Batts has arranged for some members to view the models commissioned by Rifkind Levy Partnership.'

Jenkins: 'Once we have advisers in place, discussions can start on the club's best negotiating position. If terms prove acceptable, it is anticipated MCC will commit to 50 per cent of planning costs. David Batts, the deputy chief executive, will take charge of the Masterplan project.'

Sturt: 'Lord's should remain a cricket ground. The position of the media centre has caused the loss of ten nets because of prolonged periods of shade. If the Compton and Edrich stands are raised, this might cause the loss of up to 30 nets. An extra tennis court, swimming pool and gymnasium are of little value to members with an average age of 58.'

Fry: 'A proper survey should be carried out to analyse the additional shade.'

Griffiths: 'The main benefit to members would be the total refurbishment of Lord's, without having to pay for it out of the club's own resources.'

Faber: 'I remain totally opposed to the scheme. It does not add much benefit to MCC.'

Sturt: 'RLP are briefing the press.'

Jenkins: 'Agreeing a contract with RLP would help with ensuring confidentiality for both parties.'

The committee agreed to work up a jointly funded planning application with RLP for major residential development at both the west and east ends of Lord's. Batts, a former managing director of Radisson Edwardian Hotels, took day-to-day charge of The Vision, with the official title of Masterplan project director.

Bradshaw: 'I surmised David Batts, my deputy, would be suited to handling The Vision. I found David to be a practical, reasoned team player.'

When Batts wrote to Rifkind on 26 June 2007, it was all remarkably positive, considering the previous six and a half years of stalemate. Although even at this embryonic stage of the project, Batts was making clear that the main committee had the last word:

'The MCC committee has given its in principle approval for negotiations to commence between MCC's representatives and Rifkind Levy Partnership. It would be useful for us to receive a formal proposal of the key terms of your development plans, with particular reference to the timing and nature of the benefits to be delivered to the club. It is a requirement of the MCC committee that before heads of terms are signed, it approves the details negotiated by MCC's representatives.'

Rifkind wrote back on 4 July, mentioning that there was still a lack of clarity as to what MCC wanted from The Vision:

'The various plans and brochures you have received set down the key terms of our development plans. We are happy to discuss these further once we are clearer as to MCC's intentions.'

At this stage, however, MCC were being positive and agreed at their August committee meeting to a members' survey and a number of roadshows around the country to help frame their development requirements. The decision to involve the membership came out of meetings with the communications consultant Robert Gordon Clark, who helped MCC frame the questions in their survey.

A newsletter from chairman Charles Fry, including the questionnaire and dates for the roadshows, was sent out to members on 2 August. It detailed the progress made by Sir Michael Jenkins's working party over the development options. Members were asked to grade the need for improvements on the strength of priority – high, low or medium. The sections dealt with outdoor cricket facilities, indoor cricket school, members facilities, general ground facilities and staff facilities. The roadshows would be held at Bristol, Headingley, Old Trafford, Trent Bridge, Lord's and the Rose Bowl in Southampton.

Bradshaw: 'David Batts and I spoke to more than 2,000 MCC

members around the country. We did not come across any real opposition to the plans, including the building of flats at the Nursery End.'

As part of his research, Batts also visited baseball, basketball and American football stadiums in the United States, the ECB indoor cricket facilities at Loughborough University and the All England Club at Wimbledon. Some of the MCC executive, including Colin Maynard, who had been working at Lord's since leaving school in 1975, were sceptical.

Maynard: 'Charles's ideas chimed with Keith Bradshaw, but I could never see it happening – the members would never have gone for it. You would have needed a two-thirds majority and if you know the membership of MCC, that was never going to happen. We didn't need the money. We can fund development with accelerated membership, life membership and debentures.'

Maynard's comments summed up the divide. Rifkind had found an ally in Bradshaw, who agreed with the grand plan to open up Lord's, but Maynard and the membership would be hard to budge.

Negotiations between MCC and Rifkind collapsed following the appointment of Stephen Hubbard from CBRE in place of Alistair Parker as the club's property adviser. Parker and Rifkind had formed a good relationship, even during the de Rohan years and when Parker advised the Masterplan working party. Hubbard, who had been recommended by property development tycoon Sir John Ritblat, was appointed in July 2007.

Rifkind had been adamant that the joint development for Lord's should be on a 50/50 basis, both in terms of funding the planning application and on the share of development value once permission had been granted. Parker agreed but Hubbard recommended a 75/25 split in MCC's favour, both for the Wellington Road leasehold strip and any development on Grove End Road. Rifkind was incandescent.

The joint accord set up in March had only lasted four months, during which time Rifkind had bought rights to the use of a side road near Lord's, in anticipation of lorries needing a convenient place to park during the construction period. He paid £400,000 for the private road, North Bank; its 15 parking spaces are now rented out to the Wellington Hospital for £72,000 a year.

Rifkind: 'Stephen Hubbard comes to see me. We spent an hour plus together, discussing all the models. Then he reports back to the club that the share of profits should be 75 per cent to MCC and 25 per cent to RLP and that "Charles has an obsession with this project." He used the wrong word – he should have used the word "passion". I told MCC that it would be best if Stephen Hubbard and I didn't meet again. When David Batts asked how we were going to work, I told him "You need to sack Hubbard."'

Batts reported: 'This situation is clearly most unsatisfactory from MCC's point of view. The club cannot be influenced as to whom it wishes to take advice from. But, as things stand, the project is unlikely to make any progress.'

The Masterplan working party decided to stand down Hubbard and re-engage Alistair Parker. It was reported that the U-turn was supported by Sir John Ritblat, who had first recommended Hubbard to MCC.

Parker: 'I'd been recommending a 50/50 deal between Rifkind and MCC. They might as well act in concert. It takes two to tango and neither was going to roll over. However, somebody concluded that RLP would roll over.

'I heard Rifkind couldn't deal with Hubbard. David Batts rang to tell me Charles Rifkind wouldn't talk to him, but might if I was employed again. I wasn't comfortable with the client's choice of agent being decided by the other side, but Batts was happy with it so we re-started. I sat down and told them "This is where we were. These are the issues, these are the key priorities. These are the outline terms we had, this is the paperwork." I gave them the full picture.

'I remember presenting to the committee and suggesting that we go to Alton Towers and see how they handle customer experience – that nearly caused a mass heart attack around the table! But the Lord's visitor experience is a joke – it's amateur hour. The gates can't handle the flow, and the loos around the back at the Nursery End are just a disgrace.

'There was a new drive under Bradshaw – he understood the ground desperately needed redevelopment. The catering was appalling, a lot of the stands were in a very poor shape. It needed a radical relook. I knew nothing about cricket, but I did understand large, complex developments.'

In November 2007, informal contact between MCC and RLP resumed. Batts had contacted Rifkind to discuss whether the grass on the Nursery Ground would suffer due to the shade from a residential development. Talks between them then progressed over a new financial deal that would see MCC take a 70/30 split until they had acquired £115 million from The Vision. The income would then be split 80/20 in favour of RLP, until parity of income had been achieved. Any additional income would be shared equally. However, to make this financial model work, MCC would have to commit to residential development at both ends of the ground.

By February 2008 The Vision was back on track to the extent that a panel was set up to select an architect from a longlist of 19 companies identified by RLP and MCC. The MCC committee met that month, with The Vision and the split in proceeds at the top of the agenda.

Griffiths: 'It's important to get on with making the planning application, as the climate is right for sport-associated development. In my view, a 50/50 arrangement properly reflects the contributions that both parties would make to the development and I see no reason to alter it.'

Bradshaw: 'I would prefer just to proceed with Wellington Road.'

Major: 'I see no downside in applying for planning consent and I'm overwhelmingly in favour of the new deal proposed. RLP wish to have a 50/50 split at the end of the development and I can understand why. At one stage, there was a suggestion RLP might not be totally committed to the Grove End Road development. But if the club were to insist on a 70/30 split until £115 million was achieved, Grove End Road would have to proceed.'

Batts: 'If the committee wishes to achieve the initial 70/30 split, there would have to be a link between the Wellington and Grove End Road developments. If the club are to proceed with Wellington Road only, the deal would have to be 50/50 or whatever could be negotiated.'

Griffiths: 'I feel that 50/50 should have been agreed at the start for the sake of achieving planning consent.'

Lewis: 'I was concerned the first proposal of 70/30 had fallen down, but I've been persuaded the new position is not weak.'

Wreford: 'RLP is a small company and Mr Rifkind, a man in his fifties, could be seen to be in something of a rush to achieve a return on his original investment. Wellington Road and Grove End Road should not be linked and the club should not commit to working with RLP on both projects. The working relationship between the two organisations is unknown. I think MCC should have a majority share in any development scheme.'

Gatting: 'I have a preference not to develop Grove End Road and I suggest the club look to develop the Wellington Road on a 50/50 split.'

Rice: 'I would prefer just to continue with the development on the Wellington Road.'

Fleming: 'I would like to achieve as much as possible while risking as little as possible. The club should focus on the Wellington Road but proceed with a planning application for both.'

Faber: 'I opposed the redevelopment plans last year, due to the Grove End Road element. The real tennis court is part of MCC heritage. Such features would be difficult to replicate even were the court taken down and rebuilt brick by brick. Despite that, I support a planning application for both ends of the ground.'

Vallance: 'I support a planning application for both ends of the ground, but I prefer a commitment with RLP to develop Wellington Road only.'

Stocken: 'I'm worried about the impact of bringing residential accommodation onto the ground. Residents rights are increasing all the time. I'm in favour of development at the Wellington Road only.'

Peters: 'The club should seek to agree a deal with RLP for both ends.'

Griffiths: 'My preference is to do a deal with RLP for the whole Masterplan due to the affordable housing requirement for both Grove End Road and Wellington Road.'

Fry: 'The Masterplan working party will do the best deal it can with RLP in connection with Wellington Road.'

The decision was to go ahead with the Wellington Road joint venture option with RLP. However, Grove End Road would also be included in the planning application.

The MCC committee meeting on 16 April was also Vision-dominated.

Batts: 'Work is continuing towards the submission of a planning permission for redevelopment at both ends of the ground, but the negotiations with RLP are over Wellington Road only. To allow the planning application to go ahead, an outline agreement has been put in place with a 50/50 split of the land value.'

Vallance: 'I'm surprised that as much as £4 million could be committed to the project without approval of the members.'

Faber: 'I agree. The club's redevelopment plans have been reported from time to time, but the figures mentioned have not reflected the costs to the club.'

President Mike Brearley: 'How come the club have changed their position since the last meeting with regard to the percentage agreed with RLP?'

Batts: 'The deal put forward at the last meeting would have locked the club into a commitment to redevelop Grove End Road. The overwhelming view of the committee is to go for 50/50 at the Wellington Road, without any commitment to Grove End Road.'

Vallance: 'The club can afford to take a long-term view, while RLP have less time to wait before it would need a financial return on its investment.'

Griffiths: 'The club has an agreement in principle. Planning fees are a legitimate expenditure when the total return is in the region of £140 million to £160 million.'

Batts: 'Any development without RLP would entail the club funding the entire cost of planning and development.'

An email from Batts to Rifkind after the MCC committee meeting confirmed the 50/50 deal that remained so important to the property developer. This correspondence would be used as evidence of that 50/50 agreement over a decade later.

Batts wrote: 'I refer to our discussions over MCC working in partnership with your company to evolve a masterplan for Lord's to secure a comprehensive planning permission at the Wellington Road end of the ground. On behalf of MCC, I confirm agreement in principle to move that partnership forward on the outline basis we have discussed; namely on a 50/50 financial partnership, with MCC making the planning application and both sides equally sharing the initial costs.'

The panel to choose an architect for The Vision was chaired by Sir John Egan, former chief executive of Jaguar and the British Airports Authority. It included Professor Ricky Burdett (chief adviser on architecture for the London 2012 Olympics), Rowan Moore (director of the Architecture Foundation), Sir Nicholas Serota (director of the Tate), Robert Griffiths (MCC committee member), Blake Gorst (chairman of MCC estates committee), plus Charles Rifkind and David Batts.

The five architects shortlisted were Building Design Partnership (whose works include the Wimbledon Masterplan and the Olympic tennis centres in Sydney and Athens), David Chipperfield Architects (the America's Cup Building in Valencia), Dixon Jones (the Royal Opera House refurbishment) Herzog & de Meuron (Bayern Munich's Allianz Arena and the Bird's Nest stadium in Beijing) and Hopkins Architects (the Mound Stand at Lord's and the Rose Bowl in Southampton). They were given six weeks to outline detailed plans. Herzog and Chipperfield were chosen as the final two ahead of the 11 June MCC committee meeting, which began with an update from the Vision project director.

Batts: 'The panel are due to meet again on 18 June to decide on their final choice. It's agreed to give authority to the Masterplan working party to decide whether to approve the recommendation on behalf of the main committee.'

The one person on the selection panel not supportive of either Herzog or Chipperfield was estates chairman Blake Gorst. He wanted HOK to be appointed, despite them not being on the shortlist.

Gorst: 'The Herzog scheme was too grandiose, to put it mildly. MCC wanted a 'starchitect' and Herzog fitted the bill. The undercroft would have bankrupted us – we should have stopped all this nonsense far earlier.'

Nevertheless, Herzog & de Meuron were the panel's choice – the plan was for the Swiss architects to present their design to the committee in April 2009. They called their Lord's masterplan '333', in recognition of Graham Gooch's innings against India in July 1990, the highest Test score ever made at the headquarters of cricket. An additional MCC committee meeting was held in September, so the architects could be briefed on MCC requirements. Treasurer Justin Dowley's doubts about The Vision came to the fore during the committee exchanges that month.

Bradshaw: 'There have been a number of meetings over how to improve the Nursery End facilities yet still allow cricket matches to be played on that ground. ECB's minimum criteria for first-class cricket are boundaries 50 yards from the centre of the pitch.'

Faber: 'Would the proximity of the ground to the flats pose a problem with regard to breakages caused by a cricket ball?'

Leaver: 'There would have to be a term in the lease dealing with insurance claims.'

Griffiths: 'The Masterplan working party feel it is an important principle that the development should be cricket-led.'

Brearley: 'I'm very supportive of enhancing the Nursery Ground for different forms of cricket. I don't think it would be possible to play first-class cricket on that size of ground.'

Vallance: 'The club are proposing to spend a great deal of money on upgrading the Nursery Ground for the type of matches for which the current ground is already suitable. It's more appropriate to spend the money developing a second ground away from Lord's that is suitable for first-class cricket.'

Faber: 'There is value for cricketers of all levels playing at Lord's, be it on the Main Ground or the Nursery Ground. The feeling would not be replicated elsewhere.'

Batts: 'The original plan was for MCC to enter into a co-operation agreement with RLP to achieve planning consent and then seek approval from the members. But at the last meeting, it was decided that members should be consulted at an earlier stage in the process.'

Dowley: 'One option not considered so far is that the committee may not wish to recommend the final scheme to members. The club need to be very careful in the current economic climate. I'm keen that the Masterplan working party consider the budget in greater detail than it has done to date.'

Griffiths: 'Once the co-operation agreement with RLP is signed, the club is bound to use its best endeavours to gain planning permission. The committee has already agreed to pursue this action.'

Dowley: 'I agree that the decision has been taken. But market conditions are changing more rapidly than they have done in 70 years. The committee should reserve the right to reconsider this decision due to the extraordinary prevailing conditions. The club might find itself committed to expenditure of £5 million at a time when it might not make sense to proceed with the development.'

Griffith: 'The finance committee must be involved in such an important decision.'

Batts: 'MCC is not committed to anything until the co-operation agreement is signed.'

Gorst: 'There is tremendous development potential at the Wellington Road end. But until planning permission is gained, the land has little value. The return is too compelling to ignore.'

The committee rubber-stamped the appointment of Herzog & de Meuron and agreed to a budget of £10 million for the detailed planning application. It meant both MCC and RLP would fork out £5 million each.

The next MCC committee meeting in October discussed the way forward for The Vision.

Batts: 'You all have a paper prepared by the secretariat proposing that the project should proceed until April 2009, when a presentation of the scheme will be made to the committee. This recommendation has been supported by the Masterplan working party and the finance committee, who agreed the project should proceed with caution.

'Our lawyers have received a copy of the co-operation agreement from Rifkind Levy Partnership's solicitors and a number of points are still to be settled. A further meeting with RLP representatives will take place on 23 October. The club will be represented by Jamie Ritblat, myself and Alistair Parker from Cushman & Wakefield. Mr Ritblat has proposed the agreement should be simplified and the heads of terms for a development agreement should be progressed immediately. This will flesh out any areas where there is a lack of clarity.'

Gorst: 'How much will it cost?'

Batts: 'The legal costs for drawing up a heads of terms range from £150,000 to £400,000.'

Gorst: 'This represents a significant additional cost on top of the £1.432 million budget.'

Batts: 'Every effort will be made to remain within the agreed budget, although only £50,000 has been allocated to cover legal costs up until June 2009.'

Gorst: 'The upper quotation of £400,000 seems excessive and I would be happy to sit in on discussions. It is important that the club remain in control of the timetable.'

Batts: 'RLP want to draw up an agreement with Wellington Hospital for use of the lower level of the tunnels for operating theatres. In practical terms, early development of the tunnels would require the Nursery Pavilion to be re-sited, which is not ideal, and the Olympic archery here would be an added complication.'

The proposed budget of £1.432 million up to a possible SGM in June 2009 was approved.

Rifkind: 'The heads of terms were not signed off. We couldn't agree and it was taking time. Each time we thought we got forward, we hit another issue. There were 13 drafts. We worked on the assumption that we were going forward with a mutual understanding. It didn't prohibit production of the drawings.'

For the first meeting with Herzog & de Meuron in Basel, Robert Griffiths, David Batts, Charles Rifkind and Robert Ebdon travelled to Switzerland. MCC member Ebdon, who worked for Synergy Construction & Property Consultants, was invited to become Vision project manager on the basis that he offered a discount on his usual professional prices and stepped down from the MCC estates committee. He felt privileged to work with signature architects and was initially very supportive of the Herzog scheme.

For that first meeting, Pierre de Meuron had prepared a model to meet MCC's demands. When questioned by Rifkind about the detail, de Meuron took apart the model and completely re-formed it to showcase the concept of lectern-style stands and the undercroft.

Parker: 'Herzog were a massively fashionable choice. I thought they had a bit of the "star architect syndrome" – half a million pounds for a sketch. But they put a team on it and you began to understand why they had the reputation they had. They broke the mechanics down and came up with some really elegant solutions. They had the stroke of genius in taking things underground with the undercroft. It meant that all that rubbish disappeared from view and freed up the space.

The Herzog & de Meuron design for Lord's

'The problem afterwards was that MCC went around all their departments asking what they wanted in the underground space. By the time they had finished, the undercroft had doubled in size. It was left to myself and Dave Batts to try and cut down the wish list. It was ridiculous and would have cost an obscene amount.'

The Herzog blueprint, if it was to reach fruition, would have to satisfy the main MCC committee, Westminster Council, the Mayor of London and the traditionally conservative MCC membership.

Herzog's designs were displayed in a box in the Grand Stand and in one of Rifkind's flats in Pavilion Apartments, over the road from Lord's. The extravagant undercroft utilised the space for a huge indoor cricket school that comprised 16 lanes 40 metres in length. There would also be underground shops, conference and banqueting facilities, a gym, pool, spa and six squash courts. Above ground, the Herzog & de Meuron design ensured the five rebuilt stands would allow the trees in St Johns Wood Church Gardens to be visible from the pavilion as Gubby Allen would have wished. The five residential blocks would only be visible from the top tier of the pavilion – and Sir Geoffrey Boycott was one of the first people to show an interest in buying an apartment.

Bradshaw: 'The images drawn up by Herzog & de Meuron were terrific. The blocks of flats at the Nursery End would provide the finance to rebuild five stands. Here was an opportunity that was too good to pass up, even by risk-adverse committee men. My chairman Charles Fry was prepared to be open-minded – it was only a shame that he did not remain in office. After all, the club had welcomed the financial help of Paul Getty for the rebuilding of the Mound Stand for its bicentenary in 1987. I put my signature to a 286-page booklet prepared for the Vision for Lord's, aligning myself with RLP; it need hardly be said that this did not go down well with the next chairman Oliver Stocken.'

Stocken was one of those, along with treasurer Justin Dowley and Mike Griffith, chairman of the cricket committee, who had grave doubts about the cost of The Vision, and particularly about the need for 16 lanes of nets in the underground cricket school.

Stocken: 'We had the Herzog plan, but I knew from past experience it would be vastly expensive. Did we need a 16-lane indoor school? When I put the question to the cricketers Mike Griffith, John Stephenson and Mike Gatting, they said we didn't need it. It only came back later that nobody had actually questioned whether we wanted 16 lanes. So I said to Keith Bradshaw: "Why didn't you kill it at the start?" That's where Keith's weakness came to a head – he thought other people had agreed it.

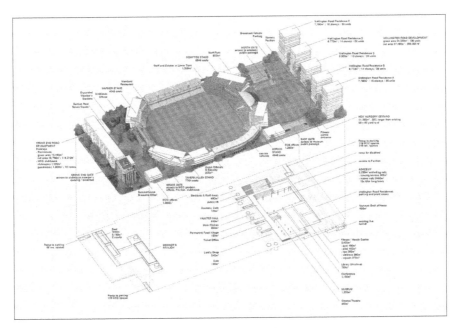

The details of the Herzog & de Meuron scheme

'We missed a lot of tricks along the way. We could have cut out a lot of wasted time if someone had said at the start that we only need six lanes rather than 16. Justin's view was that the financial figures were not realistic and Mike Griffith had concerns about the movement of the ball underground.'

Despite this high-level opposition, there was still a sufficient head of steam that a development committee for The Vision was set up. Robert Griffiths was appointed the chairman, after beating Charles Fry and Blake Gorst in a main committee vote.

The MCC committee meeting in December 2008, which endorsed Griffiths as development committee chairman, also received a presentation by Herzog & de Meuron.

Rifkind: 'Pierre de Meuron, the most senior of the architects, was kept waiting for an hour while the committee discussed a legal point which could have been kept for later. Pierre was only over from Switzerland for the day and was left pacing outside, wondering what to do. It was embarrassing.'

How Herzog & de Meuron envisaged Lord's behind the pavilion

However, The Vision was still on course, and on 18 December Bradshaw wrote to Rifkind agreeing the 50/50 venture.

Bradshaw wrote: 'On behalf of MCC, I confirm our agreement in principle to move forward with the following understanding.

'A 50/50 financial arrangement to seek planning consent for the MCC Masterplan and share equally the rewards from a redeveloped Wellington Road end.

'MCC to lead the overall planning process, but with responsibility for detail and design of the residential element to be provided by RLP and all costs to be shared 50/50.

'As proposed, I would confirm the MCC committee and any other relevant committee will be kept fully informed of progress and I would continue to ensure that, where appropriate, you are made aware of both their conclusions and any reservations as soon as any arise.

'I would also confirm our agreement to continue to run the bank account in the name of MCC, with both parties contributing a sum of

£100,000 and a mutual agreement to top up those funds as required to ensure a continuing credit balance of not less than £200,000.

'We envisage that this letter and your signed acknowledgement will record the commitment to work together in this process.

'Hopefully we will end up with an agreed masterplan, a planning strategy and a detailed heads of agreement for a development agreement that can be put to the MCC committee. And subsequently, if approved, to the MCC members.

'As ever, we are approaching this in the utmost faith, as I know you both are. However, the letter records MCC's present intent and is not intended to be legally binding and is written without liability of MCC or any officer, member or employee of MCC.

'Let us see if we can deliver something truly outstanding for all. I should be grateful if you would signify your acceptance of the terms set out in this letter by signing the enclosed copy and returning it to me.'

After Rifkind's signed acceptance, Batts sent an email on 16 January 2009 to Charles Fry, Justin Dowley, Blake Gorst, Tony Lewis, Jamie Ritblat, Mike Griffith, Sir Michel Jenkins, Keith Bradshaw, Alistair Parker, Robert Ebdon, Charles Rifkind and Robert Griffiths, inviting them to celebrate the joint venture at Lord's. It read:

'The club and RLP have both signed a co-operation agreement in the form of a letter, which sets out how the two organisations will work together going forward, as we develop a masterplan for Lord's. We (Charles Rifkind, Robert Griffiths and myself) feel that it would be appropriate to mark this event with a small dinner party at Lord's to be held on 5 February and I would be grateful if you could let me know your availability.'

The event was deemed 'inappropriate' by MCC and never took place. Even at the height of the supposed co-operation, Rifkind was being snubbed by the club's high command. And serious opposition to The Vision from five senior MCC figures – Oliver Stocken, Justin Dowley, Blake Gorst, Peter Leaver and Colin Maynard – became evident at the next two committee meetings. At the same time, new development committee chairman Robert Griffiths came to The Vision's defence at every turn. He could be guaranteed to speak out in favour of the plans and counter any criticism.

The Lord's tower at the Nursery End

The Masterplan was due to be presented to the MCC committee at their April 2009 meeting. But that was delayed until June, to allow proper evaluation of an alternative residential scheme for the leasehold land.

Rather than five blocks, this was a single giant 30-storey tower on the corner of Wellington Road and St John's Wood Road. It would increase the existing Nursery End playing area by 45 per cent and was nicknamed 'the Griffiths Tower' due to the QC's enthusiasm for this option.

There had also been a delay in the draft heads of terms with RLP, due to ongoing disagreements over the land value split and the minimum amount MCC would receive.

More doubts about The Vision were expressed at the MCC committee meeting on 15 April 2009.

Griffiths: 'RLP are not keen on the tower option because of the logistical difficulties. But they said they would act together with MCC to take both schemes forward at least until the June meeting, on the same 50/50 costs basis. It is difficult to predict the best course of action until the scheduled meetings with the Westminster planners and the Mayor of London take place.'

Stocken: 'I suggested developing one stand separately because if the planning application for the Vision for Lords is called in by the secretary of state, it's quite possible that in three years' time, there is little further to show members about progress being made.'

Gorst: 'I have my doubts about RLP's ability to deliver.'

Griffiths: 'We have investigated this. The tunnels are already worth considerably more than the original purchase price, and RLP are backed by Investec. RLP have offered to deposit sufficient funds to take the project to planning immediately, if it was felt necessary to alleviate any concerns.'

Gatting: 'I don't have any enthusiasm for the tower.'

Griffiths: 'It gives a lot more playing area on the Nursery Ground and should be explored carefully rather than rejected out of hand.'

Barclay: 'It's useful to have options and it's very good to have the opportunity to enlarge the playing area at the Nursery End.'

Leaver: 'I'm worried about taking the Vision for Lord's to planning without a commitment from ECB over the major match schedule.'

Maynard: 'If the total number of seats were increased to 38,000, the ground would be filled to capacity on only four to five days per year at most.'

Griffiths: 'This is another reason why it's important to continue with the residential development with RLP. This will ensure that much of the increased seating capacity and improved facilities will be provided at no cost to MCC.'

Peters: 'The committee took a very brave and difficult decision with the media centre, which was endorsed by members.'

Griffiths: 'We can't second-guess members.'

Heyhoe Flint: 'Where's the affordable housing element in the scheme?'

Griffiths: 'If the club creates something very special with improved facilities for the community, the requirement for affordable housing might be waived.'

A comparison showing the plans for either five blocks of residential development or a single tower

Batts: 'Westminster Council have already noted that there has been no affordable housing component in any of the proposals to date.'

Westminster City councillors were present when MCC had their meeting at City Hall with London Mayor Boris Johnson. The Lord's presentation party consisted of Rifkind, Griffiths, architect Jacques Herzog and project manager Robert Ebdon.

Griffiths: 'We presented and I remember Boris calling the scheme "fantastic". Boris is a clever bloke, very engaging and he runs with the ball. I knew that if we didn't succeed getting planning permission from Westminster, the appeal would be to Boris and I was laying the way for that. The way I presented to him was the way I wanted to present to members, but I never had the opportunity of doing that. The Vision was about bringing Lord's back to being a wonderful cricket ground, which you could see was no longer the case. It's about cricket and making Lord's a very special place, and we're doing it for London. Boris latched onto that it would be an iconic London project.'

Rifkind: 'It was a scheme bigger than for just Westminster to consider. The approach was to engage the mayor's office to improve the project in terms of enabling works. The mood at City Hall was positive that the scheme would have got accepted. MCC's planning consultants DP9 also had that view. Most of the MCC committee came to Pavilion Apartments to view the models. There were very few negatives.'

However, Stocken, replacing Charles Fry as MCC committee chairman, was not for turning. And he was going to be the most powerful individual within MCC for the next six years. Stocken also took notice of the views of the treasurer Justin Dowley, who was even more opposed to the Vision for Lord's. Dowley's concerns became evident at a combined meeting of the finance committee and the Masterplan working party (later to be renamed the development committee) on 15 June 2009.

Batts: 'The basis of the Herzog plan is to create a bigger Nursery Ground by moving the indoor school underground. The new indoor academy could provide ten or more lanes with bowlers having full run-ups.'

Peltz: 'The values being put on the residential development – £2,000 per square foot – are very high. Another new development on

Wellington Road, Embassy Court, is finding it difficult to sell apartments at £1,400 per square foot.'

Dowley: 'This meeting should concentrate on the recommendation that the club should proceed with the expenditure necessary to obtain planning permission in order to achieve a windfall of around £90 million. I'm unsure how much of that windfall could be used to carry out the proposed development plans at a time when the club is budgeting for a loss in 2010. While some of the facilities would produce revenue, many of them would increase the club's costs.'

Griffiths: 'How the resulting profits are spent is a debate for another day.'

McLintock: 'I want to be assured that achieving planning permission does not commit the club to any further action.'

Batts: 'RLP are contributing half the costs and if planning permission is achieved, they will wish to carry out the development, in order to realise their profit. If the threshold amount is reached, it would be necessary to undertake the residential development.'

Alt: 'Where are we on the development agreement?'

Griffiths: 'It has yet to be signed. RLP's share would be 50 per cent gross.'

The meeting decided it would be appropriate to recommend seeking MCC members' approval once planning permission had been achieved and the development plans were more established. Griffiths raised that decision at a fractious MCC committee meeting two days later.

Griffiths: 'To go for planning permission before consulting the members is contrary to what had previously been agreed. At this stage, we are only being asked to approve a planning application with RLP for the agreed scheme on a 50/50 cost-sharing basis. The estimate for MCC's share of this next phase of the project is £2.6 million.'

Batts: 'I would much prefer to hold the SGM before applying for planning permission, as members' approval is important.'

Leaver: 'Members should be consulted.'

Stocken: 'It is conceivable that members will need to give their approval to three stages of the project: the planning application, the agreement with RLP and how the money is spent.'

Griffiths: 'The development agreement, or at least the heads of terms, would need to be agreed before the submission of the planning application.'

Leaver: 'It is important to explain to members that the committee had considered the possibility of redeveloping the ground without entering into a joint venture with RLP.'

Griffiths: 'A financial paper had been considered at the meeting on 15 June that analyses the various options for development using the club's own resources and revenue.'

Stocken: 'I do not believe the alternative options have been considered in sufficient detail, and the secretary agrees more work is needed on the figures. This needs to be done before an SGM document could be drafted.'

Griffiths: 'The club could not fund a development which could cost £300 million on its own.'

Peters: 'According to the rules, it's not necessary to seek approval of members until it is proposed to carry out the development. But the sums involved in proceeding to planning are such that it is appropriate to seek members' approval.'

Gorst: 'The current plans are too grandiose. Serious consideration should be given to the club proceeding on its own with a smaller scheme.'

Griffiths: 'This would be a retrograde step. The Herzog plan is aspirational. It is important to establish the principle of residential development along the Wellington Road. Once planning permission is achieved, it would be possible to choose how to proceed with the development.'

O'Gorman: 'If the club tried to carry out this development alone, it could take up to 30 years to complete.'

The committee approved the recommendation from the finance committee and the Masterplan working party to make a planning application on a 50/50 cost-sharing basis with RLP. MCC's budget for the next phase was agreed at £2.6 million. It was agreed that an SGM would be held in early September at which members would be asked to approve the planning application. The date was subsequently put back, to allow for a detailed analysis to be done by the MCC secretary and for the development agreement with RLP to be completed.

Stocken would have his own negative opinion of The Vision reinforced by his closest ally Dowley's attack in a damning note sent to the chairman, his predecessor Charles Fry and secretary Keith Bradshaw. Dowley's response followed the main committee agreeing to commit more funds to working on The Vision with RLP.

Dowley wrote: 'Unfortunately I was not able to be at the main committee meeting last Wednesday. But a number of people who were there have expressed to me their concerns that the reservations about the Vision for Lord's, which were voiced at the joint finance committee/Masterplan working party meeting on 15 June, were not explained to the main committee.

'What the finance committee agreed was that:

1. It was happy that a further £2.6 million should be spent so that a planning application for residential development at the Wellington Road could be made.

2. No further cost should be incurred investigating the possibility of a residential tower.

3. The financial feasibility study needed further work. In particular it was not clear that the 'threshold amount' (currently mooted to be £92 million), below which MCC will not be obliged to proceed with a joint development with RLP, is likely to be reached.

'The case has not yet been made for spending £92 million (or whatever sum is finally decided as an appropriate threshold) on the series of facilities which form the overall Vision for Lord's.

'Clearly certain facilities will need to be renovated or replaced over time. But the finance committee is not prepared to spend a large capital sum on building a series of new facilities, the management and maintenance of which might put the club under financial pressure.

'The project is being presented in an unbalanced way. There is no real analysis of what the club could do as an alternative to pursuing a transaction with RLP. There's a feeling that we have perhaps become a little too close to RLP and are dancing to their tempo.

'There is scepticism that the numbers being used in the financial analysis are realistic. If, for example, the average sale price for the residential development of £1,700 per square foot is used (rather than the £2,000 proposed), the club's share of the profit would drop from £92 million to £58 million.

'If the financial projections are this uncertain, is it really right to carry on spending at this level, particularly at a time when spending in other areas of the club's activities are under pressure and likely need to be cut in the coming months, probably leading to redundancies.

'If we are pursuing the RLP transaction in order to build a financial nest egg (to which I do not object), we have got away from the principle originally discussed by the main committee of this being an enabling development.

'I am uncomfortable proceeding, as I think the chances of achieving a potential windfall of £92 million in the foreseeable future (by which I mean five to ten years) are low.

'In these circumstances, it may be better to spend the club's existing cash resources, with, if necessary, some borrowing, to proceed with the redevelopment of a stand, the relocating, if necessary, of the Nursery Pavilion and the development of our indoor coaching.'

Stocken: 'The finance committee had a big role to play. Justin was treasurer and then Robert Leigh took over, plus people like Tony Alt, Mike McLintock and John Varley. These are tough, experienced people. They were saying: "We shouldn't be doing this" and our numbers were not looking too bad. The asset was there for another 120-odd years. We didn't have to rush it.'

The development committee had yet to convene, but Stocken and Dowley between them had all but kyboshed The Vision. As a result of Dowley's powerful opposition, the MCC committee agreed at their meeting on 12 August to make a crucial amendment to the minutes of their previous summit in June, which Dowley had been unable to attend:

'It was agreed that no SGM (for members to vote on The Vision) would be held until the finance committee had confirmed it was comfortable to proceed; the development agreement had been signed with RLP and ECB had confirmed a satisfactory schedule of major match days.'

Effectively, this meant that MCC treasurer Dowley, who led the finance committee, had a power of veto over the whole project. He had been highly sceptical about The Vision from the start.

Dowley: 'My line was that we had to be clear on what we were going to spend the capital sum on. The idea was to increase the ground's capacity from 26,000 to 35,000, but we could only fill the present ground on six or seven days a year. It didn't make a whole lot of sense to spend so much money in those circumstances. I was also convinced that 50/50 was not the right deal for MCC. And we would only get our money when the flats were sold.'

All the negativity over The Vision came to the fore at the finance committee meeting on 16 September 2009. Griffiths, soon to chair his first development committee meeting, was a lone voice promoting it.

Dowley: 'The clear message from the finance committee is that the windfall from the residential development should not be spent on projects which had negative net present value, and a negative NPV of £74 million is the current projection.'

Gorst: 'MCC wishes to create the finest ground in the world. The club has money on deposit and is likely to achieve a windfall of £92 million from the residential development, but the current plan shows expenditure of £211 million. The wish list is excessive and alternatives need to be considered.'

Griffiths: 'My priority is to achieve a truly excellent cricket academy and I've been told this would not be possible unless it is sited underground.'

Tyrie: 'It will be difficult to present to members a project showing a loss of £74 million. Is the division of 50/50 with RLP a correct one? This ratio should be reconsidered. And with the current state of the property market, is now the appropriate time to be taking such decisions? What scope is there is for the club to redevelop the stands from existing resources?'

Alt: 'I agree about the 50/50 division with RLP. We should look at the right to call in more money in certain circumstances. We also need to understand RLP's financial position better.'

Tyrie: 'It is important not to go ahead with the planning application without the finance committee knowing the terms of the agreement with RLP.'

Griffiths: 'The development agreement has been agreed in principle and it's for the development committee to continue the negotiations.'

Alt: 'This is the first time the finance committee has seen a financial analysis of the project, yet the development agreement has been negotiated before the analysis has been completed.'

Griffiths: 'There are considerable safeguards for MCC within the development agreement.'

Dowley: 'The finance committee, the MCC committee and the members will need to see a summary of the terms of the agreement. It's the finance committee that has the responsibility of assessing and managing risks to the club, and they cannot do this without seeing the terms of the agreement.'

Stocken: 'The MCC committee support the development, but there are three conditions:

1: A summary of the terms of the agreement with RLP shall be prepared and circulated to the finance committee and the MCC committee.

2: The number of major match days should be established.

3: The finance committee has approved the investment of up to £3.6 million for a planning application.'

Dowley: 'The finance committee is not content with a project with a negative NPV of £74 million, and we will ask for the plans to be revisited.'

With Stocken and Dowley allied in such strong opposition, the newly formed development committee was up against it from the start.

CHAPTER 8

The Development Eleven

THE DEVELOPMENT COMMITTEE – DESCRIBED as the most powerful group ever convened for a sporting issue – numbered eleven members because its chairman Robert Griffiths wanted to mirror a cricket team. There had been three candidates to lead the group: Charles Fry, Robert Griffiths and Blake Gorst. A ballot of main committee members saw Gorst go out in the first round, before Griffiths sneaked past Fry in the second.

Griffiths' invitees were Michael Atherton and Tony Lewis, both former England cricket captains; Sir John Major, a former prime minister; Lord Grabiner, stellar QC who chaired the inquiry into press standards at News International after the phone hacking scandal; Michael McLintock, chief executive of insurance giants M&G; Tony Alt, deputy chairman of Rothschild; Scott Baker, a High Court judge, Sir Michael Jenkins, diplomat and former MCC chairman; Jamie Ritblat, owner of property company Delancey; Brian McGowan, co-founder of conglomerate Williams Holdings.

Also attending meetings as observers were MCC property development advisers Alistair Parker and Stephen Musgrave; lawyer Dermot Rice of Slaughter & May and Blake Gorst, chairman of the MCC estates committee, who was annoyed at not being one of Griffiths' chosen eleven.

However, the distinguished group that Griffiths recruited ended up being part of the problem. They felt that they had the expertise and knowledge to have the main say on development issues, but it is enshrined in MCC's rules that the main committee makes the final decision. Griffiths and co never accepted that – and they eventually paid the price.

Griffiths: 'I was the first chairman of a principal committee to be elected as opposed to being appointed. I chose eleven, my Test eleven. It was a nice way of doing it. When I chose them, I had in mind the difficulties I had seen with the committee structure at MCC.

'It was the pre-meetings before the meeting, so it was a stitch-up. You'd go into a meeting and hardly anyone would say anything. The chairman had already agreed with a number of people the way through. I abhor that. It's not my style, but Oliver Stocken was very keen on that approach. I didn't want my committee just to sit there and agree with what I was putting forward. I really wanted the argument tested on every point.

'Maybe the mistake I made was putting together such a powerful development committee. When you look at that committee in terms of stature and standing, including a former prime minister, and compare it with the MCC main committee, there was no comparison.

'I think I pissed them off a bit when I said "This is the committee that can take the club forward in terms of development." Behind the scenes they might have thought: "This is not right – Robert's taking over. He's got that committee, he can do what he wants."'

After picking his eleven, Griffiths had to explain some of his choices and omissions to sceptical colleagues in the committee room. Nigel Peters queried Mike Atherton's appointment, with Griffiths saying he provided a good cricketing background. Mike Griffith asked why Gorst wasn't included. Griffiths replied that, with the exception of Tony Lewis, the principal committee chairmen such as Gorst were being kept at arm's length, although all were invited to attend. Griffiths said about Gorst: 'I was concerned about his conflict of interests.'

Gorst claimed he had the greatest development expertise within the club and he oversaw its biggest asset – the estate. However, Griffiths maintained that Sir Michael Jenkins, Tony Alt and Michael McLintock provided the necessary links with the estates and finance committees.

Justin Dowley: 'Blake Gorst was right to be upset. He knew more about the property world than anyone else on that development committee.'

Blake Gorst: 'Charles Fry wanted to be chairman of the development committee to keep his nose in the trough. Instead they chose Griffiths and he knew nothing about property.'

Others on the MCC committee were not convinced that Griffiths was the right choice to lead it.

Julian Vallance: 'I don't know why Robert Griffiths was put in charge. He is adversarial by nature and had an abrasive manner. It was not a good way of keeping the MCC committee on side. They were serious people and didn't want such a confrontational person getting up their noses. He hit the wrong note too often. The development committee was the architect of its own downfall.'

Peter Leaver: 'I remember Oliver asking for people who were interested in becoming chairmen of the development committee. I would have been interested, but I had too much work. There were only two proper candidates: Robert Griffiths and Charles Fry – ignore Blake Gorst. It wasn't a great choice. Charles Fry had very little brains and Robert Griffiths was almost permanently pissed. What a choice.

'Robert held himself out as being a great planning silk. All I can tell you is that I have a lot of friends in the judiciary, and not one of them can remember Robert Griffiths. But Robert was chosen and he was given free range to appoint his own committee. He chose the great and the good. I thought it was utterly ridiculous that it was packed full of people who knew Charles Rifkind. You shouldn't have a committee so close to one of the protagonists.'

There were polar opposite opinions also about some of those that sat alongside Griffiths.

Oliver Stocken: 'Tony Alt and Michael McLintock were two good choices, sound and shrewd. Tony is a toughie, although not everybody's cup of tea. He used to be pretty shambolic, almost uncouth. A rough diamond. But whatever you might say about him, people at Rothschild, where he has spent 40 years, obviously think a lot of him.'

Lord Grabiner had a rather different viewpoint: 'Michael McLintock was an absolute prat. A finance bloke with an insurance company and supportive of the Stocken team. You could never get a straight answer out of him. Also, he was determined to make sure that nobody outside MCC made any money out of it. You never knew where he was coming from.

'Alt was a very silly man. He was at Rothschild, which you might think means a chap knows what he's talking about, but in the meetings he talked such gibberish. A very weird bloke. Absolute second-rater. He was a

Jekyll and Hyde type figure, you could have a conversation with him over a cup of coffee and think "He's not a bad chap." Then you would go into the meeting and he would come out of left field, with all sorts of crap. I think a lot of these people were motivated only by the proximity to the committee room at Lord's, loved all that stuff and loved the involvement.'

'Brian McGowan and myself were the most vocal members of the development committee. Brian is probably not as angry about it as I am. He tried more than I did to create some lines of communication, but Oliver Stocken is just a shit, basically, and I couldn't get anywhere with him. His mate Justin Dowley was a nasty piece of work as well.'

McGowan agreed with Grabiner that together they had the most to say. He said: 'It was pretty establishment, but two of the outside guys were Tony Grabiner and myself. We both spoke up a lot. We were independent. Everyone else wanted to be on the main committee – they're all cast out of the same mould. Look at them – they take a one-year sabbatical and then they're back in. It's the last bloody thing I want to do. I don't care whom I upset.

'This guy Griffiths. I went to his office chambers and he's got cricket paintings – it's an obsession for them. It's got nothing to do with commercial – it has everything, in most cases, to do with their MCC positions going forward. The guy from Rothschild, Tony Alt, was particularly difficult. I don't know what agenda he came with, but it wasn't mine. He was trying to show how clever he was as a merchant banker. He was trying to bullshit everyone around the table. They thought "He's deputy chairman of Rothschild, so he must know what he was talking about."'

Peter Leaver: 'We never really got reports from Robert. There were all these grandiose schemes of digging under the Nursery End. They didn't seem to understand that once you start digging, the cost rockets and we would never have got planning permission. It was cloud cuckoo land.'

In turn, Griffiths wasn't impressed with the personnel on the main committee: 'You had people like Mike Brearley. I always thought he was a thinking cricketer who would weigh up things properly, but I wasn't impressed with his approach. I expected a more balanced view. He sat there and let things just go over him, not wanting to get involved. It would have helped to have support from people like Brearley who are respected for what they have achieved in cricket.'

The outspoken Grabiner stood alongside Griffiths in objecting to interference from the main committee when the development group had been appointed to do a specific job.

Grabiner: 'The main committee decided eventually to develop the leasehold land. They appoint a development committee and the terms of the appointment are to identify a development partner. It was no longer an argument of "should we or shouldn't we" – the argument was who was going to be doing it. And having identified the developer, MCC would agree a plan.

'We had several meetings over 15 months at Lord's. I attended every single one. Without exaggeration, the majority of the meetings consisted of Stocken and Dowley putting forward arguments, in effect, against doing anything. We used to have 20 minutes, half an hour, of this every single time. Our task was to find a suitable developer, so please could we focus on doing precisely that?'

MCC adviser Alistair Parker was also perplexed by Stocken and Dowley's stance: 'We had a development committee set up, consisting of highly distinguished people with a wide range of skill sets. The meetings were highly professional. I remember being surprised with John Major. I had the public perception of him, probably formed partly from *Spitting Image*, but I was stunned by his accuracy and sharpness. He got it straight away.

'Stocken and Dowley sat in from time to time, and that's the bit I don't understand from what happened later. They were supportive, and Robert Griffiths on several occasions went around the table to get their views on each decision.'

Dowley's influence as MCC treasurer was clear when the main committee later agreed the change of minutes, confirming that no SGM with members would be held over The Vision until the Dowley-led finance committee were 'comfortable to proceed'. And with Stocken taking over as chairman at the start of October 2009, The Vision was now being opposed by the two most powerful officials before the development committee met for the first time on 10 December 2009.

At the end of the year, Vision project director Batts gave an update presentation at Lord's, along with Ben Duckworth of Herzog & de Meuron. It was attended by most MCC committee members, though not by Stocken or Dowley – even though they had a main committee meeting an hour later.

A further divide resulted from a letter sent by Bradshaw to Rifkind and his partner Jonathan Levy on 31 January 2010, setting out the basis for their preliminary discussions with developers. It contained conditions that were unacceptable to Rifkind; him not agreeing to them led to the breakdown of a joint venture that had never got off the ground.

The main sticking point was MCC needing to reach 'an acceptable agreement with ECB as to the future staging of major cricket matches and tournaments at Lord's'. MCC are apprehensive every time the renewal date for their major match hosting contract with ECB approaches, but Rifkind felt strongly that MCC's staging of matches was not his business. In addition, he felt how MCC spent their proceeds from the residential development should not be part of the contract. He was not prepared to keep funding a project that had already cost him around £1 million until MCC gave more clarity to the development process and were prepared to engage the members in the project.

Rifkind: 'The plan was that we should spend £5 million each on achieving planning permission. As the project started, the bills from Herzog were coming in fast. Everyone was going backwards and forwards with different ideas. When we got close to £2 million in terms of combined spend, it became clear that I needed an element of certainty if we were to spend additional funds. I wanted MCC to go to the members and receive their consent for the Vision for Lord's, but we kept being stalled and it became clear that I couldn't go on spending money without a formal commitment.

'My costs were significantly more than £1 million because I had other bills going around, whether it be the legal fees, finance deals or the internal costs of the day-to-day management. My actual spend on costs was just under £4 million.'

Rifkind officially stalled the joint venture in a letter to Bradshaw on

4 February 2010, further aggravated by two clauses MCC had inserted in the partnership terms.

'As you and your professional advisers well understand, we do not really understand the relevancy or accept as key preconditions:

"The club satisfying itself as to both the initial capital cost of the proposed extended facilities and the ongoing financial burden of maintaining them."

"The club being able to reach an acceptable agreement with the ECB as to the future staging of major cricket matches and tournaments at Lord's."

'I quite appreciate and fully support the importance of these two matters to MCC. However, how MCC determines on investing its receipts is a matter you have, quite properly in our view, reserved discretion in the draft heads of terms.

'We do not see it as a matter for the joint partnership. Again, MCC sought complete discretion on the new ground capacity, so similarly we cannot accept your staging agreements are a primary condition precedent in any form. It is not realistic to expect any party, including RLP, to expend material sums on the project if the process within the club for taking it forward remains unclear. Naturally, we would be delighted to urgently work with yourself and your lawyers to get the draft supplement letter into a form we can both sign and exchange.'

The development committee met on the same day Rifkind wrote to Bradshaw. The minutes of that meeting portray the confusion and conflict around The Vision, as well as the influence of property developer Jamie Ritblat.

Present: Chairman Robert Griffiths, Tony Alt, Mike Atherton, Scott Baker, Tony Grabiner, Michael Jenkins, Michael McLintock, Jamie Ritblat, Keith Bradshaw, David Batts plus advisers, Alistair Parker, Robert Ebdon, Dermot Rice, Blake Gorst, Simon Gibb (MCC assistant secretary, finance).

Absent: Tony Lewis, Sir John Major, Brian McGowan.

Batts: 'The finance committee are concerned about the projected negative values of the undercroft.'

Parker: 'Should MCC and RLP take on a development partner and start the process, or should this wait until planning permission has been obtained?'

Griffiths: 'If MCC/RLP are to consider submitting a planning application on their own, it might take a considerable amount of time, particularly if an appeal and a public inquiry are necessary.'

Parker: 'Many companies sounded out make the point MCC/RLP are not developers and do not have the appropriate experience.'

Alt: 'What alternative do the club have? I would like to see a financial analysis.'

Ritblat: 'The club must be completely clear what it wants, and I think this is still unclear. While this remains so, it will be difficult to enter into a meaningful agreement with a developer. The rationale for the planning permission for residential development is purely an enabling development for MCC. To that extent, an agreement with a developer would add nothing at this stage.'

Griffiths: 'What is your recommendation?'

Ritblat: 'It's the same as it was a year ago – to employ a development manager who could control the process for MCC. It's important MCC remains in control of the process.'

Grabiner: 'I agree with Jamie. Any decision should be governed by MCC. But I do not see how this should lead Jamie to conclude MCC should not enter into an agreement with a developer at this stage, provided the ground rules are in place and understood by both sides.'

Griffiths: 'The developer's input would be required in preparing the planning application. To do it the other way round, as Jamie seems to be recommending, could lead to the requirement for a larger residential development. However good the market may be, it is highly unlikely that the return from the enabling development would be sufficient for all MCC facilities.'

Ritblat: 'This is true, but the reality is that the scale of the development is already known. The risk of not achieving planning permission is not materially affected whether or not an agreement is in place with a developer at this stage.'

Griffiths: 'The benefit of having an early agreement with a developer is to ensure the planning permission was attractive to a developer. I would feel far more comfortable with the input from a chosen partner because of MCC and RLP's lack of experience in this field.'

Alt: 'I would like to understand the financial difference in signing up a development partner before or after planning permission.'

Parker: 'All companies had agreed with the calculation of £2,000 per square foot. The varied element is what reward each of the companies would require for taking the process through planning.'

Griffiths: 'Neither MCC nor RLP are experienced enough to take forward such a prestigious project, and therefore assistance is required.'

Jenkins: 'What does Jamie think about the disadvantages of signing a contract before planning permission?'

Ritblat: 'There is a great deal of uncertainty surrounding a project with such a long timescale, and it is inevitable there will be adaptions. You could think about engaging a development partner to assist in the process but with no commitment until after planning permission. I accept MCC or RLP need experience, but this could be gained far more cheaply than by employing a developer at this stage.'

Baker: 'What is RLP's view?'

Griffiths: 'They accept that they do not have the appropriate development experience and they would be supportive of engaging with a developer.'

Gorst: 'The project has become too complex. Would it be possible to look at the Wellington Road site as a stand-alone residential development?'

Griffiths: 'This would not be possible, as the residential development is only possible as an enabling development for the MCC facilities.'

Grabiner: 'I accept it is important to be careful in the choice of developer. I believe there is no argument about engaging with a developer at this stage, and receiving their full input into the planning process, bearing in mind the content of the application, should ultimately be a matter for MCC.'

Griffiths: 'I feel the consensus of the meeting is that a relationship with a prospective development partner should be explored. That's not to say Jamie's suggestion of strengthening the in-house experience should not also be followed.'

Ritblat: 'The club should not put itself into a position where it is over-committed.'

Bradshaw: 'It is important to keep the members in mind, and a development partner should not be engaged without members' permission.'

Griffiths: 'To sum up, the committee has accepted Alistair Parker's recommendation to engage with a development partner. The committee also accepts Jamie's point that more specialist input from a consultant might also be required.'

All: 'Agreed.'

Griffiths: 'MCC is a private club, but it has a public duty and should operate in an open and transparent way in the engagement of a development partner. The recommendation from Alistair Parker is that a shortlist should be drawn up and a competitive process undertaken.'

Ritblat: 'MCC and RLP should advertise for interest from developers, and then Cushman & Wakefield should draw up a shortlist.'

This process was approved.

Griffiths: 'A draft letter to RLP has been circulated to the committee. Please could you look at the two preconditions to which they object? These clauses had not initially been put to RLP, but it was the view of some senior members of the club that these conditions should be introduced. I believe if MCC does not agree to waive these conditions, the agreement with RLP will fall through.'

Rice: 'The desire to speak to developers has led to the need to regularise the arrangement with RLP. This is required to maintain goodwill and to agree the basis on which RLP and MCC will conduct their affairs. Both parties should agree to continue on a joint basis to fund work on the development. The letter would give RLP the comforts it is seeking as to MCC's situation.'

Griffiths: 'In order to persuade RLP to move forward, they have asked for some key confirmations from MCC. They are that the club is prepared to recommend either a deal with a developer or heads of terms and an understanding as to costs. They also have a concern regarding a share of any planning gain under the Section 106 requirement. If MCC are able to conclude a beneficial deal with Westminster, this should not be used to reduce the return to RLP. Apart from these issues, the draft letter is effectively in an agreed form, subject to the parties reaching agreement on the two preconditions.'

Batts: 'The two issues are set out in a side letter asking for a full disclosure of RLP's commercial position and any third party's interest in RLP's land interests.'

Griffiths: 'As the two preconditions had been introduced by the MCC committee, it will be necessary to seek its permission to remove them from the draft letter.'

Gibb: 'The two preconditions raised issues which are very important to the finance committee. I understand RLP's position, but these are areas where the club need protection.'

Alt: 'The finance committee are concerned with the long-term financial stability of the club and whether the new stands would be viable if the club are not allocated sufficient major match days.'

Griffiths: 'Everyone accepts the development will not go ahead if it's not viable. Could the committee agree that provided the minimum threshold is in place and that provided there are general provisions to the effect that the development would not go ahead unless it is viable, the two preconditions could be removed from the letter?'

All: 'Agreed.'

Griffiths: 'The committee agree to recommend these two preconditions can be removed from the letter, as sufficient safeguards already exist and the general requirement from the scheme to be commercially viable provides sufficient protection for MCC.'

Batts: 'RLP are content to start refunding the project, on the basis that a date is established for the SGM. A date in September has been identified.'

Jenkins: 'In order to have a more structured relationship with RLP, it is important there is one person who conducts the communication with Mr Rifkind. I suggest the Vision for Lord's project director should be the main contact with RLP, and that if any members of the committee speak to Mr Rifkind, they should ensure Mr Batts is made aware.'

All: 'Agreed.'

Afterwards, a revised form of letter is sent to RLP, showing the proposal to be put to the main committee has removed the two preconditions that Rifkind found unacceptable. The next MCC committee meeting on 17 February approved the change and a confirmation letter was sent to RLP. However, Rifkind, who was becoming exhausted by the process, asked for a meeting with the chief executive, chairman, treasurer and chairman of the development committee to discuss MCC's decision-making. MCC responded through their lawyers, saying they did not think it necessary to amend its processes to accommodate RLP and the club expected the letters confirming the joint venture process to be agreed and signed by 3 March.

However, exchanges of emails between the lawyers – Slaughter & May for MCC and Berwin Leighton Paisner for RLP – did not resolve the issue and the letters had not been signed by the 3 March deadline, when a further development committee meeting took place.

Present: Griffiths, MCC president John Barclay, Alt, Baker, Grabiner, Jenkins, Major, McGowan, McLintock, Bradshaw, Batts, Parker, Ebdon, Rice.

Absent: Atherton, Lewis, Ritblat.

Griffiths: 'We need to sort a number of matters, including advertising for development partners and the mechanism for working with RLP.'

Parker: 'The development partner process I recommend is that following advertisements, a longlist of companies is drawn up, with the final shortlist of three invited to make financial proposals. It should be recognised that the advertisement will trigger enormous interest, some of it from inappropriate parties.'

Major: 'If the appropriate parties are already known, is it not possible to move directly to a shortlist?'

Griffiths: 'The major players have been approached and although the level of interest is good, it did not generate 15 to 20 serious responses. Five or six companies is not sufficient.'

Rice: 'Any development partner will expect MCC and RLP to have concluded a development agreement and be acting as a joint venture.'

Griffiths: 'RLP have not yet signed the co-operation letter. Are there any insurmountable issues?'

Rice: 'Mr Rifkind has a number of concerns about the committee process within MCC and he's worried about how decisions will emerge, but the outstanding issues are minor ones.

RLP has been asked to disclose its financial structure and to indicate whether there are any founders or backers who would be expected to benefit from the transaction. It is extremely important from MCC's point of view to know exactly who has an interest in the land. It is RLP's commercial interests, which are relevant to MCC. It's already known that Investec and Network Rail have registered interests.'

Jenkins: 'This point is vital. MCC need to know what conditions Investec are likely to put on the financing of the project.'

Alt: 'Where have your reached contract-wise with RLP?'

Rice: 'A side letter which sets out financial arrangements and the minimum threshold has been agreed.'

Alt: 'It is important to know who the parties to the development agreement are, in the event of any negotiations surrounding the minimum threshold.'

Grabiner: 'It's very important this point is answered.'

Baker: 'Are MCC vulnerable to the position changing in the future, regarding those who have interests in RLP?'

Griffiths: 'This question has been asked and these two points are outstanding with RLP. It will not be possible to go forward until these points have been answered satisfactorily.'

McLintock: 'If the minimum threshold is reached but the costs of rebuilding are far in excess of what has been envisaged, would MCC be obliged to go ahead with the redevelopment?'

Griffiths: 'That would be controlled by negotiation with the planning authority and phasing of the project. The club do not want to be put into a position where it is under any obligation to carry out works which it could not afford.'

Jenkins: 'If the minimum threshold is met, then under the terms of the agreement with RLP, MCC would be obliged to allow the residential development to go ahead. This would require MCC to carry out some works – such as moving the Nursery Pavilion, indoor school and car park.'

Grabiner: 'The committee's concern is to preserve the flexibility of the club's position to cover any eventuality.'

Jenkins: 'The key question is whether the planning authority would take account of social projects to offset Section 106 requirements.'

Griffiths: 'No affordable housing is acceptable on site, but it might be necessary to identify an alternative site.'

Major: 'Are the Section 106 requirements for the Wembley Stadium redevelopment and the Olympic Village known?'

Grabiner: 'This discussion has been helpful. When the planning application is being prepared, the Section 106 requirements have to be carefully considered.'

Batts: 'MCC would use its capital receipts from the development for the benefit of cricket, but RLP would not. This might be an issue for the planning authority.'

Baker: 'The planning authority might be more sympathetic to the social obligations being met by the development of the ground if the project is MCC's alone.'

Batts: 'The intention is for RLP's contribution to be returned to MCC for reinvestment in cricket.'

McGowan: 'Have RLP signed the letter?'

Griffiths: 'I hoped to be able to report to the meeting that the RLP letter had been signed. They have been given time to consider the matter and, for whatever reason, have not responded as quickly as had been hoped.'

Rice: 'RLP only involved their lawyers in the negotiation of the letter at a late stage. Progress is being made and I will be disappointed if the letter is not signed this week.'

Griffiths: 'Charles Rifkind would like to be part of the development committee and attend its meetings. I did not think this would be permissible, as the development committee is an MCC committee. However, a mechanism should be put in place whereby the club could work closely with its partner. I suggest a small group from the development committee could become a joint venture group and meet with RLP.'

All: 'Agreed'

Major: 'It is important to give regular briefings to Westminster City Council and the Mayor of London.'

Griffiths: 'I intend to form smaller groups of development committee members to address community engagement.'

Batts: 'The RLP letter stipulates an SGM taking place by the end of September 2010. It will be necessary to undertake considerable preparatory work with members, including a series of roadshows in advance of the SGM. It should be remembered that if the members do not support the project, it will not go ahead.'

The RLP letter still remained unsigned in April, despite MCC dropping the two clauses. Rifkind decides on a different tack: realising that a joint venture will never work, he offers to sell his interest at both ends of the ground to MCC. This is seized upon at Lord's as him terminating their agreement, which he still disputes. The move brought a different dynamic to the debate, with MCC preferring to buy Rifkind out if the terms were reasonable.

Rifkind: 'I was very frustrated, so I asked MCC to come up with an offer. It never materialised – I never got a price.'

Meanwhile, Stocken laid out his feelings about Griffiths and his development committee overreaching their responsibilities in an email on 26 April that was copied to Dowley, Ritblat, Bradshaw and Batts. The email and its responses demonstrate the serious clash of personalities within MCC that had already made The Vision seemingly untenable.

Stocken wrote: 'We need to achieve a balance between your feeling that you need to have unfettered discretion to negotiate on behalf of the club and my view that we need to have in place appropriate lines of communication to ensure that we can show we have correct governance throughout. We need to operate within a similar governance structure as any corporate body would when dealing with shareholders' funds. More than one person has to be involved.

'My purpose of setting up, six months ago, the small group of you, Justin [Dowley], Keith [Bradshaw], David [Batts] and myself – now joined by Jamie [Ritblat] – was to ensure that at all times the group understood the process we were following and could have input when necessary. It would furthermore ensure that when matters were brought before the committee/trustees, there was a small group who had a united view as to the action being recommended. In this, you are supported by a strong, experienced group you have assembled on the development committee, although inevitably the number of times they can meet is limited.

'At last Wednesday's meeting, it was generally agreed that with the changed circumstances regarding RLP, three immediate steps would be taken.

1. A letter prepared by Dermot Rice would be sent to RLP by Keith, to include confirmation as to what is to be sold, the authority held by Charles to negotiate on behalf of his investors and the status of his discussions with Network Rail, the hospital etc. The letter is now ready to go.

2. Jamie would get himself briefed by Alistair [Parker] on the financial analysis done so far by Alistair and familiarise himself with any constraints etc surrounding the property under discussion.

3. You and Jamie would then sit down with Alistair to formulate the structure of the transaction which the club might find acceptable and then go through this with Justin, Keith, David and me.

'Until this has been done and Charles has replied to the letter, no further discussions should take place with Charles. In the meantime, Alastair will continue to analyse all expressions of interest received through the recent advertisements.

'The next main committee meeting is on 19 May and this will be an appropriate time for you and I to obtain agreement of the development committee as how we feel we should move forward and our respective responsibilities In the new and changed circumstance of RLP wishing to sell. I do understand that this may well have to be a different process to that which the committee agreed when the development committee was originally conceived under your chairmanship.'

Stocken also brought up the subject of his involvement with property company Stanhope, which Griffiths saw as a serious conflict of interests.

'Separately, you have raised my continuing non-executive chairmanship of Stanhope – a matter which I raised with you six months ago. Were the club to decide it wished to use Stanhope in some way, I would stand down as Stanhope chairman.

'Stanhope does not carry out major residential development, nor does it have significant funds to put into a transaction. Its role is to advise clients on assembling sites, obtaining planning permission and work alongside developers/constructors. It may be that Stanhope decides to withdraw from any further discussions or involvement, so as to remove any possible concern regarding conflicts now or in the future.

'Lots to discuss – not easy. I know you won't agree with what I am saying, but we must now ensure that everyone is clear what is the way forward. The respective responsibilities of the committee, trustees, the development committee, the executive, you and me etc.

Griffiths replies less than two hours later and was furious that Jamie Ritblat had been added to the small negotiating group. Ritblat, who had his own property company Delancey, had been a powerful voice in the development committee meetings he attended. MCC had initially asked his property magnate father Sir John Ritblat for advice, but Ritblat senior had introduced his son to the MCC battleground.

Griffiths retorted: 'I have to come back immediately on your email I have just received ahead of our meeting on Thursday. I cannot emphasis how concerned I am about Jamie Ritblat being involved in a quasi-executive capacity and having access to confidential information.

'As chairman of the development committee, I am responsible to the main committee and I would have thought, even on an interim basis, you would accept that Jamie should not be included in discussions which gives him access to highly confidential information which would be of assistance to a prospective bidder.

'I thought I could not have made it clearer in my earlier emails and in my reaction in the earlier meeting that this is not something that I can simply go along with. As far as I am concerned, he should not have access to any information of this kind. No delegated powers have been given to him to act in the way you suggest.

'In my view, he should no longer be involved in the process at all, and I believe I have the authority to remove him from the committee. If necessary, I will convene an emergency development committee meeting and explain what has happened. You, Justin and now Jamie are just riding roughshod over a matter which has been expressly delegated to me by the main committee.

'There still seems to be no recognition on your part that this is a problem. I do not, therefore, authorise the sending of the letter, and I do not give my authority as chairman of the development committee to Jamie's continued involvement in this matter. I have instructed Alistair Parker that Jamie is not to be given any further financial analysis. I am not prepared to discuss the matter with Jamie. In fact, I am considering the steps which I need to take to remove Jamie from membership of the development committee.

'As to those other matters which relate to your own conflict of interest, I still remain very concerned about your position. I also do not think it helps in these circumstances for you to phone Alistair Parker directly to inquire about your company's prospects of being considered a candidate for involvement in the development process. You must see that this is potentially an embarrassment, both in terms of your own interest and in terms of Jamie's.'

Two minutes after sending the explosive email to Stocken, Griffiths forwarded Stocken's letter and his reply to Lord Grabiner:

'Please see an email I received this morning from Oliver and my reply. He still does not seem to understand.'

The battle lines of Stocken, Dowley, Gorst and Ritblat versus Rifkind, Griffiths and Grabiner had been drawn, and it was only a matter time before it came to a head.

There were others on the development committee who were not supportive of Griffiths' leadership, one of whom was reportedly Michael McLintock.

Dowley: 'McLintock was seriously unimpressed at the way the development committee was run. He thought they were out of control from the start and were acting like they were the main decision-making body.'

Ahead of the next development committee meeting, Griffiths sent out a discussion paper updating members about RLP's stance. The conflict and confidentiality issues around Stocken's chairmanship of property business Stanhope and Ritblat's involvement in the inner circle negotiating group were his concerns.

Griffiths wrote: 'When we last met, RLP had yet to sign a letter which, although not legally binding, would have formed the framework for taking forward a joint venture arrangement. That letter was never signed by RLP and the offer contained in it was ultimately withdrawn by the club.

'A second letter, which asked for full disclosure of any other interests in the land (legal or beneficial), has not at this stage been responded to by RLP. However, it subsequently became clear through discussions that Investec had a third interest in the land. It also seems that another third party has a third interest in the proceeds.

'There was then further correspondence between the club and RLP, which culminated in the most recent letter – dated 7 May – which confirms RLP would be a willing vendor of its entire interest in the Wellington Road end. If we are unable to agree the disposal of RLP's interest, RLP would be willing to continue on a joint venture basis. There are also issues relating to conflicts of interest and confidentiality which we should touch on.'

Rifkind: 'I got to the point of absolute frustration with Keith Bradshaw and his merry men. I was dealing with different personalities, all promising everything and delivering nothing.

Selling my interest looked the only way of making it happen.'

The 11 May 2010 development committee was always going to be lively. The meeting started with Stocken declaring his Stanhope chairmanship, raised by Griffiths in their email exchange. Griffiths also brought up Jamie Ritblat's potential conflict of interests as a property developer, but didn't name him.

Present: Griffiths, Stocken, Dowley, Alt, Atherton, Baker, Grabiner, Lewis, McGowan, Ritblat, Bradshaw, Batts, Parker, Rice.

Absent: Jenkins, McLintock, Major, Ebdon.

Stocken: 'I declare I'm chairman of a company, Stanhope, whom have had initial discussions regarding the development, but it's unlikely they will proceed.'

Griffiths: 'I'm also aware that a member of the development committee has a potential conflict and this should be dealt with by a register of interests. Can Alistair [Parker] report on progress since the last meeting?'

Parker: 'Advertisements have been placed in the UK press and in Australia, the Pacific Rim and New York. The website has received 31,500 hits. There has been interest from six global companies and six premium London residential development companies. The broad consensus is that the property value is in the region of £2,500 per square foot. If this rate is achieved, the value of the residential development would be around £250 million.'

Batts: 'At one time, the development partner would have had to be acceptable to both MCC and RLP. Is this still the case?'

Parker: 'Both parties have agreed to share information about who they are speaking to, and the agreement is still in place. I believe some companies had approached RLP, with a view to buying their interest.'

Griffiths: 'Two letters have been sent to RLP. The first stated that MCC and RLP will co-operate in a joint venture to take a planning application forward. Neither party will deal with any third party without the other's consent and knowledge. RLP have not responded, so the joint venture has not gone ahead. MCC's offer has been revoked. Subsequently, RLP wrote stating a wish to sell their interest in the land at the Wellington Road. It is now for the development committee to decide whether it would be best for the club to buy that land.'

Alt: 'There is a fundamental question to be answered before considering the negotiation. Are the club bound, either morally or legally, to the 50/50 split with RLP?'

Griffiths: 'The basis for the current partnership is an equal contribution to the project and an equal distribution of the proceeds, subject to a formula for the replacement of MCC's existing facilities. And that understanding between the parties should be reflected in the negotiations.'

Stocken: 'The situation altered when RLP failed to reply to MCC's letters. I feel extremely uncomfortable adopting a 50/50 position.'

Alt: 'I agree.'

Grabiner: 'It's important to decide first whether MCC want to acquire RLP's interest and the consequences of that decision. Sir Scott Baker said at a previous meeting that the planning authority might be more sympathetic to the social obligations being met by the development to the ground if the project is MCC's alone. We should focus on whether MCC wish to buy RLP's stake or leave ourselves open to RLP negotiating a sale with a third party.'

Alt: 'The first step is to ascertain whether there is an obligation to retain a 50/50 split with RLP or whether this could be reduced to, say, 20 per cent.'

Dowley: 'The situation is that RLP has indicated a wish to sell its interest. What needs to be determined is how to purchase that interest as cheap as possible.'

Griffiths: 'It would be a considerable advantage to MCC if RLP's interest could be transferred to the club.'

Stocken: 'It is essential to buy RLP's entire interest in the ground, including Grove End Road.'

Ritblat: 'I wonder why RLP want to sell at this time. They are close to an agreement with MCC. The indications are that planning permission will be granted and the value of the site lies in the planning permission. On the basis of their unreliability, it would be unwise to do the deal for one end of the ground without the other.'

Baker: 'The committee need to establish its position if RLP refuse to sell the Grove End Road element. We should buy whatever is available. It is concerning MCC has not seen any documentation relating to the agreement between RLP and Network Rail.'

Griffiths: 'RLP have an obligation to pay Network Rail £7.5 million on the grant of planning permission, and that obligation would pass to MCC If we bought out RLP.'

McGowan: 'We should not miss the Wellington Road opportunity if the price is appropriate, even if it is unsatisfactory that RLP still have an interest in Grove End Road.'

Bradshaw: 'It is important to buy out RLP in its entirety.'

Ritblat: 'We can afford to wait and in the meantime carry out some elements of development which do not rely on RLP's agreement.'

Baker: 'How great is the danger of RLP selling to a third party?'

Griffiths: 'It's a real danger.'

Stocken: 'The MCC committee need to discuss on 19 May whether the club have the alternative of rebuilding at least one stand from our own resources. We are under no pressure and can afford to play the long game.'

Grabiner: 'What is the property situation on Grove End Road?'

Batts: 'There are some properties which belong neither to RLP nor MCC. Both parties have agreed that if any of these become available for purchase, they will attempt to acquire them jointly. The MCC committee has determined the development should only proceed in the first phase at Wellington Road. The committee indicated the club should not agree a deal with RLP for any development along Grove End Road for the time being.'

Stocken: 'The development committee has been established to take the Vision for Lord's through to the granting of planning permission. It has never been envisaged that the club would buy out RLP's interest – this is a completely new situation.'

Griffiths. 'I disagree. The chance to acquire the head lease does not change the nature of the process – it is still necessary to achieve planning permission to unlock the value of the site. The benefit of owning the head lease without any restrictions is that MCC would be in total control.'

Stocken: 'The MCC committee has agreed to the application of planning permission in partnership with RLP. The committee has not considered the possibility of buying out RLP's interest, and this would need to be considered at the meeting on 19 May.'

Griffiths: 'It is important to consider the consequence of not entering into negotiations with RLP. There is a real danger of the project grinding to a halt, with no prospect of it being resurrected. Can I ask the club chairman and treasurer, are there senior members of the MCC committee who are not entirely supportive of the Vision for Lords?'

Stocken: 'Some elements of The Vision are very good for the club. There are other elements about which I have reservations.'

Dowley: 'I'm very supportive of The Vision, but my concern is the funding. I will not support the club using its balance sheet to take a property development risk. I accept the risk would be mitigated if we enter into a funding agreement with a property developer.'

Grabiner: 'My one concern has been the existence of RLP. It is encouraging to think MCC might be able to acquire their interest, but it is disappointing that there appears a lack of an appetite for the transaction.'

Stocken: 'I'm not averse, but there might be merit in taking time.'

Baker: 'Why do RLP want to sell?'

Griffiths: 'There are a number of reasons, which might include the removal of risk that Westminster would require a very substantial payment by way of a Section 106 contribution from RLP's share of the proceeds. A sale also gives them no further liability in respect of the planning application costs.'

Rice: 'I think RLP have seen a change of attitude from MCC, which makes them believe the club is now a willing purchaser.'

McGowan: 'How real is the possibility that RLP would be able to sell to a third party?'

Ritblat: 'There is always a possibility that someone will take the risk, but not many companies will be interested. I'm keen for the Vision for Lord's to come to fruition, but MCC can afford to wait and this is not the case for RLP.'

Griffiths: 'What's RLP's position with their support from Investec?'

Parker: 'Investec felt the land had sufficient value ten years ago to support RLP financially.

Griffiths: 'MCC are currently operating the Nursery Pavilion under a lease owned by RLP, which restricts its use to cricket-related events. The revenue is around £1.4 million per year. The consequence of losing that revenue is another factor. The development committee have been given the authority to do this within its terms of reference agreed by the MCC committee. However, it will not be possible to buy out RLP for £25 million – the sum is more likely to be £75 million.'

Parker: 'RLP know MCC would not contemplate paying a figure directly related to development value and would accept an initial sum, with the greater part payable on the granting of planning permission. But they are still looking for a significant initial payment.'

Griffiths: 'They are now looking to receive a similar sum to the minimal threshold which had originally been guaranteed to MCC of around £92.5 million, plus any uplift depending on sales. On that basis, RLP would accept an initial payment for £25 million to transfer the head lease. Further tranches of payment would be required over a period of time, and the final sum would not be payable unless planning permission is granted.'

Ritblat: 'MCC would also assume all the risk of the development in this scenario.'

Stocken: 'What is the formal valuation of the land?'

Parker: 'Cushman & Wakefield would need to understand the nature of the deal before giving a formal valuation. The deal being contemplated would change from a 50/50 share of the revenue of around £200 million to an upfront sum to RLP plus a top-up balance from the development partner. This, in total, would be in the order of £75 million.'

Alt: 'This is a much better deal as far as RLP are concerned than the one originally proposed with MCC, particularly taking into account the likely capital gains tax payment and the Section 106 contributions required by Westminster City Council. I'm in favour of paying an upfront sum to RLP, but £25 million is too high.'

Griffiths: 'Can the committee agree in principle that MCC should engage in negotiations with RLP to investigate a deal that can be recommended to the MCC committee?'

Grabiner: 'The approval should be subject to three points. That it should be made clear to RLP that MCC do not believe it is realistic to assume they would be able to sell their interest to a third party. That MCC would only be interested in buying the entire interest, Wellington Road and Grove End Road. There should also be a defined period of time in which they would not negotiate with a third party.'

All: 'Agreed.'

McGowan: 'The finance committee will need to give the negotiators an indication of the sum MCC would be prepared to pay.'

Dowley: 'Jamie Ritblat has kindly agreed to carry out an analysis of the likely amount required, and I would like to see that analysis before making a decision.'

Stocken: 'The next step is for the MCC committee to discuss the matter at its next meeting, and can the secretary prepare a paper for that meeting? A small group should be set up to discuss the strategy for the negotiation, consisting of the secretary, chairman of development, treasurer, Vision for Lord's project director and Jamie Ritblat.'

Griffiths said: 'I want the development committee to be closely involved with the negotiation, so can Brian McGowan and Lord Grabiner be added to the group for their additional expertise?'

All: 'Agreed.'

Griffiths: 'There seems to be a suggestion that MCC should consider developing one stand ahead of the Vision for Lord's. I have real reservations about this, because I believe the application for planning permission should consist of the residential development, the tunnels and all the stands.'

Stocken: 'Discussions about the Masterplan have been taking place for seven years, and there is a need to show the members something is being delivered for them. The secretariat should make a recommendation about which of the stands could be developed first. It is also important to demonstrate to RLP the club has other options for development.'

Griffiths: 'This decision should not be taken without specialist advice. The new Warner Stand will only increase capacity by 1,186 seats and will cost £22.3 million. I'm also concerned that the argument of the residential development being an enabling development for the Vision for Lord's might be weakened if Westminster City Council are aware the club is capable of redeveloping a stand from its own resources.

'There has been some debate concerning the role and terms of reference of the development committee. It is a principal committee which has direct responsibly to the MCC committee by way of recommendation. It's important to guard against the prospect of a relatively uninformed lay committee ignoring the recommendation of a specialist committee.'

Grabiner: 'I have had concerns with the role of the development committee in governance terms, but the attendance of Oliver and Justin is important.'

Ahead of the MCC committee meeting in May, Sir John Major wrote a letter to Stocken. He wanted it circulated at the meeting, which he couldn't attend due to a prior engagement. But Stocken didn't do so – a decision that has reverberated down the years.

Stocken: 'Just because John Major asked me to do something, doesn't mean I have to do it. Why should I automatically do what Major tells me?'

Major wrote: 'The Vision for Lord's has been very well received. We should not readily dilute it for a smaller development. Too many expectations have been raised and, in any event, the attraction of the scheme itself calls for its full implementation.

'I do understand some members of the committee may be frustrated at the potential profit earned by RLP if Mr Rifkind is bought out. However, this is subordinate to achieving the development itself and we should therefore keep things in proportion.

'We should negotiate with Mr Rifkind, preferably through a professional negotiator in order to remove any personal irritations or frustrations he might have with MCC. Buying out Mr Rifkind is a change of plan. We should therefore advise Westminster Council of the new circumstances. I see no advantage in keeping the planners out of the loop.

'The Vision has been gaining traction over recent months. We should not lose momentum. I would not favour a delay in negotiating with Mr Rifkind in the hope of seeking a better price. Even if this were to succeed, it might be offset by rising prices and is equally likely to lead to a stalemate that might delay the development of Lord's for far too long.

'This note is dictated in haste, but I hope it covers the principal points. I wish you well in the discussions tomorrow.'

The MCC committee discussions the following day took place without mention of the former prime minister's letter to Stocken.

Bradshaw: 'RLP have been sent a letter proposing broad terms to proceed to planning and beyond on the Vision for Lord's, together with side letters about the minimum threshold and disclosure of RLP's financial backers.

'RLP voiced particular concern about how the Section 106 requirement would be handled. And, after following the matter up with RLP on at least three occasions, a decision was made to withdraw the letters.

'The club then received a letter from RLP offering to sell their Wellington Road interest. It's important to obtain a clear mandate for negotiations with RLP, and I recommend a negotiating group.

'Some figures have been mentioned already, with £75 million suggested by RLP comprising an upfront payment and then a formula for a payment structure following planning permission for the Vision for Lord's. But any proposal would need to be worked through carefully by the negotiating group. We will need feedback from Cushman & Wakefield as to the level of money potential development partners would provide.

'If we proceed with building a single stand in parallel to taking the Vision for Lord's to planning, Westminster Council will need to know the situation with RLP.'

Griffiths: 'My views don't entirely overlap with the chief executive. The club shouldn't miss out on a very real opportunity to acquire the Wellington Road land. I feel RLP's offer is a tactical move rather than a change in their circumstance. Although the legal position is that our agreement with RLP is not legally binding, it wouldn't be ethically appropriate to withdraw at this stage. There is some risk of a claim being made against the club.

'I have conducted, together with Alistair [Parker] and David [Batts] informal negotiations with RLP for some time, and there looks to be a possibility of achieving a deal for a payment of £75 million. The attractiveness of the offer to RLP is avoiding capital gains tax, no more frustrations with the club's decision-making and not having to make potential additional payments to Westminster Council to satisfy planning conditions.'

Dowley: 'I'm not against the Vision for Lord's, but I am in favour of proceeding on a prudent and tough commercial basis. Now that RLP want to sell, the club's absolute priority must be to buy the land and, if possible, their Grove End Road properties as well. We must attempt to do this at as low a price as possible, so we shouldn't do anything now which might increase the perceived value.

'We must do everything possible to reduce RLP's expectations and room to manoeuvre. We don't know what pressures they might be under. One way of doing this would be to start the process of building another stand, which will probably take three years. And if, while doing that, the land came onto the market at an attractive price, the club should buy it. Otherwise no further action is required.

'There is a risk RLP will sell to someone else, but that's unlikely, as potential buyers will know that RLP have worked hard for ten years with nothing to show for it. And in any case, if that happens, the new owner would be under pressure to turn a profit on the asset, putting the club in a stronger negotiating position.

'I am reluctant to spend the club's money on a speculative asset, although others would argue that planning permission will greatly increase the value. But I do not feel this is an appropriate use of club funds.'

Rice: 'There is a need for the ground to be modernised in some areas, but it's not an urgent need and there's uncertainty around over cricket's future. So the committee should be certain over their finances.'

Lewis: 'We have been met with great enthusiasm everywhere we went on the roadshows. The members had great interest and pride in the project – they recognise MCC leads the way in architecture. If the decision is made to go with a single stand first, I wouldn't want it to affect the overall Vision for Lord's. I'm not sure the club will be the only ones interested in acquiring RLP's assets.'

Leaver: 'The way MCC is set up has frustrated Rifkind to the extent he now wants to sell. We should continue to use this structure to our advantage in the negotiating process.

We have an asset that is worth a lot of money, and both sides are aware of this. We should play the long game. It's very unlikely RLP will find another buyer. Due diligence will show there's no quick buck to be made here.'

Griffiths: 'RLP have mentioned a figure close to £100 million.'

Leaver: 'That's wholly unrealistic. We should ask RLP to provide a proper calculation of their assets, and these discussions should be carried out by a small group rather than the whole development committee. It should include Robert [Ebdon] and Jamie [Ritblat]. Once the ownership is resolved, we can proceed with the Vision for Lord's. I don't think developing a single stand independently should be done.'

Heyhoe Flint: 'It's upsetting so little progress has been made. We must keep the focus on the cricket.'

Gupte: 'I don't think the members will like the amount of money the club would spend on acquiring the leasehold land.'

Gorst: 'I think it likely that RLP will seek a very high price, which will make negotiations difficult. The Herzog scheme is too ambitious and denies the club other opportunities. I don't think we can do a deal with RLP. We should play the long game.'

Fry: 'I agree [with Blake Gorst]. The figures mentioned are completely unacceptable to MCC, and I cannot accept a deal which will provide RLP with more certainty of a profit than they have at present. I'm sure they know what potential development partners will be thinking. The Vision is a good idea in principle, but the undercroft is just too complicated.'

Carroll: I'm greatly concerned at the sums of money mentioned. There are not many occasions when we need the increase in capacity at Lord's. And if we don't get security of major matches in future, there's no point in building larger stands.'

Brearley: 'I've never been keen on the Vision for Lords. I prefer the piecemeal option. I support trying to obtain the land, and even if members were enthused by the Vision presentation, they will understand a more sober approach.'

Peters: 'Ten years ago, we made the decision not to bid over a certain amount for the Wellington Road strip. The current situation is a comparable one. The economic outlook is gloomy, and it could get worse. There's also a lack of information about major matches from the ECB. There's no urgency to do a deal or build a new stand when the future is still in the balance. It's clearly right to do a deal with RLP, but not at the levels mentioned.'

Vallance: 'The value of the Wellington Road strip is very small on any analysis, due to the length of the club's lease. I support buying RLP's properties, but not just the Wellington Road alone. My preference would be to develop the best cricket facilities elsewhere, as there is no reason they had to be at Lord's. All is needed is the best conditions for pitch preparation and the best practice facilities.'

Dowley: 'There is a premium to the club in owning its own land and not having to deal with a third party when considering redevelopment options.'

Lewis: 'I would support anything which did not abandon the Vision for Lord's, including building a single stand within the overall planning permission.'

Griffith: 'The club has reached the current position due to RLP being difficult – there is no need to deviate from the current strategy. RLP would lose all their risk if MCC purchased their interest, including a release from any commitment to Section 106 planning conditions. Unfortunately, I've come to the conclusion that the Nursery Ground would never be suitable for the staging of first-class matches, but I want to retain the area as an excellent practice facility. The indoor school is already an extremely good facility and should not be an overriding consideration for going ahead with The Vision, which I still support.'

Wileman: 'The committee must focus on what the club wishes to achieve, rather than blocking RLP in what they wish to achieve.'

Dowley: 'If a deal can be struck with RLP, then we can proceed to discussions with potential development partners. But if that's not possible, we will simply spend the reserves on redeveloping the single stand and make it clear to RLP that the club's funds are committed elsewhere.'

Stocken: 'The strong feeling of the committee is that the club should attempt to acquire RLP's total interest at Lord's.'

Griffiths: 'The advice from Alistair Parker is that the RLP interest is worth in the region of £100 million.'

Stocken: 'That is a valuation, not the result of a negotiation. If MCC can buy RLP's interest, it will be in the interests of the club to do so. It would be preferable to obtain all of the properties.'

Bradshaw: 'I will get the negotiating group into place quickly. We will obtain a valuation and then work with the finance committee to establish the financial parameters which would then form the brief for the independent negotiator.'

Batts: 'The negotiation could continue for some time, maybe two years or more, which could bring the price down.'

Griffiths: 'The consensus of the meeting is to play the long game and wait and see how the situation develops. In that case, there should be no further incurring of fees.'

Stocken: 'The next step is for the chief executive to write to RLP, stating MCC's interest in buying all his properties in and around Lord's. We must request RLP put their suggestions for how to proceed in writing. This reluctance to commit their views to paper is of continued concern.'

As instructed by the main committee, Bradshaw wrote to RLP on 27 May 2010:

> 'I think we both now agree that the best course open to us is for MCC and RLP to enter into an agreement under which the club agrees to acquire your interests at Lord's. On that basis, we believe the most productive next step would be for you to set out in writing the commercial terms that you would wish any such agreement to contain.
>
> 'I can confirm the MCC committee has authorised me to lead any negotiations with you. Whilst MCC does not wish to pre-empt our discussions, I think it is only right to make it clear the club would expect any agreement reached between us to cover not only Wellington Road, but also your interests at the Grove End Road of the ground.
>
> 'It may be a very considerable time before anything happens at Grove End Road. but the club believes any agreement reached between us must deal with both. I would be grateful if you could let me have a reply within two weeks from the date of this letter.'

Rifkind, who at the start of this saga was responding on the day, took until 11 June to reply. He said: 'I was exhausted and frustrated – it was basically one man against an institution. I had had enough.' He also didn't put a figure on how much he wanted, which Stocken thought might happen. Instead he wanted MCC to quote him a price.

Dowley: 'Robert Griffiths was telling us that Charles would sell for £75 million. I said that £7.5 million was more realistic. Without planning consent, it was just a property gamble.'

Rifkind wrote back to Bradshaw: 'As discussed, RLP are prepared to discuss a potential acquisition of RLP's interest in the Nursery End, although RLP continue to have a preference to work together within the agreed heads of terms of July 2009 in a joint venture.

'There is not a simple formula to place an outright value on RLP's interest. RLP are naturally concerned that placing any figure in writing may have an adverse impact for any future sales to a third party other than MCC. To determine a sale value, RLP would naturally look at the residual land value. RLP understand that both MCC and RLP's agents have advised that would be in the region of £200 million to £250 million. As agreed in the heads of terms, any distribution would be calculated on a 50/50 basis.

'If MCC were to acquire RLP's interest now unconditionally, RLP would be prepared to negotiate with MCC on the sum payable. However, it is RLP's understanding that this figure would exceed the amount MCC would be willing to pay to acquire RLP's interests.'

The stand-off with RLP once again dominated the next MCC committee meeting on 7 July.

Bradshaw: 'RLP do not wish to compromise their position by confirming a figure in writing.'

Dowley: 'Now that there is no agreement with RLP, we should stand back and take a long view. The project is being presented in an unbalanced way. There is no real analysis of what the club could do as an alternative. We have become a little too close to RLP and are dancing to its tempo.

'There are three options: collect £125 million by accepting a development partner, develop the ground more slowly on our own, or look again at developing on the club's own land, where the club would receive 100 per cent of the profit and therefore could potentially make do with a smaller residential development.'

Major: 'The club's reputation will not be enhanced by playing the long game.'

Parker: 'The club has received 20 responses to the global advert for a development partner and five have been shortlisted. They are Almacantar, Capital & Counties, Native Land, Grosvenor and Londonewcastle. Almacantar has already put in an offer proposing to buy the RLP land for £85 million. They have been asked to resubmit the bid according to the criteria, but their offer shows there are third parties out there willing to buy out RLP.'

Stocken: 'The committee's agreement has always been subject to the overall financial viability of the project. The executives are concerned about the number of days a larger Lord's will sell out.'

Dowley: 'I don't think RLP will sell its interest to someone else. It's a speculative position, without an agreement with MCC to develop the land.'

Gorst: 'The club are forecasting a loss in 2010 and could be in a similar position in 2011. Upgrading facilities will increase overheads without guaranteeing income. The undercroft destroys the financial viability of the Vision for Lord's. We should look to develop on our own land.'

Ritblat: 'I am doing a valuation report on MCC doing a development on their own land. It is worth considering.'

Batts: 'The negative value of the undercroft could be reduced if it included just the facilities MCC needed – museum, indoor school, better circulation and enlarged Nursery Ground.'

The development partner shortlist was then reduced to three – Almacantar plus Capital Counties and Native Land, who also put forward their proposals. Almacantar had the support of Rifkind, who was delighted to be able to take a back seat. But at the same time, MCC were considering other options. Rifkind discovered this on 23 July and immediately complained to MCC adviser Alistair Parker, who in turn emailed Batts:

'Had a call from RLP first thing this morning. Charles Rifkind has heard about an exercise to relook at MCC developing their freehold land, in order to avoid developing on his land. He regards this as a fundamental breach of the mutual understanding underlying the Vision for Lord's. As a consequence, he's very much inclined to now close his own deal with Almacantar and to refuse to engage with Capital Counties or Native Land. As agreed, will seek to persuade him to hold.

'Yesterday's meeting was the first I had heard that MCC were re-looking at an old issue. This was comprehensively explored through plans by various architects in 2003, 2004 and 2006 – and I thought consistently rejected by MCC on the grounds of a loss of a substantial part of the ground freehold. Indeed, I even did sketches (September 2002) and we revisited the issue again in June 2008.'

Mike Hussey, chief executive of Almacantar, also wanted more information from MCC about how the tender is progressing. He wrote to Bradshaw: 'I believe we have complied fully with your request and indeed have submitted a robust and generous offer that should lead to delivery of the Vision for Lord's.

'We have stated our rationale for selection of Almacantar as your chosen development partner and would like to know the formal process that you will now undertake. This project requires significant energy, drive as well as substantial financial commitment. To keep us engaged, I would encourage a swift and clear timescale for the next stage.'

Rifkind was equally frustrated at being kept in the dark about the development partner process and MCC working up other alternatives. He wrote to Alistair Parker:

'Further to our numerous conversations over the last few months concerning MCC's wish to introduce a development partner to the agreed Vision for Lord's, I would be grateful if you could confirm the following:

1. Who are the development partners that have been selected by MCC?

2. The terms upon which MCC have asked the shortlisted development partners to make an offer.

3. The date MCC expect to confirm their preferred development partner.

4. The date MCC expect to enter into a development

agreement.

5. Is the Vision for Lords the only proposal being considered? RLP have learnt alternative proposals are being considered which exclude the Wellington Road End.

'RLP understood the Vision for Lord's, designed by Herzog, had been agreed by the main committee in June 2009. Fees in excess of £2.5 million have been spent between RLP and MCC to obtain the agreed Vision.'

Parker wrote back: 'In response to the points you raised, I would confirm as follows:

1. The shortlisted development companies are Capital & Counties, Almacantar and Native Land.

2. The invitation to make a financial proposal (terms attached) was sent out on 12 August.

3. The deadline is 30 September, with a final selection made during the first two weeks of October

4. The intention is to enter into an agreement as soon as practical.

5. I have no instruction to consider alternative proposals although, as you may appreciate, our report will set out recommendations having considered all alternatives available to MCC.'

Rifkind wrote back seeking updates on 4 October, 19 October, 16 December and 3 May 2011. There were no replies.

While MCC were keeping Rifkind out of the loop, he was trying to bring more people into the MCC circle. He proposed a London-Amsterdam-Brussels charity bike ride, to be arranged under the MCC banner. The club turned him down, so Rifkind approached the Wellington Hospital. They embraced the idea, and the event raised £1.5 million for the British Red Cross and the Juvenile Diabetes Research Foundation. The cyclists included Robert Ebdon, who four years later become MCC's assistant secretary (estates and ground development).

Rifkind: 'All the time I was trying to bring people into the MCC fold, but I was always being met with resistance.'

In parallel to the three shortlisted development companies submitting their final bids by the end of September, Jamie Ritblat's company Delancey were examining MCC's options to develop on the Lord's freehold land. Stocken and Dowley wanted to properly examine what Ritblat could produce as an alternative before committing to a Vision for Lord's development partner. Separately from the Ritblat project, there were shenanigans at play that have still to be properly explained. Astonishingly, Almacantar's MCC bid turned out to be the only one of the three that was compliant with the design brief. The other two shortlisted proposals excluded all or part of RLP's leasehold land, sparking allegations that pressure had been applied not to keep within the guidelines.

One person involved in the process said: 'There was interference from somewhere, telling the two companies that it was in their interests to put in non-compliant bids. There is not a shadow of doubt about that in my mind, and I work in the shadows. A senior figure at Capital & Counties told me afterwards that he was furious to have been misled in such a way.'

Bradshaw: 'To this day, it remains a mystery why Capital & Counties and Native Land put in non-compliant proposals. Rumours of interference abounded. One advocated the development solely on MCC's freehold and the other presented on the basis of only part-development on the leasehold land. It was extraordinary that two companies should ignore the request of the development committee. The obvious inference was that someone had interfered with the process.'

Grabiner: 'It was really quite shocking that two of the three bids bore no relation at all to the invitation to bid and were for that reason rejected. The only one compliant was the one from Almacantar, which was a top-notch firm and backed by the Agnelli family.

'We never had any explanation why the two other bids were non-compliant. My own view is that both the other bidders were told to make sure they didn't comply. I think that is precisely what happened. It wouldn't work with Mike Hussey at Almacantar – if it had been tried, Hussey would have told whoever it was where to go.'

Parker: 'I knew something had gone on because the brief to which the three shortlisted developers had responded was crystal clear: "You build on that site only, just on the Nursery strip." MCC would not entertain any proposal for land outside the strip. Yet three designs come in and two out of the three had development outside the strip. I asked them what the hell they were doing. They told me they thought it was better suited. I smelt a rat, so I rang people in their teams casually and found out they had been guided. Someone had been round misleading them.

'I've never seen anything like it in 30 years in the business. If you do that on a local authority tender, you would have to go and see the constabulary. It's contrary to law, misleading a formal bidding process. But MCC is a private members' club, bound only by its articles of association.'

Capital & Counties and Native Land both declined to be interviewed for the book.

Griffiths: 'There were awful politics. I said to Charles before Christmas, "Are you giving up on this?" He said: "Never. I will never give up."'

CHAPTER 9

Ashes to Ashes

WHEN MCC HIRE OUTSIDE CONSULTANTS, money seems to be no object. It was certainly the case when property expert Stephen Musgrave, a former chief executive of Grosvenor Estates in UK and Ireland, arrived at Lord's in September 2010, to give advice on the three short-listed development partner bids and come up with a recommendation. He helped Keith Bradshaw, David Batts and Alistair Parker prepare a lengthy report.

Musgrave was understood to have been paid around £500 an hour, which would have made him one of the highest paid sports administrators at the time. A *Daily Mail* story revealed that Musgrave was being paid, pro-rata, more than a Premier League footballer.

'I found that very amusing,' said Musgrave, 'but I think it was a sensible decision by MCC to employ outside assistance in order to produce the best possible report. I think I gave them value for money during the time I was there.'

The three offers being considered were from Almacantar, Capital & Counties and Native Land, though Almacantar's was the only one that was compliant with the advisory brief. Almacantar are best known for transforming the unloved London skyscraper Centre Point into 82 luxury flats.

Bradshaw: 'I don't think I've ever worked harder than I did on that 100-page report. I was very proud of the quality of the output. Every paragraph had been written, rewritten and rewritten again. The report was factual, concise despite its length and came up with balanced and credible recommendations.'

It recommended building a relationship with Almacantar, with the aim of increasing their offer and refining the scheme. The Almacantar proposal also dealt with RLP, as Rifkind had his own agreement in place with the development company.

Bradshaw also canvassed the views of the cricket committee. Mike Griffith wanted matches still to be played on the Nursery Ground. Mike Brearley was uncomfortable with any residential development at Lord's. And Mike Gatting was worried about shadows from the residential build harming the grass and preferred two blocks of flats, one in each corner.

There was written advice from MCC's lawyers Slaughter & May over the club's concern at having to repay the £1 million spent by RLP in building up The Vision if it transpired that MCC had breached the partnership agreement. The repayment of that seven-figure sum remains an issue to this day.

Bradshaw's report concluded: 'Entering into exclusive talks with Almacantar seems very much the most rational and reasonable thing to do. The competition has produced a very clear front-runner and it will look very odd if the club are to abandon the process at this very late stage without entering into proper discussions.'

However, the chairman Oliver Stocken was unimpressed with Bradshaw's findings.

'I remember Oliver reading it late one evening in my office for the first time,' said Bradshaw, 'I sat silently at my desk overlooking the ground, doing my emails, and I could hear Oliver sitting at the board-room-style table in my office, grunting, moaning and dropping his pen down over and over again as he skimmed over the report, showing his immense displeasure.

'As part of our research we found that the MCC committee had passed a general resolution not to allow any non-cricketing development on the Lord's freehold land. Stocken was incredibly angry, and questioned me over and over again. "Why did you put this in the report? Why is it relevant?" This went on for days.

'I couldn't work out why Stocken felt so strongly about this particular point. When I reread it, I understood why. Stocken, when he was treasurer, had put forward the resolution that freehold land should not be developed on; now he was promoting that very action himself as a possibility. It was quite embarrassing for him that the MCC committee then had to backtrack on what he had initially recommended. I think he thought I had resurrected this on purpose to make him look silly. I hadn't. Despite our differing views on redevelopment, it was always my job to support the chairman.'

There followed a critical meeting of the negotiating group on 22 November 2010, at which the conflict was laid bare once again. Stocken had wanted that historical freehold resolution changed because he wanted to explore a residential build on MCC's own land, as opposed to RLP's leasehold. Musgrave was keen to pursue the Almacantar option. In his short time working at Lord's, he had been horrified at the subterfuge over the two non-compliant bids and the desire to look at other alternatives behind RLP's back.

Musgrave: 'Certainly there were strange things going on behind the scenes. It is just speculation why Native Land and Capital & Counties put in non-compliant bids. Perhaps they thought it was a better solution. But any interference by MCC representatives would have been highly unprofessional bordering on immoral.

'It was completely wrong for MCC to be considering other alternatives at that stage. We had a compliant bid on the table after a vast amount of work to reach that stage. I made it very clear that I felt it was not appropriate to talk to the architects Squire's at that time. It was not ethical to be looking elsewhere. We were in the middle of a process, which we either had to complete or start again.

'What I found extraordinary about the negativity was that we were not recommending a full acceptance of Almacantar's offer – it was just the start of a process, to see if we could work it up into something both sides found acceptable. There were tons of things that had to be done. All we were doing was agreeing to go to the next stage. The Herzog scheme was too big and there was a chance with Almacantar to work up something quite a lot smaller. I found it all very difficult, but I was only a consultant and I was made very aware that was the case.'

The negotiating group consisted of Keith Bradshaw, Oliver Stocken, Justin Dowley, Lord Grabiner, Robert Griffiths, Jamie Ritblat and

David Batts. Also at the meeting were a trio of MCC advisers, Alistair Parker, Dermot Rice and Stephen Musgrave.

Musgrave: 'This is a tremendous opportunity for the club and should be seen in a positive light. This process had been exhaustive and a very important stage has been reached. In whatever way the bids are measured, the numbers are good and represent an extremely good deal for the club.'

Parker: 'We have analysed all three proposals. The most critical parameter within the brief had been maintaining the Nursery Ground at its current size.'

Rice: 'There are significant reputational issues. Two of the submissions are not compliant – MCC can only consider the Almacantar bid. It would be a difficult position for the club to accept a non-compliant bid.'

Ritblat: 'I believe the two companies who have submitted non-compliant offers have done this because RLP has a relationship with the principals of Almacantar.'

Parker: 'All the developers had meetings with RLP. It has been made clear that they had two options – making their own arrangements with RLP, or MCC dealt with RLP. It's not possible to keep the existing size of the Nursery Ground without encroaching onto RLP land, so any plan which moved the Nursery Ground onto the freehold land alone would mean a smaller Nursery Ground.'

Stocken: 'Stephen Musgrave should meet with Jamie Ritblat and his colleagues to look at the detail of the alternative plan exclusively on MCC's land.'

Ritblat: 'The initial work on the alternative shows it is possible in principle, subject to detailed work on refinements. It has not yet been possible to carry out the detailed work, and this will require more interaction with Keith [Bradshaw] and David [Batts].'

Bradshaw: 'We agree it should be recommended to the development committee that the two non-compliant bids should be rejected and MCC proceed in detailed negotiations with Almacantar. But before we proceed, the following steps are required:

1. Further examination of the Squire & Partners proposal

of residential development (solely on MCC freehold) should be undertaken by the executive and advisers in conjunction with Jamie [Ritblat].

2. Further financial analysis of the Almacantar proposal and its financial implications for MCC.

3. A financial appraisal and report to be produced on option B as an alternative to the full Vision for Lord's scheme, which is the development of a single stand.'

Grabiner: 'I want it formally confirmed that the purpose of this meeting is to make a recommendation to the development committee as to the way forward. I don't want opponents of the Vision for Lord's to sidetrack or divert the talks.'

Dowley: 'I'm uncomfortable with the club having only one bid to consider. The alternative bid, which is being worked up by Jamie Ritblat's company, has not been considered in sufficient detail. We need to know what size and shape of development might be possible on our freehold land with the size of the Nursery Ground remaining the same, and what profit that development might produce. This would give a comparison for the Almacantar deal to see whether it is, in fact, good enough.'

Batts: 'An analysis has been carried out with roughly the same residential land value, but this would not address the problem of the leasehold land.'

Stocken: 'It is essential to be in a position when a recommendation is made to the MCC committee to say that all possible alternatives had been investigated and the proposal put forward was the one believed best for the club.'

Dowley: 'Tony [Grabiner] has proposed and it has been agreed that it should be recommended to the development committee that the two non-compliant bids should be rejected. It's also been agreed MCC should not proceed to any negotiations with Almacantar until further financial analysis of their proposal and its implications for MCC has been completed and until further discussion between Stephen Musgrave and Jamie Ritblat on the alternative proposal has taken place. So it's agreed that no discussion with Almacantar is therefore likely until after the 11 February MCC committee meeting.'

There is still disagreement on this final point. The furore around the timing of when Almacantar were to be informed was one of the major factors that led to the development committee being disbanded.

A lot of the same faces were around the table in the Lord's pavilion for the development committee meeting a fortnight later on 9 December – although critically, Stocken and Dowley were not in attendance. It turned out to be the last time that the development committee ever met.

Present: Griffiths, Alt, Grabiner, Major, McGowan, McLintock, Bradshaw, Batts, Parker, Rice, Musgrave, Gorst.

Absent: Martin-Jenkins, Stocken, Dowley, Atherton, Baker, Jenkins, Lewis, Ritblat.

Musgrave: 'The decision of the negotiating group is that Almacantar is still seen as the preferred partner, compliant or non-compliant. But it will be necessary to seek clarity with Almacantar on certain points and to keep up the negotiating tension by not publicising their preferred partner position. All bidders have been very patient, but any further delay could raise questions about the credibility of the project.'

Grabiner: 'There has been a unanimous decision from the negotiating group to shelve the two non-compliant bids. There is no purpose in investigating how or why these bids were non-compliant.'

Major: 'There are some members of the development committee who still have reservations. Those reservations have to be considered and addressed to achieve maximum unanimity.

My fear, as someone who has been actively involved in considering the redevelopment of Lord's for the last seven years, is that if we were to return to the market, the one compliant bidder will disappear. And if MCC withdraw from the current process, the club would not have acted in good faith.'

McGowan: 'The analysis has shown Almacantar are the best bid in every respect.'

Alt: 'There remain serious uncertainties about the club's finances. The lack of competition for TV rights is not healthy. I do not feel it is appropriate to proceed with a preferred development partner at present.'

Griffiths: 'The MCC committee has made it clear they would not contemplate reduction in the size of the Nursery Ground, so it's difficult to see how an alternative scheme on the club's freehold could be made to work.'

Parker: 'I agree. The site is not wide enough.'

Griffiths 'The last plan submitted by Squire's showed there would be a 16 per cent reduction in the Nursery Ground.'

Alt: 'Is it possible to talk to Almacantar about building solely on the club's freehold?'

Griffiths: 'Yes, but Herzog had considered the use of freehold alone without success.'

Bradshaw: 'Jamie Ritblat believes such a scheme is possible. He is waiting for further information from the architects Squire's.'

Musgrave: 'We've met with Squire's. Their sketch proposals are based on very little information. They did not have a copy of the Vision for Lord's. We provided them with some parameters, like the required size of the Nursery Ground and the need for natural light for the indoor school.'

Alt: 'The chosen developer does not necessarily have to proceed on the leasehold land option.'

Parker: 'Almacantar's bid is made on the basis they would deal with RLP.'

Musgrave: 'Mike Hussey has indicated that his other investors are bigger and more significant than the Agnelli family, but he's not prepared to reveal his information until Almacantar are agreed as the club's preferred development partner.'

Alt: 'On the basis that money comes into the company and the club understand the processes of how Almacantar's backers made their investment, the financial background issue would be satisfied.'

McLintock: 'I'm not completely opposed to doing a deal with Almacantar, but there are a number of grey areas. There should be a proper financial analysis done. I feel that the views of the finance committee are in a minority on this committee and are therefore getting lost in discussions.'

Major: 'It would be wholly improper for the development committee to have made decisions of this type without the involvement of the finance committee. The financial implications of a project with Almacantar are not fully known yet, and would not be known until the club begin discussions with them.

'The scheme may change once the club start talks with the potential development partner. And until a legally binding agreement is reached, MCC is not committed to it. It's better to consider and answer concerns now rather than proceed to a point and have the finance committee reject the scheme.'

Alt: 'There has been much discussion as to how realistic the Squire proposal will be. But if it is found to be practical, the development partner should consider it in the same way as the Vision for Lord's.'

Batts: 'I have had letters from Sir Michel Jenkins and Sir Scott Baker, who can't be here tonight. They both support taking discussions with Almacantar to the next stage.'

Griffiths: 'I'm going to go around the room, asking for everyone's views. Should we appoint Almacantar as the club's preferred partner?'

Alt: 'I'm content to proceed.'

Musgrave: 'MCC's reputation is resting on this process, and the club must enter into the next stage with its preferred partner in good faith.'

Grabiner: 'Agreed'

Major: 'I agree, if the club is not legally bound.'

McLintock: 'I agree, provided the club is not legally committed and a proper financial analysis is carried out.'

Gorst: 'I'm not comfortable proceeding to the next stage. The club is making loses and the financial outlook is bleak. Planning will not be easy and there are problems with Section 106 requirements.'

Griffiths: 'The intention is to get the club into a position where we can start negotiations with Westminster and gauge their reaction.'

Grabiner: 'There has already been a unanimous agreement by the negotiating group to proceed to the preferred partner stage.'

McGowan: 'It is not yet known how the project will develop. There are some aspects of the non-compliant bids that are good and could be incorporated into the final scheme.'

McLintock: 'There is much enthusiasm and momentum behind the project, but there are problems with RLP and development committee meetings are infrequent. It means that members are not always up to speed with the latest position.'

Alt: 'Other options can still be looked at that do not risk the fortunes of MCC – like developing only on freehold land.'

Musgrave: 'I would like to have a few days to talk further to Almacantar, without the non-compliant bidders having been stood down.'

Griffiths: 'Letters will be drafted to each of the three bidders.'

Major: 'The club have an obligation to tell each of them the position fairly soon.'

Alt: 'I'm concerned about any public statement at this time.'

Griffiths: 'Nothing will be said until after the three parties have been notified of the decision to proceed with Almacantar.'

Charles Rifkind was still on the outside, despite having paid 50 per cent of the cost of the development plans. He wrote to Bradshaw: 'RLP wants clarification by MCC as to whether the Vision for Lord's is the only proposal that is being considered by the club. We are now led to believe through the marketplace that architects have been instructed on behalf of MCC to consider an alternative scheme on MCC land only.'

Rifkind: 'I knew nothing about these other plans. As far I was concerned, MCC had committed to a joint venture of which I was paying half the costs. I am an honourable man and I thought MCC were a gentlemen's club. How wrong I was. I only found out about the alternative Squire's plan when Mike Hussey sat next to Michael Squire at a dinner. MCC also sent me a bill for some of Squire's work.'

Christmas arrived in 2010 with the redevelopment project up in the air and the main protagonists scattered around the globe. Almacantar were still unsure whether they would be working with MCC. Mike Hussey wanted official documentary evidence from Lord's to show his board that the partnership had been rubber-stamped, but it was not forthcoming. Almacantar's shareholders included Rolex, Chanel and the Agnelli family, and Hussey had already hosted a private dinner for them in the Long Room.

Rifkind spent Christmas in Kenya, while Musgrave was in India on a holiday arranged before his Lord's involvement. Meanwhile, Stocken,

Leaver, Bradshaw and Peters were part of the MCC contingent that headed out to the 2010/11 Ashes series in Australia. It was a victorious trip for Andrew Strauss's England team on the pitch, while the MCC backbiting was taking place off it. The main issue was whether the development committee or MCC were in control of the proposed development of Lord's.

Bradshaw: 'Stocken and Dowley were blindsiding the development committee to an extent Griffiths considered intolerable. An illustration of the way the chairman would change his mind and decide policy on the hoof came during the Ashes. One night, following a meeting of MCC's World Cricket committee in Perth and feeling constantly frustrated at being told not to engage Almacantar as a development partner by Stocken, I poured my concerns out to Tony Lewis and John Stephenson.

'I did send the chairman a letter about all this, and to my surprise he informed me that I could go ahead and take on Almacantar. I felt ecstatic. Reason had finally been seen to prevail and we could, actually, achieve something. I clearly recall taking the call on my mobile outside the lounge where the MCC World Cricket committee staff had been working. A celebratory drink duly ensured. We were there.

We were going to announce it the next day. That morning, I got the quote from Mike Hussey at Almacantar to go in the press release. I sent it to Oliver to approve. Then I received the phone call, saying we were not doing it. Oliver didn't give a reason, no negotiation, no debate – he just told me it wasn't happening. I was told that Peter Leaver was to write the letter that was to go to Almacantar and that I should meet with him in Melbourne.

'I was concerned about this, not to say a little suspicious. I had breakfast with Nigel Peters at the Hyatt hotel on the first morning that I was in Melbourne and shared my worries with him. He was supportive, although I discovered later that was only in a very superficial way and he was no use to me whatsoever.

'Leaver's letter caused the whole project to come off the rails. I hoped he would construct a letter to kickstart the project. It was not, however, the sort of correspondence you would have with someone you are engaging. It had no substance, it gave no guarantees – it wasn't worth the paper it was written on. There was no way a backyard builder would begin a project on this basis. It was just a stalling tactic. Almacantar chief executive Mike Hussey was understandably distraught and angry.

'I then spoke to Stocken, who was then still in England, and with Peters. He may have agreed with my position, but he was not going to be someone who would fight my corner. Peters agreed to attend a meeting on the first day of the Sydney Test with myself, Stocken and Leaver. This was quite a frank and open discussion in which I aired my concerns. I was effectively shot down and undermined by the chairman. I was told what was going to happen.

'It was during this Test that Stocken, referring to the letter I had written to him, said: "It is better not to put some things in writing." Oliver decided that he would sit down with Mike Hussey and discuss what was or wasn't going to happen.'

Peter Leaver: 'It was in Perth. We wanted to kick it as far into the long grass as possible. I think I was asked to write the note because of my legal knowledge. I drafted it on my knees in the pavilion at the Waca during the Test match.

'It was no work of art – just a few lines informing Almacantar that it was MCC's main committee that decide such things and their next meeting was in February. Almacantar were pushing for a quick decision. They were businessmen, why wouldn't they?'

Images of Almacantar's proposed Nursery End scheme then appeared in *The Times*, ahead of any official word from Lord's about a development partnership. This caused huge ructions inside an organisation paranoid about media leaks. Griffiths, who was often blamed by committee colleagues for talking to the press, sent an email to Stocken, Dowley and Leaver. It was copied to Keith Bradshaw, Lord Grabiner, Sir Michael Jenkins, Brian McGowan, Alistair Parker and Stephen Musgrave.

'I have had some further thoughts overnight. For my part, I cannot believe that the leak (if there was one) would have come from Almacantar. Why should they release information that it was not in their interest to disclose to the press? The more likely explanation is that the press knew that Native Land and Capital & Counties had been told by Oliver prior to Christmas that they were unsuccessful bidders and drew their own conclusion that Almacantar were successful.

'This is the problem that flows from MCC not having made a press release and not sending an appropriate letter to Almacantar. I do not believe it is helpful at this stage to have any further negative communications with Mike Hussey. My view is that Oliver should not speak to him until we have resolved these issues.

'It seems to me essential that there should be an urgent meeting between the officers of the club, the executive and those members of the development committee who have been actively involved.'

Shortly after the Griffiths email was sent on 9 January, Grabiner replied to all in a damning fashion about the way the Almacantar decision has been stalled.

'This is all very unsatisfactory and the sooner we have the meeting suggested by Robert, the better. It's pretty obvious that the present state of affairs has been caused by the failure at our end of the story to comply with our own process.

'It was agreed many months ago that the steering group (negotiating group) would go through the exercise of studying the presentations, interviewing and then (if thought appropriate) recommending the favoured developer to the main committee. It was also agreed that the development committee would make its own decision as to which of the applicants (if any) it would appoint. All the developers went into the process on that basis.

'In the event – and for reasons which have never been explained but which to my mind are plain and obvious – two of the three finalists put in non-conforming bids. The steering group and the development committee unanimously decided to reject these two and also decided to go with Almacantar. The advice from the property and legal professionals totally supported both these decisions.

'Thereafter, I believe the losers were rightly advised (I think by Oliver) that they were out of it, but for some reason Almacantar were not advised they had been successful and that the decision had been taken to proceed with them. That was a key failure of process and it was a decision taken without any or any proper consultation with a number of people, including me, who were, even at the level of ordinary courtesy, entitled to know what was going on in their name.

'As far as I can tell, and I've only seen bits of the email traffic, there were meetings and discussions in Australia, as a result of which, it was decided to keep Almacantar in play alongside another exercise being pursued with Delancey and some people called Squire. This was flatly contrary to what was agreed unanimously by the small group and the development committee.

'What we agreed was that in the exclusive, non-legally binding discussions with Almacantar which were expected to follow, all suggestions for the content of the final version would be considered, whether they came from Delancey, the schemes put forward by the losing developers or our own improved thinking.

'The process failure has been compounded by the facts that a) people who should have been consulted/copied into emails have been ignored and b) others, who have never previously been in the process, have been introduced into it. This is a classic recipe for a mess.

'The suggestion made in some of the emails I've seen to the effect that the "leak to the press" must have come from Hussey/Almacantar is, I think, nonsense. Why would they imagine that was a prudent or sensible step to take? The most likely explanation is that the losing developers spoke to the press. And they, as well as the press, drew the obvious conclusion. I think also that great care should be taken before making accusations about leaking and breaking confidences. We could easily find ourselves on the wrong end of defamation proceedings.

'The short point is that if we had followed our own process, we would not now be in the potentially embarrassing situation we are in. I sincerely hope this can be salvaged, because there is a great deal at stake here. I believe we need to have a meeting asap to thrash this out in a sensible and grown-up way.'

Grabiner's development committee colleague Brian McGowan followed up with an equally hard-hitting email:

'I have been in business now for nearly 50 years, and I have never experienced anything like this. I have not spoken to Tony Grabiner for several weeks, so there is no collusion or connivance between us, but I agree with everything he says in the email This process is a disgrace. And to hide behind the argument that this is how private clubs operate is probably inaccurate and, if true, it is about time they, and in particular MCC, changed their ways.

'A process was set out a year or two ago creating a so-called prestigious development committee to deal with the detail of the development, but always subject to the parameters set by the main committee. Eventually to be approved by the main committee and, for obvious reasons, the finance committee.

'The development committee was deemed to be too large and unwieldy to deal with the detail (rightly so, in my view) and accordingly a smaller negotiating group was formed, made up of some members of the development committee, but crucially including the chairman and the treasurer. In my view, the people holding those positions should always have been included in any meeting where recommendations or agreements relating to the development were being made.

'Eventually the small group put forward a recommendation to the development committee, which, after a lengthy debate, was agreed. A minority, who were also members of the finance committee, had reservations. But once assurances and safeguards for their fears were given, there was unanimity on the committee to proceed with Almacantar.

'Part of this agreement was that we would amend the original Vision to include changed circumstances, financial constraints and good ideas proposed by other bidders. Always there was the obligation that anything finally 'agreed' had to be further approved by both the finance and main committee.

'What has happened since beggars belief. Just about everything agreed has been overturned, to the extent that there is a real risk of losing Almacantar, who in my opinion are already paying too much. Talk of avoiding paying money to Rifkind would only result in a seriously substandard development that future generations of MCC members, would, quite rightly, find appalling.

'As I have said before, there is an unhealthy objection to paying anything to Rifkind, despite him holding most of the cards. I find it incredulous that at the last meeting, one of the executives, who was guilty of failing to buy the tunnels all those years ago, was actually allowed to argue the case for doing nothing so that Rifkind did not benefit.

'The press leak is unfortunate, but I bet it did not come from Hussey. It is not in his interests, but it is in the interests of his rivals or those who are opposed to the whole idea of The Vision. Any who doubt this should remember there were plenty of leaks long before Hussey came on the scene.

'I am very unhappy with where we have ended up. For two pins I would resign, but this is too important for that. It is also regretful that I feel obliged to write this type of note. The sad thing is that I believe we all want the same thing but seem incapable of discussing the way forward without the mistrust of others' views. Can I please request an urgent meeting of the small negotiating group to agree the way forward without rancour? Is that too much to ask?'

Rifkind's team next complained to MCC about the way they had been treated via their supporter John Botts, an American investment banker. Botts sent a letter to Keith Bradshaw bemoaning the lack of communication from RLP and pointing out the shambles of MCC billing RLP for work examining other schemes. He wrote: 'I am extremely concerned about the process for taking our project forward, equally the complete lack of information from MCC is unnatural and unprofessional.

'The last communication was Alistair Parker's 19 August reply to RLP's request for information, in which Parker said that no "alternative proposals are being considered at present by the working group". Our request was prompted by learning from other sources that alternative proposals are, in fact, being considered which exclude the Wellington Road end. For the past six years, RLP have negotiated in good faith with MCC and have jointly spent in excess of £3 million developing The Vision.

'Our agreement was based on the understanding that MCC had ruled out alternative schemes which excluded the Wellington Road end. We have consistently made clear that we are not prepared to invest into a joint scheme with the possibility that at a later date, MCC decide to develop their own land excluding the Wellington Road end.

'As far back as 2009, RLP reiterated this point at a meeting with Dowley and Stocken. The RLP offer of £100 million in receipt of planning permission was based on this understanding.

We understand further Squire and Partners have effectively been commissioned by MCC to consider alternative schemes avoiding Wellington Road.

'We also do not understand an MCC request for payment by RLP of 50 per cent of the attached invoice dated 31 August 2010. It refers to "liaison with Delancey and setting up a confidentiality agreement". Why is RLP being asked to fund this cost, and on what basis is Delancey participating in this transaction, since they were not on the bid list? Almacantar's offer is well in excess of the £92 million threshold required in the heads of terms and both the steering and development committees and advisers have recommended acceptance.

'We are concerned that the lack of communication with RLP, the recent publicity about this project and the overdue formal MCC response to Almacantar will jeopardise the transaction and result in Almacantar withdrawing. Inevitably, this will require RLP to take stock of our in-principle joint venture with MCC. There has been no response to RLP's request for information in August and October. Might we please yet again request one and receive an answer?'

The negotiating group meeting that Grabiner and McGowan had urgently requested took place on 19 January. Yet McGowan and Ritblat, whose involvement with Delancey was at the centre of the controversy, were absent. The minutes of this fractious meeting were never agreed or circulated.

Present: Bradshaw, Stocken, Dowley, Grabiner, Griffiths, Batts, Parker, Rice, Musgrave.

Absent: McGowan, Ritblat.

Bradshaw: 'The purpose of the meeting is to review the current situation and decide how to proceed with regard to Almacantar. There are three possible courses of action: stand-by-stand, Squire's carrying out the development on MCC freehold land and the Vision for Lord's.

'At first sight, Squire's is an inferior plan that would encroach further onto the Nursery Ground and has issues with entry to the ground. It is not an iconic scheme appropriate to the area, and more work needs to be done. I hope it will be possible to agree at this meeting to proceed with Almacantar in a period of exclusivity on a non-binding basis to work up the Vision for Lord's, on both the leasehold and portions of MCC freehold land.'

Dowley: 'There has been a lack of clarity regarding exactly what had been agreed at the last meeting of the negotiating group on 22 November. In the interests of working together, I hope this can be clarified. Can Oliver explain what he and I thought had been agreed?'

Stocken: 'I feel Mike Hussey of Almacantar has misunderstood the process. Decisions are made by the MCC committee and not by principal committees, unless they are specifically authorised to do so. And that has not been the case. The MCC committee need to agree any proposal. It has a scheduled meeting on 16 February and two reserve days on 9 and 16 March set aside to consider the proposal.

'There will be no more important decision taken by the committee during the involvement of anyone present. It is vitally important that the MCC committee fully understand the implications. I hope it will be possible to meet with Mike Hussey to ensure he understands the process.

'When the debate began in July 2008 as to whether or not to enter into discussions with RLP, it had been agreed that on the granting of planning permission, MCC would receive £92.5 million in cash plus the additional cost of replacing Lord's facilities, estimated at £23 million.

'At the moment, the offer from Almacantar is for only £60 million in cash plus £40 million in kind, the majority of which would be spent digging out the undercroft. It would be nice to have the museum there, but it's not ideal to have conference and banqueting facilities underground, nor the indoor school.

'At the last MCC committee meeting, the former cricketers questioned whether there was any necessity to improve the current indoor school. I want to set up a meeting with Almacantar to advise them that their bid requires substantial improvement.'

Griffiths: 'I'm very much against meeting with Almacantar before we agree an exclusive negotiating period.'

Grabiner: 'So am I.'

Bradshaw: 'The feedback from Hussey is that there is an opportunity to improve the bid.'

Grabiner: 'Is there any objection to members of the negotiating group attending MCC main committee as people entitled to speak but not vote? Some main committee members have no detailed understanding of the project and it is important as much information as possible is made available to them before coming to a decision.'

Stocken: 'That will be possible.'

Griffiths: 'The development committee agreed to enter into a period of exclusivity with Almacantar. It had also been agreed to convey that decision to Almacantar and to let the two non-compliant bidders know that they had been unsuccessful. Where confusion had arisen is that all of the further work required outlined by Oliver would normally be carried out during the period of exclusivity. However, Oliver has implied these discussions should take place prior to the period of exclusivity. This issue needs to be sorted out.'

Dowley: 'I believe what was agreed is to inform the two non-compliant bidders that they had been unsuccessful, and to tell Almacantar that they are the only bidder but not to make any commitment to them until after the MCC committee meeting on 16 February. That committee will also consider the other two alternatives.'

Grabiner: 'I agree that the highest decision needs to be made at the highest level. But to insist this decision must be taken by the MCC committee would frustrate the agreed process and have the decision taken by those without detailed knowledge of the issues.'

Stocken: 'Neither the negotiating group nor the development committee have authority to take decisions.'

Grabiner: 'Oliver, your approach has undermined the process – it does not respect the functions of either the negotiating group or the development committee. It is not possible to have abstract financial discussions with Almacantar. This is only possible in the context of a scheme which proved acceptable to both Almacantar and the club.

'We should agree to enter into an exclusivity period with Almacantar on a non-binding basis, to examine matters that give cause to concern and see if it's possible to arrive at a scheme which satisfies both parties.'

Musgrave: 'The club entered into a process when it advertised for a development partner, and that process needs to be completed – not doing so would leave the club at risk of professional criticism. Almacantar can be asked to test all the options on both the freehold and leasehold land.'

Dowley: 'Almacantar have been selected because the other two bidders had been rejected as non-compliant with the brief. If the club were now looking at a wider scheme, other developers might have been interested.'

Parker: 'The invitation to tender had been very carefully framed. It was put to the market that MCC wanted a bid within the existing Vision for Lord's and that a clear understanding already exists with RLP. I agree with Stephen – it's important to complete the process.'

Rice: 'The club moving into a period of discussion with Almacantar would not only complete the process, but it would also improve the situation with RLP.'

Bradshaw: 'The heart of the disagreement is the timing of entering into the exclusivity period. Some feel it necessary for the MCC committee to take that decision, others feel the negotiating group should be able to agree to move on with the process.'

Stocken: 'I believe that should the club decide to undertake residential development on other than the leasehold land, a retendering process should occur.'

Grabiner: 'Would it be possible for the negotiating group to agree unanimously that MCC should embark on a period of exclusive negotiations with Almacantar on a non-binding basis?'

Finally, the negotiating group decide unanimously to recommend the following to the MCC committee.

'That MCC should embark upon an exclusive negotiation initially for a period of three months with Almacantar, without any obligation on either party to proceed to the conclusion of a binding development agreement. The negotiation will focus on all options on both the freehold and leasehold land.'

Later, Dowley asked for an additional paragraph to be added to the recommendation. The minutes state: 'Mr Dowley said that it was quite possible that after such a period of discussion, MCC might well decide not to proceed, and that Almacantar needed to be made aware of that. He was concerned, as ever, that MCC should not get gradually sucked into an unattractive position.'

The minutes have never been approved, and nor do they record that during the heated debate Grabiner called Stocken 'a 'f******** c***'.

Griffiths said: 'I think that might be slightly over the top.' Grabiner replied: 'No, it's not – he's a c***.'

At that meeting, Musgrove agreed with Bradshaw that it would be best if they parted ways, and that was the end of his involvement with MCC.

Musgrave said: 'When I came back from India, I found there had been zero dialogue with Almacantar. I thought that was appallingly bad form. They had been working in good faith. It was obvious that I wasn't going to have any positive influence on the outcome. The powers that be had made up their minds to kill the project – they didn't want it to happen. And in those circumstances, I didn't want any part of it. I clearly remember telling Keith: "I don't have a role here anymore." It was sad. Keith was a very honourable person with whom I had a very fond working relationship.'

Bradshaw said: 'So many perceived obstacles were strewn in our path to attempt to divert us. It was suggested that we should just develop on the freehold land, even though the square footage of residential housing would not provide anything like the same financial returns. As one firm of architects after another came in and repeated that, so they'd be thrown out and the next ones through the door would say the same.

'Jamie Ritblat had his own agenda. Squire's designed probably the most ugly architectural edifice I saw envisaged for the Nursery Ground. They proposed two parallel residential blocks on St John's Wood Road and on Wellington Place. This was an old concept rejected by the MCC committee in 2004 because of the reduction in size of the Nursery Ground, which would look like a housing estate.

'Ritblat then withdrew his proposal because the numbers didn't add up. He kept on saying: "We can do the development on our own land and earn more money, so why wouldn't we go ahead with this? Rifkind wouldn't be able to do anything at all." This was always the undercurrent. It became more important to them to halt Charles Rifkind than to achieve the best result for the club.

'We really struggled over The Vision. The development committee would agree a particular course of action, and people like Blake Gorst or Dowley would support it. Yet when that recommendation was brought to the main committee, they would then speak out against it. This went on and on.'

CHAPTER 10

Blood on the Carpet

'One Saturday morning in January, I opened my emails and discovered the issue had reached crisis point.'

Christopher Martin-Jenkins was an unlikely figure to move into a central role in the redevelopment conflict. He was at the top of his profession as a cricket broadcaster and writer, which resulted in him becoming MCC president in October 2010. But CMJ's term in office came at the height of the MCC civil war, during which he was ill-equipped to play a presidential role.

The first of the emails that CMJ found on his laptop had been sent at 11.38 a.m. on 20 January 2011 by Oliver Stocken. It also went to Keith Bradshaw, David Batts, Justin Dowley and Robert Griffiths, and announced that Stocken had changed his mind about allowing a few extra people into the next main committee meeting on 16 February, when the Almacantar decision was due to be made.

Lord Grabiner had asked for that to happen because he wanted the MCC committee to hear from those with a deep knowledge of the development saga, and Stocken agreed to the request at the time. But now he wrote: 'On further reflection, I do not think we can invite all members of the negotiating group to the main committee meeting, as I would then have to extend a similar invitation to the members of the finance committee and possibly the cricket committee. I have therefore sent a message to Tony Grabiner to this effect, saying we would have no invitees at the meeting, nor advisers at this stage.'

Griffiths emailed back to Stocken three hours later asking him to reconsider and copied Grabiner, Musgrave, McGowan and Dowley.

'The reason why I believe it is important for the non-executive members of the negotiating group to be invited is that it is obviously important to have informed debate at the committee meeting. I thought that was something that you and Justin [Dowley] would want to ensure. It would not set a precedent for inviting members of the finance or cricket committees, because they are not members of that group and are not privy to the discussions we have had.

'I do not think increasing the numbers attending by a maximum of three results in any practical reason why they could not be invited to attend. I also note that your view is that no advisers should attend the meeting. Does that mean that Stephen Musgrave is not going to be invited? Surely his input is extremely important, especially as we have recently engaged him as a specialist consultant.

'I would therefore ask you to reconsider the decision. With respect, I think your initial view that they could attend was the correct one.'

There is no reply from Stocken, but his chief ally Justin Dowley increased the tension a week later, on 27 January. He wrote to his finance committee: 'We had been planning to have a special meeting on 2 February to review progress on the possible development and provide a recommendation to the main committee which meets on 16 February.

'I have agreed with Keith [Bradshaw] and David Batts that we postpone the finance committee meeting for the following reasons.

'We have three alternatives. Proceed with Almacantar and try to increase their bid to develop on the leasehold land. Pursue a scheme, worked up at no cost so far to MCC by Jamie Ritblat's company Delancey (which would have no part in any development project) and the architects Squire's which involves development on MCC's freehold land. Or leave residential development alone at this stage and pursue a single stand option funded by our current reserves and probably some modest bank borrowings.

'The finance committee needs to consider these alternatives when armed with accompanying financial analysis, which is not yet ready.

'As you all know, my concern since the last analysis was prepared in the summer of 2009 has been that we crystallise a large windfall through residential development, only to spend it on an expensive-to-build, expensive-to-maintain and non-cash-generating undercroft.

'In the last couple of weeks, the cricket committee has decided that it would prefer an indoor school of similar size to the current one and above ground. It is also clear that a banqueting facility underground would not be ideal. We could probably find another place to put the museum, which is the other key proposed tenant of the undercroft. It is not clear, therefore, that an undercroft, certainly of the size which is being contemplated, makes sense, and the executive need some time to reconsider their plans.'

Stocken replied to Dowley: 'A really excellent note to the finance committee, for which many thanks. I am meeting with Keith to ensure we are clear on the points which we need the committee to address initially on 16 February and the steps we would recommend taking.

I will then meet up with Robert [Griffiths] to ensure he is fully briefed.'

That same afternoon, Griffiths replied to Dowley in a powder-keg email that led to his beloved development committee being disbanded. He rashly called for Stocken and Dowley to stand down because of their opposition to The Vision and shared his views with a number of MCC committee and development committee members.

Those copied in the email included Oliver Stocken, Charles Fry, Michael McLintock, Robert Leigh, Roger Pilgrim, Russell Cake, Tony Alt, Vicky Griffiths, William Maltby, David Batts and Keith Bradshaw.

Griffiths wrote: 'Thank you for your email re postponing the finance committee meeting. Given the planned meeting of the main committee on 16 February, I agree with your decision.

'As to the rest of your email, I'm afraid that I cannot agree with your summary of the choices before us. Indeed, what you say bears no relation whatsoever to what was agreed at the last meeting of the development committee and negotiating group.

'We agreed unanimously to recommend to the main committee the appointment of Almacantar on an exclusive basis. The resolution of the development committee on 9 December was:

1. The club would enter into a period of exclusivity with Almacantar to test the design and all the MCC requirements.

2. Almacantar would be required to take into account all different proposals received.

3. Almacantar would be notified of this decision.

'Furthermore, as you know, at the meeting of the negotiating group last week, both you and Oliver and the rest of the group yet again unanimously agreed to recommend to the main committee that we enter into a period of exclusive negotiations with Almacantar.

'This would not be legally binding and Justin, I recall you specifically agreeing that there could be no good reason for not doing this. It was again unanimously agreed that a letter to that effect would be sent out to Almacantar. This letter has still not been sent.

'Your summary plainly ignores all that and suggests possible approaches which explicitly reject the Vision for Lord's. None of this reflects the views of the executive or any of the professional advisers or the development committee. You and Oliver (I have just seen his email) are pursuing a personal agenda. The process for dealing with this critically important issue for cricket and the future of MCC, which was agreed and authorised by MCC at the outset, is just being ignored.

'For those members of the finance committee who understandably have no personal knowledge of the deliberations of the development committee/negotiating group, your email must have produced an entirely false picture of what is going on. This is most regrettable and in my view is very damaging to the club, the interests of the membership and cricket generally.

'In these circumstances, and it is sad that it has come to this, I believe that you should both consider your positions as chairman and treasurer of the club.'

An MCC committee member calling for the heads of the chairman and treasurer was always going to provoke a strong reaction, and so it did.

Stocken: 'Robert Griffiths sent round this email accusing us of all sorts of things. I thought "This not acceptable." So I contacted the president, Christopher Martin-Jenkins and said: "This has been put in writing, I can't chair the club with a member of the committee who feels like this. The matter has to be resolved. I can't have a member of the committee doubting the standing of the chairman and his colleagues. We have to bring this to a head."

'Robert had made the mistake of copying about 15 people. If he had only sent it to Justin and myself, we might have been able to sort things out between us. But when it went to all those people we had to bring it to a head, and quickly. It wasn't Christopher's scene, so he brought in the MCC trustees, Mike Brearley, Sir Tim Rice and Anthony Wreford, to investigate.'

Dowley: 'After Robert had written his email and the trustees were brought in, there was such a divide. Either the trustees backed Oliver and myself and disbanded the development committee or they supported Robert, which would have meant Oliver and I standing down.'

Christopher Martin-Jenkins: 'Matters came to a head in late January. Robert [Griffiths] was frustrated at the lack of progress. Unwisely, he suggested to the chairman and treasurer that they should consider their position. I decided to call on the trustees to take an independent look at the reasons for Robert's frustrations and whether or not there had been unreasonable delays on the part of the executives and senior committee members in their dealings with Michael Hussey, the boss of Almacantar.

'In the period before the next crucial committee meeting in mid-February, the trustees spoke to all concerned and came to the conclusion, as I expected, that Oliver Stocken and Justin Dowley had acted with no more than reasonable caution. Neither was against the idea of entering into negotiations with Almacantar, but neither could they go forward with someone whom they believed to be pursuing his own agenda.

'Knowing how one journalist in particular, my *Times* colleague Ivo Tennant, had been given confidential information from previous committee meetings by a source never definitely identified, I was concerned there might be a further damaging leak before the committee met.

'I persuaded the trustees that the proposed way forward should be kept a total secret between ourselves until the meeting started. Although Oliver was to chair the meeting, we had to tell him nothing about the main item on the agenda.'

Dowley: 'The trustees interviewed Oliver, myself and Robert. I remember it taking place in the bar at the top of the pavilion, which is normally a very convivial place when big matches are on.'

The eyewitness accounts from that day give a fascinating insight into one of the most momentous and acrimonious episodes in MCC's long history.

Bradshaw: 'The Vision was scuppered at the most fractious and unpleasant meeting I have ever attended. Stocken and Dowley said to me before the meeting that Griffiths must go or they would stand down.

'The night before, I rang Robert to tell him I was entirely supportive of him and his development committee. I asked him whether he had heard from Anthony Wreford and told him there were factions at work that I could not control. I told him there would be blood on the carpet in the committee room. "What colour is it?" said Robert. "Will it stain?"

'Wreford was supposed to have rung Robert to warn him that the future of the development committee was due to be discussed. That call was never made and the likelihood was that the decision to wind it up had already been taken.

'Robert was upset when he arrived at Lord's to find the development committee would be on the agenda, having not had time to discuss the issue with his members. Although I agreed with Robert's position, I also knew my job was in jeopardy because I was taking an opposing view to my chairman. My expectation and my hope was that Oliver and Justin would be cautioned by the trustees.

'I was really surprised when the trustees declared that the redevelopment should proceed without the development committee. Griffiths would lose his place on the main committee as a consequence.

'In the days beforehand I'd met up with Robert several times and he was clearly highly emotional. He looked stressed and ragged as if short of sleep. The agenda had been structured so that the matter could be dealt with towards the end of the meeting. Robert told me: "I'm not having any of this – I'm going to get stuck into this right from the start." The meeting started and Robert said the issue needed to be dealt with straight away. The trustees then asked that I, along with the chairman, the treasurer and Robert, be removed from the meeting, which was adjourned.

'We were taken to the members' lounge and the trustees handed us the findings of their inquiry. Wreford had not turned up, citing another engagement.

'Griffiths told Brearley and Rice that all the work done by the development committee was now being discarded without a proper and open debate. He also told the trustees they were weak, had no bottle and were the lapdogs of Stocken and Dowley. Brearley responded that Griffiths was being paranoid. Griffiths spent about two minutes skimming through the trustees' findings, declared they were rubbish and stormed out. I thought Robert had left the building.

'We then spent the next 15 to 20 minutes talking through the report. To me, it felt like a charade. But if I made a stand, I knew that was the end of my job. Having been divorced twice and with four children and two stepchildren, I was not financially well-off enough to be out of work.

'We went back down to the meeting and I was surprised to see that Robert was in the room. Then the real battle commenced. I have never seen a more nasty and aggressive interaction than I saw that afternoon. Robert had been vilified, and yet there was little support for him. He believed he had been stitched up by not having been given notice that the development committee would be the focal element and that a decision to get rid of it had already been made.

'The debate over The Vision was handled in a shambolic manner. CMJ had to take the chair. He was emotional, and to some extent the meeting was deteriorating to the point at which it wasn't being chaired at all. Committee members were shouting and holding discussions amongst themselves. Robert told CMJ he was not chairing the meeting dispassionately, believing him to have been too easily influenced by Stocken – a remark he took personally.

'CMJ was accustomed to reporting cricket meetings, not chairing them, and commercial knowledge was not his strong point. He asked Robert to leave the room while conclusions were reached. Robert, supported by David Faber, objected to this but did so.

'Then Stocken offered to stand down. He was on his way out of the room, when Sir John Major opined that it would be too embarrassing for the club to lose its chairman and treasurer.' Major declared that there was no other option but to retain them in office, so the decision was taken to disband the development committee.'

Stocken said: 'Ahead of that meeting, I said to the trustees, "Are you going to ring up John Major to tell him what's coming up?" They said they didn't think they should and that all the committee should find out simultaneously. John was a bit shocked. I didn't find out about the trustees' findings until they reported to the committee. All this crap about threatening to resign – that's not my style. All I said was that I couldn't chair something when you had a member of the committee who was publicly in disagreement. That's not resigning – they had to choose one course or the other.'

Griffiths: 'I sent an email which used the language "consider your positions". I don't know necessarily I was saying they should resign. "Consider your positions" seemed to be a reasonable thing to say in the circumstances.

'How can I have the development committee continue doing the work it's doing if behind the scenes, the MCC chairman is behaving in this way? Clearly at that time he was trying to get rid of the development committee. I'm glad I wrote that because I really wanted to make him realise that what he was doing was pretty serious stuff. He was preventing the development committee set up by his own MCC committee from engaging in work that I still believe would have benefitted the club enormously.

'I was asked to leave the main committee meeting. When I came back, I was told it was a fait accompli. In my world, you talk about people having the right to defend themselves, natural justice. Any concerns about the development committee should have been put to me in advance. I should have been given the opportunity to address the concerns. If they had said there was a fundamental flaw, we could have addressed it. But it was nothing like that – it was all superficial stuff. It was an argument based on personal matters.'

Ivo Tennant: 'Robert had to go and stand outside the meeting at one point. But he had left his glasses on the committee room table. Brearley brought them out to him. Robert told him: "I think this is very unfair." Brearley gave him one of his steely looks and said: "No, it's not."

'I spoke to Robert that night, when I think he was being consoled by Charles [Rifkind]. He'd had a drink.'

Charles Rifkind: 'The night of the vote, Robert Griffiths went berserk with me. He'd had a few drinks. He thought I could have somehow manoeuvred the MCC committee. I helped get him membership of the Garrick, but I couldn't influence MCC to that extent. Bradshaw changed sides on the day of the meeting – he didn't want to lose his job.'

Christopher Martin-Jenkins: 'I was quickly obliged to take the chair and reluctantly cross swords with one of the sharpest barristers in the land, who had given a lot of time and expertise to The Vision – completely unpaid, of course.

'Robert was understandably crestfallen, but he had misjudged the mood by challenging the senior officials. Eventually the committee, helped by the balanced views of a former prime minister who had seen more momentous conflicts than this in Downing Street, came to a unanimous decision that the development committee should be disbanded and that a smaller negotiating group, led by Justin Dowley and Keith Bradshaw, should be appointed to begin negotiations with Almacantar that did not prejudice other means of developing new stands.

'This was, at least arguably, a natural end to the development committee's work, although its chairman emphatically did not agree. MCC's press officer issued a statement that evening that made no mention of any offers to resign, but that side of the story appeared under Ivo Tennant's name the next morning.'

The MCC statement announced that the club were to enter into a period of exclusive discussion with Almacantar and dissolve the development committee in the process: 'Almacantar's appointment completed the work of the club's development committee and further negotiations will now begin immediately, led by the executive with assistance from a smaller team of experts.'

Mike Atherton: 'The development committee received this email from Oliver saying our services were no longer required. I thought it was a little perfunctory. It was just two lines: "Thanks for your time. You are no longer required." I thought given the fact that John Major and others had given their time, it could have been a little more expansive. That was it. I never really spoke to these guys again.'

Blake Gorst: 'I kept telling Oliver after every meeting that we should disband the development committee. It was out of control, but Oliver was a very affable non-executive and wanted to be fair to all sides. Eventually, after he had disbanded the development committee, he sent me an email saying I had been right all along. I told the main committee on the day the development committee was terminated that it had been appallingly mismanaged. John Major was furious. He banged his fist on the table and said he had never heard such an outrageous comment.'

After the demolition job on the development committee, Bradshaw wrote to Rifkind and Levy about where it left their relationship with MCC. His letter contained the only gratitude RLP ever received from Lord's.

'As you know, we now intend to enter into a period of non-binding, exclusive discussions and negotiations with Almacantar. It is something of a statement of the obvious that the journey we have all been on to arrive at this very positive juncture has been a long and sometimes trying one.

'I did want to put on record, however, that the club has always been, and remains, sincerely grateful for the key contribution that you have made over a significant period. Your willingness to engage and to discuss what have often been difficult issues in an open and constructive manner has been a vital part of getting us to the point we have now reached.

'I'm also conscious that you have often maintained this constructive attitude during periods when it has not been all that obvious to whom at the club you should be talking. Although we are still a fair way from reaching a definitive position with Almacantar, what I did want to make clear is that the position we have now reached brings to a conclusion any historic arrangements or understandings between the club and RLP as to the joint marketing or disposal of our respective interests in the leasehold land.

'We have held a global competition and we have selected a clear preferred bidder from that competition. And, as we understand it, you have reached a separate arrangement with Almacantar, to which we are not privy. Almacantar is dealing with each of us entirely separately. We are content with that and we have assumed that you are too. Any future discussions, if they are ever needed and if we decide between ourselves to hold them, will start with a blank sheet of paper.

'There is no intention here to promote any kind of disagreement with RLP – all we wish to do is to make the position as we see it entirely clear. In saying this, I am, of course, conscious that there are certain outstanding matters relating to the club's leasehold interest and its relationship with you as our landlord, which do need to be properly put to bed.

'The other matter we need to cover is the settling of a final account between us in relation to our previous cost-sharing arrangements. Whilst my understanding is that the amounts outstanding here are small in the great scheme of things, I do think for good order we should reach a final sign-off on it.'

Rifkind is still waiting for RLP's share of joint costs building up The Vision, which amounted to over £1 million.

Keith Bradshaw: 'Justin Dowley and I were charged with selecting a replacement committee. It wasn't formed until 24 May because of the difference of opinion over the selection. I wanted Grabiner, Justin wanted Jamie Ritblat.

'Ritblat had a huge conflict of interests, in my opinion, as a property developer himself. Justin claimed he was not conflicted because he had maintained he would never be the club's development partner. For some reason, Ritblat's company Delancey's view seemed to carry huge weight with Dowley and Stocken. They constantly wanted to use Jamie in a non-official capacity.

'As for taking on property experts, it was the classic case of "If we don't like what you're telling us, let's get someone else in." Alistair Parker's recommendations to go ahead with The Vision were such that I was instructed by Justin Dowley to get rid of him. I told Justin that he would be exposing the club to litigation, as the club had an agreement with Cushman & Wakefield whereby they would receive a substantial pay-out if the project was stymied.

'Justin said: "OK then, put him on time and materials, but don't use him. I had a very difficult conversation with Parker in my office. He was never going to receive all the payments owing to him. It was much the same with Stephen Musgrave. He drew the same conclusion as Parker – that the finances stacked up with the RLP partnership – and I was told to get rid of him as well.'

Alistair Parker: 'Keith Bradshaw was hugely apologetic and utterly embarrassed, but I understood where he was coming from – he was just carrying out committee instructions.

I would never work again for an organisation that can change its mind that erratically. The Lebanese are a byword for government mismanagement, but I was doing work in the souks in Beirut, and I thought the quality of governance there was a lot better than in St John's Wood.

'As far as my own involvement, we succeeded, but MCC terminated it. I had a legal case. We could have sued, but my partners at Cushman & Wakefield didn't want to and instead came to an agreement with which I had to abide. A significant number of the partners were MCC members, and two of them lived in Century Court overlooking Lord's.'

Almacantar had waited months for their official confirmation as MCC's development partner. Now there was a further delay on an exclusivity letter detailing the terms being agreed between them. The impasse went as follows:

18 March: With all parties preparing a three-month work plan, Almacantar reports it has verbally agreed with Bradshaw that the costs will be 100 per cent underwritten by MCC until the exclusivity letter is signed.

22 March: Mike Hussey emails Bradshaw to say he has agreed the exclusivity letter wording. Bradshaw responds, saying he will 'turn the letter round.'

29 March: Almacantar's lawyers Berwin Leighton Paisner chase MCC's lawyers Slaughter & May to see if the exclusivity letter is finalised. They respond, saying the delay is due to Bradshaw's father being

ill. Both parties continue to work on the basis that the terms are agreed.

26 April: As well as the exclusivity letter still not being signed, RLP are unhappy with the invoices they are being charged by MCC.

Bradshaw wrote: 'I think the best course of action would be for us to sit down together and go through the various payments and invoice details. My understanding is that Charles Rifkind had agreed those with David Batts through the course of the project. However, I am aware, following a recent conversation with Charles, that RLP is not comfortable with all the payments.'

24 May: Another Masterplan working party is formed to replace the dissolved development committee. It consists of Keith Bradshaw, Sir Michael Jenkins, Angus Fraser, Garri Jones, Michael McLintock, Brian McGowan and Justin Dowley. It never meets.

4 August: Almacantar chief executive Mike Hussey emails Bradshaw, reminding him that there is no sign of the elusive exclusivity letter.

24 August: The confusion is further increased when Bradshaw resigns as MCC chief executive following the death of his mother and the need for him to return to Australia to help care for his brother, who has special needs.

26 August: Bradshaw writes to RLP, telling them to deal directly with Almacantar over development issues, without mentioning his resignation.

Bradshaw writes: 'Given that RLP's interests now effectively form part of Almacantar's bid, it is, I think, more appropriate for RLP to speak to Almacantar about these matters rather than to the club direct. This is not motivated by any desire on the club's part that RLP should not be privy to what is going on, it is simply having two lines of communication brings with it the risk of confusion.'

1 September: Property consultants Savills produce a report commissioned by MCC on potential return from different types of development at Lord's. High-density residential on leasehold land is rated 'high-risk', in planning terms.

Bradshaw said: 'The conclusions they reached after six months ignored the benefits of The Vision. I raised it with Savills and they produced another report, but yet again this Vision element was missing. I questioned them about why this was the case and later they didn't recollect the conversation. I could only conclude that there was interference from within the club.

8 September, 13 October, 25 October: Further meetings take place between Almacantar and MCC, to work up a smaller design for the Masterplan.

21 October: Colin Maynard, acting MCC chief executive, announces that the Masterplan working party set up on 24 May has been disbanded without meeting. The reason given is that the club wanted to see the report from Savills and by the time it was completed, Bradshaw had resigned.

A smaller ground working party was formed instead, consisting of Oliver Stocken, Robert Leigh. Colin Maber, John Stephenson, Colin Maynard, Justin Dowley and Blake Gorst. They went to Almacantar's offices in Marble Arch to look at the plans. The revised scheme had four rather than five blocks of flats along the Wellington Road, with the expensive undercroft abandoned.

Almacantar's view was that this cheaper and smaller blueprint had a better chance of achieving planning permission than the grandiose Vision for Lord's. The offer of £110 million to MCC remained. Chief executive Mike Hussey wanted to present to the MCC committee, but the club said it was sufficient to put his proposals to the new ground working party.

On 30 November, *The Times* published Almacantar's new images. The article was timed to coincide with a MCC committee that day, at which a number of potential schemes were being presented by the new ground working party.

Christopher Martin-Jenkins: 'I had serious personal doubts about the Almacantar plans, and I knew they were shared by many members who had been given a rather partial view of the future in various unofficial leaks to the press. Those huge new buildings would tower over the northern end of the ground, where the trees of St John's Wood churchyard still give Lord's the feel of a cricket ground rather than a stadium.

I felt that this need not be the inevitable price of progress. There was also a question mark over the long-term sustainability of a ground with greater capacity.'

The MCC committee meeting on 30 November saw the partnership with Almacantar disbanded by 18 votes to two, in just one hour of talks.

The press release read:

'The MCC committee met today at Lord's and considered a number of enhancement schemes put before it by its ground working party. It has decided to focus on developing Lord's on a stand-by-stand basis and on the club's freehold land only.

Oliver Stocken, MCC chairman, said: "As reported at the AGM earlier this year, the club has committed £3 million since 2008 on this complicated project. During this period, the economic climate has changed substantially. However, the club was awarded the platinum package of major matches by the ECB in September 2011, and that has provided the committee with the confidence to fund a redevelopment scheme on the club's freehold land, on its own. This is the course of action that the committee has today decided to pursue. MCC would like to thank Almacantar, the property developers with whom we have been working over the last few months, for their work in presenting possible development options to the club.

"Ultimately the committee agreed on the way forward for the long-term redevelopment of Lord's, probably beginning at the Pavilion End with the rebuilding and enhancement of the Tavern and Allen stands, which will provide significantly improved amenities."'

Mike Hussey, chief executive of Almacantar, replied to a media inquiry at 9.33 p.m. with the following email:

'The mandate from the members of MCC was to deliver a vision, following a global competition. Real cricket fans would have been dreaming about the benefits of a wonderful experience visiting Lord's from 2015 comparable to Wimbledon today, with Henman Hill and the total tennis offer.

'It would have buzzed with excitement and vitality, showing the general appeal of cricket, beyond the fortunate MCC members who get into the Main Ground on the day and the privileged few who can buy tickets or have corporate access. The venue would be brought into the modern age and be truly accessible and rewarding for all cricket fans, year round.

'Above all, I feel for the members who set their committee a task to deliver a vision and may be feeling a little underwhelmed right now. Unfortunately, in the nine months since our selection, MCC never managed to produce an exclusivity letter for us. So we will be taking up the club's offer to reimburse our costs in full in due course. I estimate they will be about £750,000. That is small consolation when you consider the lost opportunity for all parties.'

At 21.37, Hussey forwarded his email and the MCC press release to Rifkind with the message 'FYI'.

At 21.46, Rifkind replies equally succinctly. 'Where are you?'

21.51, Hussey: 'Cloud cuckoo land?'

22.34, Rifkind: 'Best place to be.'

22.51, Hussey: 'What a fiasco.'

That same night, Rifkind bumped into MCC committee member Anthony Wreford at the opening of The Delaunay restaurant in Covent Garden. Wreford had come straight from the main committee meeting which had terminated the Almacantar partnership.

Rifkind: 'What's happened? What's going on?'

Wreford: 'Why don't you come and talk to me?'

Rifkind: 'There's no point. We've been down that road before, and the decision has been made by MCC.'

Charles Fry: 'It was only Sir John Major and myself who were against terminating the Almacantar partnership. It was a great pity that the club basically turned its back on £150 million. I was always in favour of development, but during my time as chairman, Charles's dealings were mainly with Maurice de Rohan, and he was set against it from the start.'

Bradshaw: 'The very last meeting I had at MCC was with Mike Hussey and Oliver Stocken in the committee room. The meeting went incredibly well – I couldn't believe how it finished up. Mike Hussey would develop up the plans and if they weren't taken up, he'd walk away and there would be no charge. I documented that meeting and everyone shook hands. Despite everything that had happened, I could go home to Australia with the process still on and everybody understands where everyone is.

'But f*** me, it didn't go anywhere. It beggared belief. I just couldn't work out how such a complex project could be cancelled in such a way. The only two people to vote against The Vision being scrapped were Fry and Major. I expect Stocken worked the committee room, as they were the last two to be called for their opinion. By then, the vote was 18-0 against carrying on.'

Stocken and Dowley were never prepared to treat Major any differently from the rest of the committee, and they were underwhelmed by Major's financial acumen.

Stocken: 'John Major, although he was a Chancellor of the Exchequer, is not really a financial man. He's a politician. He did not have a very strong financial background – it's frightening that the cricketers on the committee seemed to have a better grasp of financial matters than him. He was just another human being. My thoughts were always for the club, not John Major.

'I told John that we didn't have a cash problem, we didn't need £100 million. Why should we give away our birthright if we don't need to and we're still in that place? Major replied that this was a once-in-a-lifetime opportunity. I said: "But John, these guys are property developers. They'll come back, and it will be with a higher offer."

'He would never accept that argument, but they came back five years later with £130 million. And we still have a long lease. I would have got rid of the development committee earlier, if MCC had been a City business.'

Dowley: 'John Major didn't seem to know the difference between £50 million in cash and £50 million paid over a number of years. And he would have taken £50 million, even though it was £100 million on the table. I had the embarrassing job of explaining to a former Chancellor of the Exchequer net present value, which is the difference between the present value of cash inflow and the present value of cash outflow over a period of time.

'NPV is used in capital budgeting and investment planning to analyse the profitability of a projected investment or project. Ministers do not really deal with it – they have an annual budget and have to work within that. That is the nature of government.'

Stocken said the following about the meeting that called time on the Vision for Lord's and led to the shock resignation of Major from the MCC committee:

'I went around the room, asking people for their views. Most of them thought we should discontinue the talks with Almacantar. John always sat in the same place, to the right of the chairman, president and chief executive. I started the conversation going around the other way. When we got to John, he said: "I'm going to express my views, but I expect the committee will not accept them. If the committee goes in the direction I think it will, I will support the decision publicly."

'John came up to me afterwards and asked to see the draft minutes. I told the person doing the minutes to make sure they recorded John saying he would support the committee decision publicly. I sent the minutes to him. Then, ten days later, we get his bloody letter resigning. He said he resigned because of the process. Then an article appeared in the *Telegraph*. That's Major all over.'

'For me, cricket has been a lifelong and enduring passion and it will remain so,' Major said in a statement on 14 December. 'The solace the game has given me in good times and bad, the friendships I have made and the sheer joy of the game will never fade. My decision to resign from the committee of the world's pre-eminent cricket club has been reached with very great sadness and I wish other members of the committee well in their future deliberations.'

MCC said it had accepted his resignation – which was due to 'fundamental disagreements over the direction of policy on the Vision for Lord's; the manner in which decisions have been reached, and their wider implications for the club' – 'with great reluctance'.

Phillip Hodson had replaced Christopher Martin-Jenkins as MCC president two months earlier. He recalls: 'John Major was simply part of the committee. He didn't help matters. Like a lot of politicians, he has never been in business. He was always in favour of taking the money, although some of the figures looked nonsensical to me.

'After he resigned, I went down to his flat in Vauxhall and had a cup of tea, trying to explain the MCC position. I told him we didn't need £50 million and that there was a very long lease.'

There were mixed feelings about Major departing the MCC committee in the way he did.

Maynard: 'I was very surprised when John Major resigned. I didn't think he was the type who resigned from anything.'

Leaver: 'I was astonished when John Major went public with his resignation. I was very surprised and disappointed.'

Dowley: 'I wasn't that surprised at what happened. John Major is a politician, after all, and politicians often do change their minds.'

Gorst: 'The way Major left the committee was a disgrace. He told the chairman and myself that he disagreed with the committee decision but would abide with the collective responsibility. Then he resigned.'

Griffiths: 'His resignation was not a surprise to me. When I spoke to him about what was going on, he said these people were impossible to work with. His view was: "Why should I attend these meetings and be all enthusiastic, singing MCC's praises at what an opportunity this is, when people behind the scenes are traducing me?"

'It was demeaning for a former prime minister that no one respected his view. And rather than have an out-and-out battle with those against the development, he chose to go. That in itself is a hell of an indictment against the club, and subsequently they haven't tried to win him back. He would have been the first prime minister to be president, but we lost him and treated him badly. Whenever I've seen him at various functions, I feel guilty at having got him on the development committee.'

Bradshaw: 'Major's frustrations had smouldered over some months. He had written a letter to the chairman about speeding up the redevelopment, which was not read out as requested. It was later agreed that it would be released to committee members, but it was included along with a number of other documents so didn't carry the same weight. And coming after the committee meeting in question, it had lost its relevance. This demonstrates how scurrilous and dirty the process had become, and the fact that an ex-prime minister had cause to resign validated my feelings.'

Colin Phillips, Major's private secretary: 'If you had all the experts in the room, Major would listen to them all and take the best advice he heard. That was why he was so good on a committee. He marshalled all the facts and then came up with the sensible option. It was his whips office training – he filtered out the rubbish very swiftly. He wasn't an intellectual, but he was bright enough.'

Grabiner: 'John Major could have done more. We tried very hard with him, but he was just not prepared to put his head over the parapet. My view – and I've said this to him – is that he was not prepared to take them on publicly and so he resigned, making it perfectly clear he wasn't happy. If he had gone to an AGM or SGM of MCC members and had done what I was prepared to do, to get stuck in, it might have been a different result, but he was not prepared to do that.

'Actually, it was a bit like his time as prime minister. He's a fantastic bloke and a smart guy, but when it comes to it he quite often backs down and disappears. And that's what happened here. He's the only one who really could have done something – the rest of us were just shouting in the wind, really.'

CHAPTER 11

The Major Fall-Outs

THE FALL-OUTS AFTER SIR JOHN Major's resignation began with Lord Grabiner venting his feelings about MCC's leadership on Channel 4 News on 17 December 2011.

Grabiner said: 'The future of Lord's resonates far beyond just a limited MCC membership. There is a national interest in sustaining an outstanding cricket ground. If this transaction, or a similar transaction, were to happen, it would provide a really significant social benefit for the community at large, nationally and internationally.'

Asked about the MCC fuss in the year of a home Olympics that had sparked the building of new sports facilities, Grabiner said: 'It is ironic and rather depressing, and I'm afraid driven in my view by entirely the wrong motives. I think we all know that if you run organisations as if they were in your hip pocket, ordinary governance rules simply don't apply.

'And when I say ordinary governance rules, I mean modern-day governance rules, where decisions are reached on a proper basis and where there is absolute transparency in the decision-making progress. I do not believe that is what has happened here. The reason they have put forward is the current financial climate. The trouble with that argument is that it is nonsense. The reason it's nonsense is that the developer would take the financial responsibility for doing the work and that money would go one way, namely into the pocket of MCC.

'They prefer to stop the transaction rather than allowing the transaction to happen to benefit MCC, cricket, kids generally and all the rest of it. I think that's because they focused on the wrong issue. They are much more concerned about their ruffled dignity and that of their predecessors than about the current genuine long-term interests of MCC and its members.

'What I think is shocking is the possible deprivation to future generations of the opportunity to play good-quality cricket. There are young kids out there who would be perfectly excellent at the game, and they don't get the chance because their schools have sold off grounds or because there are not facilities locally available to them. If they can display real talent, it is possible that it could be organised at Lord's.'

MCC responded to Channel 4: 'We have always made it clear that the project was subject both to the financial viability of the proposed development as a whole and reaching agreement with the ECB on the number of major matches to be played at Lord's in the coming years. The club have not ruled out redevelopment at the Nursery End in the future.'

Sir John Major and Lord Grabiner also made a strong point by proposing and seconding Robert Griffiths for his successful election to the MCC committee in October 2012. He had lost his place following the disbandment of the development committee in February 2011.

MCC responded to the Grabiner broadside by emailing a question and answer guide about the redevelopment conflict to members. It was candid by MCC standards, including the names of the two main committee members – Charles Fry and Sir John Major – who had not supported the ditching of Almacantar.

Q: Why did the committee decide to pursue a revised development plan?

A: Since 2008, the economic climate has changed substantially. But the club's award of a platinum package of international matches in September 2011 provides the committee with the confidence to fund a redevelopment scheme on the club's freehold land on its own.

Q: How much money was on the table from Almacantar, and can MCC really afford to turn it down?

A: Almacantar in its tender indicated £100 million available to the club as a result of residential development at the Nursery End. At the end of February 2011, Almacantar suggested the figure might be £110 million. Having spent time during 2011 working with MCC's executive and having reconsidered the likely scale of residential development which might be approved by the local authority, Almacantar reduced its estimate of possible proceeds to the club to around £50 million to £60 million in October 2011.

Q: What does this mean for the Vision for Lord's?

A: The committee are unanimous about long-term development, starting with the Tavern and Allen stands.

Q: Does MCC owe money to Almacantar or anyone else involved in the Vision for Lord's?

A: MCC has committed £3 million since 2008 on this complicated project. The club believes, and is advised, that it does not owe any further money on any aspect relating to this project.

Q: Will there ever be any development at Lord's at the Nursery End?

A: The committee concluded to work on a stand-by-stand basis, but the club has not ruled out any development at the Nursery End. Should the club want to look at residential, we will approach Almacantar first.

Q: 'How large is a very large majority? Was there a vote?

A: There were only two votes against the new proposal – Sir John Major, who felt The Vision should proceed, and Charles Fry, who felt that more work should be done to determine the financial benefits of residential development.

Q: Can you quantify the supposed positive reaction from members over not continuing with Almacantar?

A: MCC has had an overwhelmingly positive response to its new proposal, and this has been fed back in a variety of ways – letters, phone calls, emails, posts on the club's online forum and comments at MCC functions.

Q: Did Keith Bradshaw resign, or was he forced to resign because of disagreements on the Vision for Lord's project?

A: No, Keith had to resign for family reasons. He enjoyed a very productive and harmonious association with the MCC committee. He had an excellent working relationship with the chairman and treasurer.

Q: What is the evidence that planning consent may not have been given?

A: MCC commissioned Savills to conduct an independent assessment of its real estate options and to summarise the Vision for Lord's project to date. One of their conclusions was that the original Herzog plans would have been unlikely to achieve planning consent. This was confirmed by Almacantar at a separate meeting.

Q: Why was the Masterplan working party disbanded without ever meeting?

A: The club wanted to wait to see the report by Savills. By the time it was completed, Keith Bradshaw had had to resign. The club therefore needed to change the composition of the group, which it did so with the creation of the ground working party. The chairman and president both felt this group struck exactly the right balance – two from estates, two from finance and two from the executive.

MCC hoped their Q&A would quieten the noise around the issue, but it was the unlikely figure of past president Christopher Martin-Jenkins who kept the controversy at full volume, with a one-sided comment piece in defence of Stocken and Dowley in *The Times* on 9 January.

He wrote: 'There comes a time when distortions, repeated often enough in the media, start to be accepted as fact. When that happens, bad decisions can be made and the wrong people can prevail. By the same process, honourable and innocent men can be disparaged and the great institution that they represent, in this case MCC, gets spattered by mud quite unnecessarily.

'Declaring an interest as an MCC committee member and last year's president, I feel bound to warn that these things could happen as a consequence of one-sided, and misguided, press reports on the long debate about how Lord's should be developed to maintain its unique prestige.

'This is the same MCC whose chairman and treasurer have been repeatedly sniped at by a disaffected group who did not like decisions taken by huge committee majorities last year on the issue of the future development of Lord's. They have behaved like batsmen refusing to walk when given out.

'It has to be stressed in fairness to the two vilified non-executives that both the finance and estates committees believed The Vision to be financially risky and unrealistic in the changed economic circumstances.'

CMJ omitted to mention that he had chaired the main committee meeting in which the development committee had been axed. His *Times* colleague Ivo Tennant said: 'It was an ill-advised piece. Major asked for a retraction and was given it. Robert Griffiths threatened to sue. And *The Times* were not happy that the *Daily Mail* revealed CMJ's own role in that crucial MCC committee meeting.'

Major received a retraction in *The Times*, stating that CMJ had not intended to imply that the former prime minister had sniped unfairly at the chairman and treasurer or that he had acted in any way other than honourably and for the good of the club.

Private Eye reported: 'CMJ was always likely to run into difficulties by continuing to work for *The Times* while serving as a president of MCC. He achieved the impressive feat of upsetting Sir John Major, Lord Grabiner, Robert Griffiths and the *Daily Mail*. In his *Times* column on 9 January, CMJ implied the trio [Sir John Major, Lord Grabiner and Robert Griffiths] had acted "like batsman refusing to walk when being given out", after the MCC committee on which he sits rejected the Vision for Lord's.

'He omitted to mention he chaired the meeting in which the development committee was axed. Nor did he mention that on breaking the news to Griffiths, he said: "I'm sorry Robert, but this club cannot afford to lose the chairman and the treasurer."

'Grabiner sounded off furiously in the *Daily Mail*, which had been criticised by CMJ for 'one-sided and misguided journalism'. 'Paul Dacre's organ, never one to bear a grudge, took exception to having its MCC coverage rubbished and has run no fewer than six retaliatory blasts by sports columnist Charlie "Charles" Sale in the past fortnight. As a further torment, CMJ had to suffer sharing a press box with Sale during England's equally lamentable performance in the first Test against Pakistan in Dubai.'

On his return from the UAE at the end of the England series, CMJ was diagnosed with cancer. He died of lymphoma on 1 January 2013, aged 67.

The start of 2012 also saw a new dynamic in the redevelopment saga. Rank-and-file members of MCC became involved online, first through the official MCC forum set up by Keith Bradshaw, and when that was closed down, through the Members' Independent Online Pavilion, introduced by James Mitchell in July 2012. Only a fraction of MCC's membership posted regular comments, but those that did made their presence felt. One of those committed from the start was Nick Gandon, a schoolteacher who became a director of the Cricket Foundation, where he set up the Chance to Shine charity.

Gandon had bumped into Charles Rifkind at a reception at 11 Downing Street hosted by chancellor George Osborne's wife Frances. Following their meeting, Gandon had a long session at Rifkind's Tea House during which he learnt about the conflict. And in January 2012, Gandon wrote to MCC president Phillip Hodson with questions about the process and asked for an independent inquiry.

'The purpose of my writing is to raise concerns directly with you in your capacity as president of MCC. Would it not be reasonable to read Sir John Major's resignation from the committee, while simultaneously nominating Robert Griffiths for election back to the MCC committee, as a thinly veiled expression of no confidence in the club's governance and its handling of matters relating to The Vision?'

As a result of the correspondence Gandon had an hour's meeting with Hodson, who later told him he would not be implementing an inquiry.

Almacantar had made a revised offer, increasing their bid to £100 million in cash plus a £10 million contribution towards supporting young cricketers, subject to planning permission. But the MCC committee on 8 February rejected the offer, maintaining that the building of four residential towers would not be supported by members, irrespective of the cash offered.

But the committee did want to bring the matter to a head with the membership. A statement said: 'The amount of money involved is such that the members must be allowed to properly contribute to this debate, and for that reason a resolution will appear at this year's AGM. The outcome of the resolution will guide the club in its future plans and determine whether or not members would permit residential development within the ground at the Nursery End during the foreseeable future.'

Stocken was hoping to kick any residential plans at the Nursery End into the long grass. But then, MCC president Hodson's letter to members, in which he attempted to explain the club's stance on ground development, caused serious upset – not least from Sir John Major.

Hodson wrote: 'The public debate in the national press and elsewhere surrounding the redevelopment of the ground has been unhelpful to the club. Members should be aware that the vast majority of articles regarding the Vision for Lord's or Masterplan have neither been authorised nor promulgated by the MCC committee. Members should always be the first to know what is happening at MCC, and incorrect statements together with incorrectly attributed comments are nothing other than harmful.

'The committee's view as to how the ground should be redeveloped has changed during the past three or four years, and some members have said that the committee has spent large sums of money unwisely. The total amount spent on the redevelopment project since the beginning of 2008 is £2.92 million. This expenditure has not been wasted, but instead has allowed the committee to undertake the most comprehensive examination of the ground that has ever taken place.

'A large sum of money and the provision of facilities at the Nursery End had been offered to the club. But the committee agreed that the preservation of Lord's as a cricket ground was more important than a windfall of cash. Of equal importance was the committee's belief that members would not be inclined to accept such a scheme.

'This stance led to the resignation from the committee of Sir John Major – a very regrettable consequence. On the committee's behalf, I should like to take this opportunity to thank Sir John for the very wise and thoughtful contributions which he made during the period of his committee membership.'

Nick Gandon posted his reaction to Hodson on the members' forum: 'If ever there were a letter written which has achieved the polar opposite of what it intended, then I am sorry to say that the president's letter stands out as an exemplar. Rather than create confidence in the MCC committee and its decision-making, the letter serves to highlight an extensive list of contradictions and seemingly to expose its incompetence. Furthermore, it also invites us to speculate as to its motivations, which seem much more obviously driven by personal agendas rather than by the objective long-term needs of the club.

'And by the way, does the president consider his predecessor's article in January in *The Times* as authorised or promulgated by the MCC committee "unhelpful or harmful"? Is it only the committee view that has any legitimacy? And what are we to make of Sir John Major's resignation? Is it conceivable that a man of Sir John's standing would have resigned without his wishing members to sit up, take note and ask questions?

'Besides, did not Sir John say that his resignation was as much about the manner in which decisions were being made as it was about the decisions itself? What does he know about the process behind the decision-making?'

Gandon's post sparked an intriguing response from a whistle-blower inside MCC, whose identity remains unknown:

'I am employed by the club and sit on a couple of sub-committees. So if the contents of this letter were ever to come to the attention of the secretariat and suspicion fell on me, my position (and possibly my livelihood) could be in jeopardy. So please respect my confidentiality, but feel free to use any of my suggestions as your own.

'It is no secret that since the departure of Keith Bradshaw, there is an atmosphere of fear and suspicion within the club. I am very much in favour of the original Vision. However, I firmly believe that any decision taken to adopt The Vision, or abort it, must be taken by all the membership. Furthermore, this decision cannot be made until all the members are fully acquainted with all the facts.

'So, whatever my personal opinion may be, I will abide by a decision arrived at by the membership ... not by Stocken, Dowley and the other MCC committee members.

'Right up to that infamous February 2011 meeting, the committee had voted almost unanimously in favour of The Vision. The so-called change of mind and the disbanding of the development committee was a direct result of the threat by Stocken and Dowley to resign. I understand from a member of the committee that it was the nastiest, most vicious meeting he had ever attended.

'Why did the committee change their minds … simply because they did not want the public humiliation and press publicity if the chairman and treasurer were to resign.'

Major was furious with Hodson's portrayal of his reasons for resigning from MCC. He wrote to the beleaguered president on 2 March, copying the letter to all members of the main committee and demanding it be circulated to all members. It was also leaked to the *Daily Telegraph*. It fully exposes Major's falling out with MCC over their leadership and governance. It also follows Major telling chairman Oliver Stocken he would fall in line with the committee over their decision to terminate The Vision.

Dear Phillip

I have read your letter of 13 February, addressed to the full and senior members of MCC. Whilst I am grateful for your kind words about my contribution to the club, I fear that your letter totally misrepresents the reason for my resignation from the MCC committee.

You wrote:

'the committee agreed that the preservation of Lord's as a cricket ground was more important than a windfall of cash. Of equal importance was the committee's belief that the members would not be inclined to accept such a scheme. This stance led to the resignation from the committee of Sir John Major…'

This – emphatically – is not true. If I may, I will repeat

(some of) the points I made in my resignation letter, dated 9 December 2011.

I did *not* resign over the decision to abandon the 'Vision for Lord's', even though I do believe it is a serious mistake the club may come to regret. I resigned due to the manner in which the decision was reached.

During the last four years, we have spent a huge amount of time, money, energy – and cost – discussing "the Vision for Lord's", which was endorsed by the main committee on many occasions – often overwhelmingly, but sometimes with a minority of very committed opponents.

I sat on the development committee for The Vision, until the main committee was informed that our work was done and it was disbanded. Since our work was not done, the decision came as a surprise to me and other members of the development committee. However, in the interests of harmony, I accepted this peremptory dismissal.

When a new committee: the 'Masterplan working party' was subsequently set up. I was reassured when Sir Michael Jenkins – who chaired the working party which had developed the original Vision for Lord's – was included as a member. Yet this committee was disbanded without ever meeting.

A ground working party was then formed to carry matters forward. The composition of its membership was entirely biased *against* the plans in The Vision.

As the chairman of the working party conceded to me in committee, this working party contained *only* opponents of the scheme: not one single member had *ever* expressed any support for the comprehensive development of Lord's.

Nevertheless, I was hopeful that they would take an open-minded look at the wider opportunities offered but – as I ascertained in committee – they failed to even discuss any outcome other than a piecemeal redevelopment over many years, funded from our own resources.

Moreover, the argument put forward in the working party report (conducted by Savills) was tendentious. We were told we might not get planning consent; that the additional seats could not be filled; that the members of the club were moving against a residential scheme at the Nursery End (whereas in the past we had been advised precisely the opposite).

It seemed as though this report had been drafted in such a way as to justify a pre-determined outcome. As a result, the working party report unceremoniously ditched many years of work on the Vision for Lord's.

I concede, of course, that the committee has every right to change its mind – even as comprehensively as it has done. But this episode has been damaging to the MCC purse, and our reputation. This is not the way our club should be run.

The converse is, I believe, that we have missed an opportunity to raise an absolute *minimum* of £50 million for the club, which would have greatly strengthened our financial resources; enabled us to improve facilities for members and hold (or even reduce) their annual fees in what is a very difficult economic climate; and make, if we wished, a larger contribution than at present to the wider world of cricket.

I do not argue for the *maximum* Vision, since the economic times have changed, and we have to take account of this: that is why I agreed that removing the undercroft from the scheme was sensible. But I do believe a plan could – and should – have been approved that would not have damaged the ambience of the ground.

I agree with those members who argue that we are first and foremost a cricket club. But this argues for a sensitive development of Lord's, not for the lengthy, fragmented approach that now seems to be in operation.

When I resigned from the committee I did so after much deliberation, and with great reluctance. At that time, the chairman asked me not to make any public comment. In the interests of MCC I agreed, and have remained true to my word.

However, although I have kept my counsel, others have not. I have found the reason for my resignation repeatedly misrepresented in the media, and now in your letters to members.

It gives the impression that I did believe cash was more important than the preservation of Lord's whereas this is not, and never has been, my view.

Unsurprisingly, such an impression has generated a reaction from people who have been misled. At the time of my resignation, I told the chairman – orally and in writing – that if my position was traduced, I would not hesitate to correct the record.

It is for that reason that I am copying this letter to all members of the main committee, and would ask that you copy it to all full and senior members. That way, there can be no further doubt about the reason behind my resignation, nor my personal and lasting commitment to MCC, the wider world of cricket and the upholding of the spirit of the game.

I would be grateful for your early confirmation that this will be done.

Yours sincerely,
John Major

Hodson did send Major's letter on to all members as requested, along with a covering note in which the MCC president describes the process that dismantled The Vision as 'flawed'.

'Further to my letter to members on 13 February 2012, Sir John Major did not think my words reflected the true reasons for his resignation. Whilst he is in favour of a development at the Nursery End, the abandonment of this project in November 2011 was not the cause of his resignation; rather it was the flawed process which led to this decision.

'Accordingly, since the agenda for AGM will include a discussion and vote on the committee's decision not to accept Almacantar proposals for residential development on the club's leasehold land, I have agreed to attach Sir John's letter of 2 March.'

The AGM literature, in a pack that also contained Major's letter, asked members to consider and, if they thought fit, approve the following resolution: 'That members ratify the decision of the MCC committee not to permit any residential development on the club's leasehold land at the Nursery End of the ground.'

It was Stocken's attempt to put a lid on the residential debate for the foreseeable future.

Ahead of the AGM, Almacantar called in their lawyers over their costs on the aborted Vision, which MCC were not intending to pay. Berwin Leighton Paisner wrote to acting chief executive Colin Maynard and cited Sir John Major's letter to support their concerns, along with their own president Phillip Hodson having calling the process 'flawed'.

'Our clients are disappointed and frustrated by MCC's failure to address the issue of its abortive costs. In light of the lack of progress which has been made, we are now instructed to take this matter forward. Accordingly, please treat this letter as our client's formal letter before claim.

'Whilst our client has no particular desire to sue MCC, regrettably your approach to date suggests that MCC does not share our client's desire to avoid litigation. As set out below, unless a satisfactory response is forthcoming within 21 days (9 May 2012), our client will have no option but to commence proceedings for the recovery of these costs.

'It is our client's primary contention that it has a contractual claim against MCC for recovery of the sum of £400,598.20 plus VAT, being the professional costs which were rendered abortive by MCC's decision to abandon the Vision for Lord's redevelopment in November 2011.

'Regrettably MCC's letter of 20 December 2011 to our clients and its letter of 13 February 2012 to its members contain an inaccurate and misleading account of not only the relationship between the parties but also their conduct towards each other during the relevant period. Whilst there is much we disagree with in those letters, we do not consider it would be productive to rebut each and every point in this letter.

'By March 2011 the exclusivity letter was agreed, save for a small point in relation to VAT. Importantly, payment of abortive costs was agreed in clause 4 of the exclusivity letter. Notwithstanding the exclusivity letter not being formally executed, the parties proceeded to work on the basis terms were agreed. Our client has extensive correspondence with MCC during the relevant period (including text messages with Mr Bradshaw), corroborating and detailing this. Regular updates and cost estimates were provided by our client.

'Ultimately on 30 November 2011, MCC decided to abandon its plans for the redevelopment and subsequently made it clear that it did not consider that it owed our client any money whatsoever, only its "gratitude". Not only was this a disappointing and surprising remark, it was legally incorrect.

'Sir John Major, in his letter to members of 2 March 2012, makes it abundantly clear that he resigned from the main committee because of the manner in which the decision to abandon The Vision was reached. His view that the working party report had been prepared to justify a pre-determined outcome (ie the abandonment) is worrying and requires investigation.

'Indeed, we note that MCC now agrees that its conduct was unacceptable. Mr Hodson has now forwarded Sir John Major's letter to the members and, in his covering letter of 2 April, admits "Whilst [Sir John Major] is in favour of a development at the Nursery End, the abandonment of the project in November 2011 was not the cause of his resignation; rather it was the flawed process which led to this decision."

'It is plain MCC received a benefit from the extensive advice and service which Almacantar provided. What was created with Almacantar's assistance was a revised and scaled-down scheme which was arguably more sympathetic to the existing setting of the ground and more likely to gain planning consent.'

Also ahead of the AGM, Rifkind's supporter Simon Elliot wrote to MCC grandee Sir Michael Jenkins, outlining RLP's major concern about the upcoming resolution to prevent flats being built on the leasehold land:

'Since we talked, I have debated what to send you, and I have decided to give you access to everything. You will make your own conclusions. But the overwhelming impression is that you have a president [Phillip Hodson] who is backing his chairman [Oliver Stocken] and finance director [Justin Dowley] to the hilt. And in doing so, he is seriously misleading the membership to the extent he is trying to halt any open discussion over the future of Lord's.

'The resolution which he is personally promoting "not to permit development on the leasehold land" is dishonest at best. It does not disclose his knowledge of the Wellington Hospital possibility, of which the membership should be informed.

'I can assure you that an approach from the Wellington is serious. It would be ridiculous not to entertain a serious negotiation on the leasehold land; the president's resolution would not allow this to happen. Surely the trustees, with their responsibilities over land transactions, would be concerned about rejecting this out of hand?'

The pressure over the Nursery End land resolution increased further when six MCC members – Nick Gandon, Paddy Briggs, Geoffrey

Glazer, Steve Hollis, Derek Zissman and Laurence Dillamore – sent an open letter to Stocken.

'The issues that MCC has faced surrounding The Vision/Masterplan are the most consequential the club has faced for a very long time. The surrounding controversy is not, as the president said in his radio interview with Jonathan Agnew on 28 March 2012, "much ado about nothing".

'To date, what has been gained is negligible. What has been lost – money, time and reputation – is significant. As rank-and-file MCC members, we have received from the club a range of explanatory letters and statements, listened to radio interviews and read articles in the press – which, rather than offering clarity and reassurance, have served to contradict, obfuscate and raise alarm.

'Our concern is compounded by the resolution the committee is asking members to support at the imminent AGM on 2 May, namely: "That members ratify the decision of the MCC committee not to permit any residential development on the leasehold land at the Nursery End of the ground"

'The resolution is wrong on every count. To allow it to pass through unopposed would be equally wrong … This open letter is a last resort to alert members to concerns and encourage them, prior to the AGM, to oppose the resolution for the following reasons:

'The resolution is in direct contradiction of the club's statement (development Q and A, posted online in December 2011): "The club has not ruled out any development at the Nursery End in the future." … The committee's aiming to pass a resolution that will be determined inevitably in its favour by postal voting without offering a credible counter-argument is undemocratic and morally questionable.'

The AGM on 2 May 2012 brought matters to a head. Hodson was chairing the meeting in his role as president. And, much to the dismay of Stocken and Dowley in particular, he withdrew his resolution before the vote, following questions from the floor.

Stocken: 'Justin and I had spent a long time rehearsing answers to all the possible questions we might get asked. A question was raised from the floor about the resolution not being appropriate. Phillip panicked and withdrew the resolution. Justin and I were livid. That night at the AGM dinner, Phillip had one or two too many drinks. The next morning, we were meeting at 9 a.m. to review things. Phillip said: "I think you're not very happy with me?" "You're bloody right," we replied. We could have killed the whole thing dead then.'

Hodson: 'I felt it was the right decision to drop the motion because of the opposition from members. Oliver and Justin were fuming, but I took advice from Mike Brearley. I was very emotional about it at the annual dinner afterwards and the following day, but I had to take the heat out of the situation.

'Our finances were strong and I don't believe in selling one's birthright. Charles Rifkind would have done better if he had aligned himself with different people. Some of them were not very pleasant and did him a disservice.'

Paddy Briggs: 'I took the lead at the AGM. I said at the meeting: "When it comes to the redevelopment of Lord's, there are not two options, one with and one without residential development. There are a whole range of options." Hodson replied that he would have a little chat with his colleagues. He then decided to withdraw the motion. There was a ripple of laughter around the room. It really was preposterous. They withdrew something that would have been extremely difficult to manage – managing the future.'

Peter Leaver: 'Phillip panicked. I was in despair.'

Rifkind: 'The resolution was a clumsy way of the club being spiteful to my situation. Why else would you put forward such a resolution?'

At the AGM, Derek Brewer, the new MCC chief executive and secretary, inherited the issue that would dominate his five years at the helm. Hodson had told the AGM that Brewer would have a free hand to consider all options. So the Gandon group of six wrote to Brewer, welcoming him to MCC and asking for a dialogue to start. They met with Brewer at the end of May and sent a follow-up letter on 11 June:

'You ask us to be patient and to await the plans of the ground working party to be communicated early in July. But as we emphasised in our letter to you on 3 May, whilst we have no particular entitlements relative to any other members, we do know that we speak for an increasing number of members who share our concerns. This matter was handled very skilfully at the AGM with the withdrawal of the contentious motion. But there still remains a significant body of members who are prepared to call an SGM to seek a full and independent inquiry.'

Rifkind, not known for his patience, waited two months after the AGM before contacting Brewer, the third MCC chief executive during the tunnel saga.

'I wanted to allow you reasonable time to settle into your new role before making contact. However, now that you have been in place as CEO for eight weeks, I thought it would be an appropriate time to write to propose a meeting.'

It took a further eight months for that meeting to materialise.

Rifkind: 'We had very formal letters going between us. There was no room for any form of relationship. Derek Brewer became a shadow of himself. He realised that a relationship with me was untenable. It took him ten months to come and see me with Colin Maynard. He had been given a remit to look at the whole of the estate, so I'm not quite sure why there was a stalling process of ten months.

'When he did eventually come to the Tea House, he had three hours of me talking to him, telling him the history. He became uncomfortable because his knowledge was very limited. He was frightened of Oliver Stocken and adhered to everything his chairman said.'

The suspicions about Rifkind and those who supported him swirling around Lord's at that time were highlighted in an email from Stocken loyalist Anthony Wreford to Gandon: 'Please could you answer a perfectly straightforward question to ascertain whether your views are truly independent or may, in some way, be linked to other interested parties?'

Gandon replied: 'If you are questioning whether either Paddy Briggs or I are in any way raising issues around development at Lord's because we might personally benefit through some sort of back-hander from RLP and Almacantar, you should know that any such speculation is entirely groundless.'

Paddy Briggs had similar questions put to him: 'Nick Gandon and

I had a meeting with Oliver Stocken and he said to us: "Now come on, what is it between you two and Charles Rifkind?" Stocken assumed what we were doing was part of some largesse from Rifkind. Charles bought us breakfast once in the Wolseley, but that's the beginning and end of it. For Oliver to hint or suggest fairly strongly that we were in Charles's pocket was fairly offensive.'

It was at that meeting with Briggs and Gandon in September 2012 that Stocken claimed RLP 'withdrew unilaterally' from the process and that he had a letter confirming this to be the case. This was the reason, according to Stocken, that the club had neither a moral nor legal obligation to return the £808,000 paid to the club by RLP.

The talks with Stocken had not appeased the Gandon group's disquiet about the way MCC was being run. On 16 October, Gandon gave Brewer notice of their intention to raise enough backing from members – 180 signatures – to call an SGM to vote on their proposed resolution for an independent inquiry into how Vision for Lords had been handled. Their concerns included the resignation of Sir John Major from the main committee, the president having to withdraw an MCC resolution at the AGM, Almacantar's legal action and the lack of information to members, including no mention of Wellington Hospital's proposal for using the tunnel space at the Nursery End.

The MCC civil war was becoming more fractious by the day. In December 2012 MCC made a secret pre-planning application to Westminster Council for a four-block residential development on their freehold land, where the indoor school and ECB offices now stand. Even some main committee members were unaware of it. It was almost a year later that the *Daily Mail* revealed the initiative and quoted an MCC spokesman, who said: 'We were examining all options and this one didn't stand up.'

Peter Leaver, who closely aligned himself with Stocken, made a rare posting on the Members' Independent Online Pavilion on 2 January 2013 to counter a comment made by Nick Gandon. He wrote: 'Your suggestion that I have said things as a result of my determination to be loyal to chums in the establishment is gratuitously offensive, as it implies that I have deliberately said things that I know to be untrue.'

By March 2013, the reformists had the necessary 180 signatures to call an SGM. They wanted an independent panel to investigate and report to members about the process followed by the MCC committee leading to their rejection of the Vision for Lords.

Briggs wrote to Hodson in a highly confrontational manner: 'My own intervention at the AGM was sincerely meant and I genuinely accepted that you were clear (because you said so twice) that Derek Brewer would have a free hand to consider all options at Lord's. It seems now this is very far from the case. Frankly I feel betrayed because I took on trust something publicly stated by the president of our club which emphatically is now not being delivered.

'The case for considering residential development on leasehold land has always been strong. However, for reasons wrapped up in a range of personal agendas, the best interest of the club and its members are clearly being sacrificed. This is unacceptable. If I might dare to say as much, you and the committee seem delusional in not accepting that the potential consequences of events surrounding The Vision are significant in the extreme – in terms of cost, damaged reputation and lost confidence.'

The MCC committee are further aggravated when Gandon, Briggs and co access a database used for selecting club members to play in MCC matches to drum up support for their SGM resolution. Mike Griffith, Hodson's successor as MCC president, sends out an email to members.

'You may have read in the press in recent weeks that some members are campaigning to requisition an SGM calling for an independent in-quiry to look into historic events concerning the redevelopment of the ground. All members, of course, are within their rights to scrutinise the club's activities and, if they desire, requisition an SGM. It is nonetheless disappointing that the SGM requisitionists have chosen to correspond with certain members using a database that is reserved for recruiting playing members for MCC matches. A number of members have com-plained to the club at having received that email.'

Gandon owned up on the online forum that he had access to the playing membership contact details:

'Since I am almost certainly responsible for contacting playing members of the club regarding the call for an SGM, allow me to comment as follows: I fully apologise to any member of the club who has received an unwelcome communication from me on behalf of the MCC Reform Group. It wasn't intended to be a nuisance but rather – in the absence of the club allowing us (or actually refusing us) the means by which to communicate with our fellow members – to enable members to be made aware of matters that some at least might consider important. As a former match manager of MCC matches, I have access, alongside all other match managers, to a handbook which provides contact details of all playing members.'

Gandon also replied to Mike Griffith in a similarly aggressive tone to his colleague Briggs:

'Your email gives an entirely one-sided and highly questionable slant to the matters it refers to. This is particularly regrettable, as it is likely to be the first that many members will have heard of the SGM call. If I might be so bold, it appears a clear attempt by you and the rest of the MCC leadership to undermine this initiative.

'The withholding of means by which requisitionists can give every member an equal chance to participate in the club's democratic process does not sit well, merely serving to strengthen a perception that the club's leadership is prepared to go to any length in order to prevent members from accessing information that would better enable them to hold the club's committee to account. It creates an inference that the committee wishes to bury the past and will resort to Kremlin-like control to obstruct any endeavour that might help to shed light.'

However, supporters of land development calling the MCC committee 'delusional' and accusing them of adopting 'Kremlin-like' tactics will not have helped Rifkind's cause when he was offered an opportunity to make a presentation to the ground working party chaired by Colin Maber on 3 April 2013.

Rifkind was given an hour in the committee room to explain his latest plans, including Wellington Hospital's involvement. Those in front of him included Stocken, Dowley, Brewer, Leigh, Gorst and Maynard, all strong opponents of residential development at the Nursery End. So it was no surprise when, a week later, the MCC committee rejected Rifkind's latest proposal, instead opting for the club's masterplan to upgrade the ground over a 15 to 20-year process.

Mike Griffith's email to members afterwards stated: 'The committee is totally focused on ensuring that Lord's is in the most advantageous position possible to secure major matches in the future and no development at the ground should put that position at risk. Accordingly, the RLP proposal was rejected for the reasons stated below.

'The committee believes the size of the Nursery Ground is sacrosanct, both for the staging of cricket matches and as a practice area of international standard.

1. A development such as that proposed by RLP would lead to a loss of operational space essential for the running of the ground on major match days.

2. The visual and environmental impact of the proposed RLP scheme would damage the character and ambience of Lord's.

3. The committee received a presentation from the chairman of the ground working party, Colin Maber, on the progress of the club's Masterplan, part of which was a presentation from the treasurer Robert Leigh on the funding of that plan. The committee supported both presentations.'

Griffith's comment about the size of the Nursery Ground being 'sacrosanct' was to be conveniently forgotten when MCC came to consider the design of the new Compton and Edrich stands four years later.

The discord between the two sides became even more apparent when Rifkind met the MCC trio of chairman Stocken, chief executive Brewer and treasurer Leigh for a breakfast meeting at the Wolseley restaurant on 24 July.

Stocken stressed that MCC were concentrating on their Masterplan of a stand-by-stand development, while Rifkind outlined his reasons not to close the door on the leasehold land opportunities. Such were the differences that Rifkind emailed Brewer the next day, asking to see the notes from the meeting.

'Thank you for taking the minutes of the discussion that took place yesterday with Oliver Stocken, Robert Leigh and yourself. Can you let me know when the minutes might be ready for collection?'

Brewer replied: 'This is the mother of all weeks, with something every evening (T20 tonight). So it's likely to be next week, and I'll send the minutes through when ready.'

When Rifkind received them, he found that they only reflected the views expressed by the MCC contingent. Being frustrated at every turn, he turned to his most influential supporters, including Lord Grabiner and City grandee Sir Simon Robertson, chairman of Rolls Royce. Robertson had been brought on board by his close friend Simon Elliot, who was convinced Rifkind had been subjected to a gross injustice by MCC.

A meeting with Stocken, at Robertson's office in St James's Place, Mayfair, was arranged at the start of September. Stocken was accompanied by Mike Griffith and Brewer. After the meeting, Sir Simon wrote to Mervyn King, chairman of the Bank of England, to drum up support for Rifkind.

'Dear Mervyn, I hope you are well and enjoying New York. I had a meeting last Thursday with Oliver, Mike Griffith and Derek Brewer. The atmosphere was tough but cordial. I felt at the end Oliver and his team were more uncomfortable than when we started.

'What would make Oliver really have to pay attention is if I could get a few more names of support. I have spoken to David Gower, who has said to me privately that he is supportive and I could put his name in if there were other names also. I am trying John Major, too. What has been going on at MCC over the last few years is really very unsatisfactory. I really worry for the inevitable train wreck if Oliver cannot be persuaded to change tack.'

Brian McGowan, who sat on the disbanded development committee, wrote in a similar vein to the Rifkind camp:

'The key will be bringing on board high-profile names, as they will dramatically affect the reactions of the members. David Gower's reaction is typical of people in a similar position. They are happy to put their names to a cause in which they believe, but not if they stand alone.

'Can we not use a little subterfuge on the back of David's comments by pulling in other high-profile names, by saying David is putting his name to the letter? If no one else joined we could obviously not leave David high and dry, but I bet we will pull in at least one other with this tactic.

'John Major is a big prize, but Mervyn King would be not far behind. Charles Fry would be good to have on this list. A team of John Major, Mervyn King, David Gower and Charles Fry would be unbeatable.'

Mervyn King wrote back to Robertson: 'I arrived in New York only yesterday, having been out of touch while at sea. It is disquieting to learn of developments at MCC. But I do not feel I know enough at this stage to take part in what will inevitably be seen by Oliver and Derek as an attack on their leadership.'

Major was also not prepared to put his name on the letter.

Colin Phillips: 'John Major's view was "once you're out, you're out". "If they don't want me, that's fine." He's not a backseat driver. He was a member at Surrey first, not MCC. He was nervous to intervene as the knight in shining armour. He's very pragmatic. And with all that stuff about him and Edwina Currie, he wanted to keep his head down.'

Stocken: 'I remember watching something Tony Grabiner did on television and then Simon Robertson got involved. Simon had been a long-term member of MCC, but had not been to Lord's for a long time.'

Ahead of the SGM in October, Robertson wrote to Stocken, outlining his misgivings at the way MCC ran their affairs.

'Dear Oliver, I have received the SGM papers. The MCC recommendation in red and bold on the front page reinforces my concerns over governance, which I have reflected in my correspondence with you.

'You have told me that the way proposals are put to members and then voted on are like any public company. They are, except in one crucial respect: nobody apart from the MCC committee is able to communicate with members, as you are not obliged to provide a list of members. As a result, nobody can seriously mount a contrarian view to that of MCC.

So your emblazoned recommendation shows to me the unbalanced nature of how the SGM is being conducted.

'I am not aware of any occasion when MCC members have been

asked to vote specifically on development choices available to MCC and therefore its members. I repeat what I have said before. My contention is that the members are entitled to have the full facts put before them in a balanced way. Frankly, the production of some slides at the AGM does not do it for me.

'May I suggest that you reconsider the approach to the SGM, by advising the membership that they will be written to after the meeting with a full presentation of the discussion at the SGM and an assessment of the original Masterplan and the new MCC plan, and crucially they will be asked to reaffirm their vote.

'Unless you are prepared to consider something along these lines, I fear that public scrutiny will not go away and further SGMs will be called for.'

Robertson signed off by saying: 'I would like to attend the SGM, but I have destroyed my membership card as I felt I would have no further need of it now that the cricket season has ended. Could I please ask you to arrange for me to attend the SGM without my membership card?'

Stocken responded: 'Your letter reached me while I am on a visit to India. I will call you on my return next week. In the meantime, arrangements will be made for you to receive a replacement membership pass.'

The SGM on 17 October 2013 resulted in an inevitable defeat for the Reform Group's resolutions for an independent inquiry over the demise of The Vision. Robertson caused a furore by reading out a coruscating letter from Grabiner, who was unable to attend. Rank-and-file MCC members felt the letter went over the top in its personal attack on Stocken and Dowley, and that if Grabiner felt that way, he should have been there to make his comments in person. The requisitionists only showed Grabiner's letter to MCC shortly before the SGM, giving them no proper chance to respond.

Grabiner's letter read as follows:

'Unfortunately I am not able to attend the meeting because of a prior longstanding engagement. I write this letter in my capacity as an MCC member and as one of the 11 members of the development committee appointed by the main committee in October 2009, for the purpose of identifying a suitable development partner.

'From the outset, it was obvious to me and other members of the development committee (including, in particular, Robert Griffiths, Sir John Major and Brian McGowan) that the two key MCC officers, Oliver Stocken and Justin Dowley, were absolutely opposed to The Vision and the task which was supposed to be performed by the development committee.

'Both were members of the smaller negotiating group of eight and they took every opportunity to try to deflect the group from the task by engaging debate about what they claimed were the deficiencies of The Vision. That was not our job.

'It was recognised by everyone else at the table that when a suitable partner had been identified, it would be necessary for the development committee and MCC to sit down with the chosen developer, in order to formulate a planning application to be made to Westminster Council. The planning application needed the approval of MCC and would have to work in all respects, financially.

'Oliver and Justin were, and I believe still are, motivated by a strong sense of irritation, driven by the fact that in 1999, when the strip of land within Lord's adjacent to Wellington Road was put up for auction by Railtrack, it was purchased by RLP rather than by MCC.

'I have no personal knowledge of the 1999 events, but the talk around the club – and I know this view is shared by people with firsthand knowledge – is that the estates committee made a bad error by not authorising a higher offer which might have secured the land for the club.

'Indeed, I believe the 1999 documents show that Railtrack offered the land to MCC before putting it into auction, but for some unfathomable reason the offer was ignored or declined. Oliver and Justin were not prepared formally to admit that this was their motivations, although I and others of the committee repeatedly made that point to them in our meetings and the charge was never seriously denied.

'As a result, I believe Oliver and Justin proceeded at all times on a deeply flawed basis. Instead of focusing exclusively on the correct question, namely how should the development committee best proceed by reference to the interests of the club, they were rather more concerned to sweep under the carpet the abject failings of the 1999 estates committee.

'They also made it plain that they were absolutely determined that no money should end up in the pocket of RLP, even if that meant the club would or might lose out on a massive financial windfall. It is for this reason that I believe these gentlemen have failed to discharge their duties to MCC and why, in a television interview a year or so ago, I called for their resignation.

'In their various attempts to undermine The Vision and to seek to justify their behaviour, Oliver and Justin, in effect as the public face of the club, have picked holes in The Vision and have suggested that to proceed with it would involve grave financial risk for the club. Both points are bad. It was never the task of the development committee to evaluate The Vision. We were never asked to undertake that function, and we never did. Our job was to find a suitable development partner for the club, and then together they would scrutinise The Vision and make any appropriate amendments to it, before submitting a planning application.

'As to the financial risk point, this was always a piece of scaremongering, because the proposal put forward by Almacantar (the selected developer) made it plain that they, and not the club, would bear that risk.

'In a fairly palpable attempt to divert the attention of MCC members away from the debate about the potential development on Wellington Road – which is and always has been an eyesore and a large underused part of the estate – Oliver has focused on and made public suggestions for possible piecemeal improvements elsewhere in the ground.

'As a result of all these machinations, the development committee proceeded at a snail's pace but eventually we identified five leading developers each of whom we interviewed. On a unanimous basis, we then selected three of the five and invited each of them to make a formal proposal in response to the specification provided to them by the committee.

'Events then took an astonishing turn because two of the three selected developers, without any explanation of any kind whatsoever, submitted non-conforming proposals Only Almacantar's proposal was conforming. The development committee was satisfied (again unanimously) with the choice of Almacantar as having the necessary expertise and financial clout (backed by, amongst others, the Agnelli family) to do the job and be the partner of MCC.

'No explanation has ever been provided as to why two highly reputable developers thought it appropriate to submit non-conforming proposals. Given the background and all the circumstances, MCC members may feel able to draw their own conclusions as to what went on behind the scenes at the time. For my part, it left a very nasty taste in my mouth.

'Thereafter, the development committee and the smaller negotiating group were, without more ado, informed that they had been disbanded, although common sense suggests they would have been better left in place to monitor the progress of discussions between Almacantar and the club.

'Another committee to which I was not appointed – The Masterplan working group – was set up in May 2011, to perform this monitoring task. My understanding is that there were negotiations with Almacantar which were conducted by Oliver on behalf of MCC but the new committee was never involved. Indeed I believe it never met, even once. The negotiations came to nothing.

'This is a depressing story for cricket lovers because it reveals a scandalous state of affairs so far as the governance of MCC is concerned. Decision-making is done in a high-handed, undemocratic and secretive fashion by one or two people, and the potential damage to the club and cricket generally which could result from this particular episode is enormous.

'It is a matter of public record that Sir John Major resigned from the main committee because he was unhappy with the procedures which had been adopted on this important matter. He would not have lightly taken this step. A key aspect of the whole sorry story is that the vast majority of MCC members are wholly ignorant of what has been going on because the details have been suppressed.'

Grabiner's attack on Stocken and Dowley had little effect on the vote: MCC members elected not to back the SGM resolution by the margin of 6,191 to 1,556.

Robertson: 'The hostility was very strong. You could feel the atmosphere in the room. It felt like 99 per cent were against what I was saying, and a lot of people I knew through business thought I was wrong. I got a huge volley from Tony Alt, who was absolutely incensed with what I said. I had to leave the meeting before the end, and the eyeballs were pretty intense. We didn't want to give them the letter because we didn't trust what they were doing. I just didn't trust them. They did get a copy, admittedly, very close to the meeting.'

Grabiner and Robertson were criticised from all quarters, as were the Reform Group's lack of preparation for the meeting.

Dowley: 'It was pathetic. Robertson lost it. It was like an eight-year-old prep school boy reading out a letter. I don't know what possessed him to do it. It was so embarrassing and went down badly with everybody.'

Leaver: 'That was utter nonsense. Very strange. Who knows what was going on – I certainly don't. I'm not going to cast stones.'

Even those on the Reform Group were mightily unimpressed. Brian McGowan was scathing: 'It was a complete shambles. As a prospective bit player, I did my best to bring some order to proceedings, but the damage was done already in the way the meeting had been set up. Inevitably we lost, but the way in which we lost upset me.

'The requisitionists met at 4 p.m. in a hotel close to Lord's on the day of the meeting, just two hours before the start. There was no leader. Most of the group had not met each other before, and no one knew what the other requisitionists were going to say. There was no order agreed for making a presentation – the format had not been agreed with MCC.

'Tony's letter was only seen by the MCC committee 30 minutes before the meeting started. There were copies of our slides, but no one had agreed with MCC if these could be handed out. As it happens, they refused.'

McGowan: 'The MCC's raised stage was enormous. Seated there were the chairman Stocken, treasurer Dowley and president Gatting hosting the meeting, plus Brewer and Maynard.

'On both sides of the central team were 16 seats, four rows of four.

On one side were the MCC committee and on the other, the MCC executive. It was a formidable and impressive demonstration of who was in charge and running the show.

'And where were we? We had been allocated five seats on the front row, right on the side of the hall. We were up against an incredibly well-organised establishment and we didn't even know our batting order. We were lambs to the slaughter.

'We were given 30 minutes to make our presentation, and we took 35. I think Tony's speech was too personal and I expect that had he been there to deliver it himself, he would have toned it down as he went along.'

Robertson: 'Of course, Brian is right. It was not well organised and we are all responsible, but I thought his outburst was totally unnecessary and unfair to Nick [Gandon] and Steve [Hollis].'

Stocken: 'They gave us no notice. If you are going to do something like that, you at least give those you are writing about 48 hours' advance notice to give them a chance of responding. It was bizarre – Simon Robertson lost so many points that day. He just played into our hands.'

Andrew Beeson: 'Simon Robertson is a great friend of mine, but reading out Tony Grabiner's letter went down really badly. It was a mistake, standing up at an SGM reading someone else's letter.'

Former MCC communications director Neil Priscott: 'Why didn't he deliver it himself? Members thought "What the hell does this guy think he was doing? What atrocious behaviour by both of them." If you feel that strongly, surely you present the case yourself?'

However, MCC didn't escape criticism following the SGM. Mike Hussey, boss of Almacantar, claimed the club gave its members 'misleading and inaccurate information'. MCC had stated one of the main reasons for not building flats at the Nursery End was the lack of space for a TV compound; Hussey said the Almacantar scheme rejected in 2011 would have included provision, either above ground or in the tunnels. And he didn't hold back in a letter to Brewer:

'We have until now happily refrained from any involvement in the chaos your committee are creating around this whole unfortunate episode, but you must stop dragging us back into it.

We didn't force ourselves upon your organisation. You invited submissions in a global marketing campaign for a development partner and you selected us from a very large list of interested parties.

'You seem to feel it necessary constantly to look to blame us for a process that you started, you briefed, you mismanaged. And you stopped. It is somewhat ironic that MCC continues to behave in such a way with no proper governance and yet expects MCC members and the world of cricket to respect your position as arbiters of fair play, respect for the opposition and honesty.'

MCC said in reply: 'MCC's business with Almacantar has been concluded. We have had a very encouraging postbag following the SGM.'

But MCC were sufficiently worried about the Almacantar legal action to send Brewer to Adelaide to seek reassurance from former MCC chief executive Bradshaw that he wouldn't support Almacantar in court.

Bradshaw: 'At some point Mike Hussey had made a comment to Oliver Stocken that I had signed or was prepared to sign an affidavit about Almacantar's role and what had happened. Derek Brewer phoned me up to say that he was off to New Zealand for a World Cricket committee meeting and was going to pop over to Adelaide to have a look at the new Oval and say hello. When he arrived, I asked him how New Zealand was. He said: "I didn't go."

Bradshaw: 'So you've just come to Adelaide? That's interesting.'

Brewer: 'I just want to know – have you signed an affidavit for Mike Hussey over the Vision for Lord's?

Bradshaw: 'What?'

Brewer: 'Have you signed an affidavit?'

Bradshaw: 'No I haven't. Is that why you're here?'

Brewer: 'Yes. Oliver has sent me to eyeball you with that question.'

Bradshaw: 'So you've flown 10,000 miles to ask me that one question?'

Bradshaw added: 'They were so worried that I would do that – that's why they were so worried about my book.'

Bradshaw had planned to write a book about his time at the MCC helm, and the news went down badly at Lord's when it was first reported in the *Daily Mail* in April 2013.

Bradshaw: 'When they heard I was doing it, Giles Clarke [chairman of the England Cricket Board] went off his nut, apparently, and phoned Oliver. My chairman at South Australia Cricket, Ian McLoughlin, is a very powerful heavy hitter, a legend around here. He came to see me and said: "What's this about the book?" His words to me were along the lines of: "There's no future in that. If you release that book, you will never work in cricket again. Don't write the book – I repeat, you will never work in cricket again."

'This guy was my boss. He made it clear if I write the book, I'm out of here. He told me people were really upset about it. The feeling was very strong.'

The Reform Group were debating bringing up the way Bradshaw's book had been blocked as part of their doomed SGM presentation. But in an email to his fellow activists on the eve of the fateful SGM, Gandon wrote: 'I haven't made any reference to Keith Bradshaw's book and endeavours to suppress its publication. Perhaps that would be a step too far.'

A few copies of Bradshaw's book were printed in its draft form. There were claims at the start of 2018, during the Ashes series in Australia, that it might be published later that year, but it never happened. Bradshaw, who has been fighting cancer for 12 years, still works as CEO of South Australia Cricket.

CHAPTER 12

The Spy Who Loved Lord's

MCC REMAIN PARANOID ABOUT LEAKS. At one time during the re-development saga, chief executive Keith Bradshaw was thinking about bugging the committee room to try and discover who might be responsible for unwanted stories appearing in the media. Yet for three years from October 2011, MCC had a real-life spy on the main committee. Mark Williams, who entered the diplomatic service after being in the Royal Navy, worked for MI6. and accompanied the Soviet defector Igor Gordievsky on his world tour of political leaders.

Williams has an important role in this story, as the first MCC committee member prepared to engage with the rank-and-file membership. He was responsible for encouraging the Reform Group to carry on campaigning, after their motion for an independent inquiry into the Vision for Lord's had been heavily defeated at the 2013 SGM.

As well as interacting with members, Williams tried to find out what had gone on with The Vision. He looked at files, asked questions, visited Westminster planners and talked to the MCC consultants. It was at the penultimate meeting of his three-year tenure on the MCC committee that Williams finally challenged Stocken over the way he had terminated the development committee and abandoned the Vision for Lord's.

Williams had been to see Charles Rifkind before he joined the committee to receive a briefing on the development situation. He was nervous about going to Rifkind's Tea House office near Lord's, for fear of being seen. So they met, along with Williams's girlfriend, Penny Barnard, cloak-and-dagger style at a London restaurant.

Following his three years on the main committee, Williams led the MCC Reform Group in putting forward four more resolutions. It took at least six months of hard work to formulate them. It was a day-and-night project for Williams, and it put such strain on his relationship with Barnard that they separated in the spring of 2015.

Penny said: 'Mark was obsessed with MCC – there's no other word for it. He always carried around a briefcase packed full of documents relating to MCC. When he was with me in St Lucia, he would take calls day and night about MCC. Even when guests were arriving for dinner, he would be on the phone.

'I got bored of the talk. It affected our relationship. He just couldn't let it go. I told him it wasn't just a one-sided matter. I knew Oliver as well, and I told Mark that Oliver was trying to act in the best interests of the MCC members.'

MCC Reform Group member Andrew Lloyd: 'Paddy Briggs and Nick Gandon got me involved – they were involved in the first resolution put forward at the October 2013 SGM. I was sucked in. Briggs and Gandon were struggling to get their numbers up and it didn't get off the ground – it wasn't the right time. Then I was approached by Mark Williams. He understood that I didn't think much of how MCC had dealt with the development issues. There had been numerous mistakes over the years.

'A number of like-minded people got together under Mark's banner. There was myself, Tom Page, John Hegarty, Sir Ian Magee, Sir David Metcalf, Nick Gandon and Paddy Briggs. It started with Mark and the issue gathered momentum. With Nick and Paddy at the helm, there had been no momentum. I met Mark at Lord's. We gathered in the Bowlers' Bar in the pavilion. There were eight of us, and I felt we had all been invited by Mark for a drink with a purpose.

'Mark had his faults – he was like a cultured bull in a china shop, but he was a very principled bloke. He loved MCC and hated the way it was being run. He felt, like me, that MCC was like a comfortable armchair – very reliable and wouldn't make any bad decisions. Then you find a spring sticking up your backside and you realise it's not quite as comfortable as it was, and then another spring comes up.'

After his three-year spell on the committee ended in October 2014, Williams immediately put himself forward for election to return after the required one-year break for elected members. But Stocken, not wanting Williams asking difficult questions about his regime from inside the main committee, made use of MCC's starring system. This allowed the MCC committee to recommend, or star, those on the candidates list they considered best suited for election. Those starred over the years were inevitably successful in the members' ballot. To block Williams returning to the main committee, Stocken starred four other candidates for the four vacant places. The furore that followed resulted in the starring system being disbanded.

Tom Page: 'I went along to watch the fireworks at the October 2013 SGM. One thing that struck me was the club's view that at the end of the Wellington Road lease, MCC would find a way of keeping the land if the law changed.

'But the law will never change, as it would fundamentally destroy the entire UK estate industry. The principle is the landlord owns the land and the tenant rents it. And when the lease ends, it reverts back to the landlord. That's never going to change.

'After the meeting, Mark Williams came up to me and introduced himself. He had got together a group to discuss the development future. The starring of four candidates invigorated us – the blatant attempt to keep a dissenter off the committee triggered off the resolutions.'

The shock within the MCC membership at Williams being snubbed by the starring system was compounded by the fact that he had been proposed by Sir John Major and seconded by Mike Atherton. But that didn't mean as much as it seemed. Atherton said: 'The only reason I seconded Mark was that I happened to be in the MCC library when he asked me. MCC committees are not something that I give a great deal of thought to. I didn't know Mark well – I simply said yes because I didn't want to say no. I never spoke to Mark again. He had been quite critical about the treatment of Graeme Hick when I was England captain.'

MCC trustee Andrew Beeson: 'Using the starring system for all four vacancies was a definite mistake. You might star one, or maybe two, but not four. I said as much at a committee meeting. Mark used to come to committee with a very thick pile of papers. He was like a dog with a bone, and anyone who has that sort of mentality eventually becomes a bit tiresome. That was the general feeling, although it was very sad when he died.'

When Williams came back to London from the Caribbean following his split from Penny, he wasn't well and within six months of his return, he died of cancer.

Rifkind: 'The work on the MCC resolutions totally obsessed him. He went into the most forensic detail. The pressure of preparing those resolutions put such pressure on Mark that I think it precipitated the illness that led to his death. He had created a change, in that MCC members were now publicly challenging the governance of Oliver Stocken and his cabal. His tenacity and perseverance highlighted the club's embarrassments.'

MCC member Philip Banham: 'I met Mark twice at dinners here. He was treated appallingly. After one of those dinners we came up to the members' lounge and he opened up his briefcase which was full of documents. After he sadly died, I wrote to his daughter Charley. She told me that she and her mother had gone through all Mark's MCC stuff and destroyed it.'

Robin Knight, an MCC member since 1973: 'Mark Williams was in MI6. I didn't trust him. He was in a minority of one on the committee, and they all started blaming him for leaks. He almost campaigned for re-election. He tried to change the MCC mindset, but nobody changes the mindset.'

However, the formation of the Members' Independent Online Pavilion gave MCC members a forum to talk about change. MCC had shut down the official site set up by Keith Bradshaw after John Fingleton, briefly a committee member, had used it to describe supporters granted access to the Lord's pavilion for a Twenty20 match in 2012 as 'the great unwashed'.

Bradshaw: 'One of the issues members repeatedly raised was communication. They felt they weren't communicated with well enough and they weren't able to share their views with each other. I fought long and hard to introduce the members' forum online, and I was greatly disappointed to see it shut down. The main committee didn't like members commentating on the club's affairs and used John Fingleton's comments as an excuse to close down communication.'

Only a small percentage of MCC's 18,000-strong membership use the MIOLP, but the MCC high command take notice of it even if they don't admit to doing so. By November 2013 – just a month after the resounding SGM defeat for the Reform Group – Williams was posting support for RLP from within the inner sanctum:

'I don't think it is betraying any confidence to state that I am already on record as saying that I believe that the Lord's Masterplan can be significantly improved. But it is hard to see how the club can do this without re-establishing its former close relationship with RLP, who are our landlords at one end of the ground and our neighbours at the other.

'We occupy a very small site at Lord's. It would be a wonderful legacy if we could ensure that future generations yet to be born were able to enjoy an enhanced garden space behind the pavilion, as well as a Nursery Ground no smaller than at present, with some view of the trees beyond in perpetuity.

'Wimbledon has worked wonders in recent years, expanding their small site to provide an extraordinary experience for All England Club members and the public alike to enjoy a day at the tennis. We can surely do the same for cricket at Lord's.'

Almacantar had finally settled their legal battle with MCC out of court for a £125,000 payment. The agreement gave RLP more ammunition to recoup their near £1 million costs, but RLP were prepared to waive their claim if MCC put in place a proper process for members to vote on the Vision for Lord's with the MCC committee remaining neutral.

In December 2013, Tom Page made his first contribution to the MIOLP: 'My point at the SGM was that Oliver Stocken was simply wrong to suggest that the current Masterplan does not rule out future options on the leasehold land. He implied that we may have another opportunity to revisit this whole issue in five, ten or twenty years' time.

'The whole strip, if developed, is currently worth £300 million, with £100 million of development costs and £100 million each for the leaseholder (MCC) and the freeholder (RLP). If we delay a decision for ten years, we may get £10 million less in today's money.

'The committee needs to swallow its pride, forget the past, not re-investigate decisions that have already been taken, but look at options with a clean slate. It needs to put aside personal prejudices against RLP and its determination to stop them making a profit, even at the expense of members' interests.'

Page joined the Reform Action Group in helping to draft the resolutions, but they were outwitted by the MCC secretariat. The club persuaded the requisitionists to work with them in drafting the resolutions, which ultimately meant they ended up heavily diluted.

Page said: 'I got involved in the requisitioning, which we divided up between us. The club need to approve the resolutions so they knew what we were doing. They duly approached us and asked whether we were willing to tweak the wording. We had a number of meetings with Derek Brewer, Robert Ebdon and Colin Maynard, and changed the wording. Inevitably the wording of the resolutions was not quite as desirable as we might have wanted.

'We had to accept compromises. Without the club's support, we were a very long shot at getting anywhere and it would just end up as a noise-making exercise. Outmanoeuvred? Yes and no. We were never going to have control of a review. The club were going to have to commission the report and pay for it. And he who pays the piper calls the tune – that was inherent in the process. So the committee-approved resolution was reckoned to be a better way to do something rather than nothing. We continued to meet Brewer, Ebdon and Maynard, to discuss what form it should take, but they basically ignored us and did what they were going to do anyway.'

John Hegarty: 'The club looked like they were doing everything we asked. It was only later that it dawned on us we were being outmanoeuvred.'

The ever-resilient Rifkind had come back to MCC with another scheme in February 2014. It had been designed by David Morley, an architect well known to Lord's. Rifkind had been introduced to him by Robert Ebdon at a clay pigeon shoot the previous year.

Sir Simon Robertson was used by Rifkind as a third party to approach Oliver Stocken, despite the fiasco when he read out the Grabiner letter four months earlier still being fresh in the mind. Robertson wrote to Stocken: 'I have been kept informed about the conversations with David Morley, Derek Brewer and Robert Ebdon. From these discussions, I had been led to believe that many of your objections to the Vision for Lord's contained in the original Almacantar proposal have been satisfied.

'I was also told that the amended proposals would be considered at the MCC committee meeting on 12 February. I gather now that you feel it will not be possible to consider the amended proposals at the meeting this week, as there will not be sufficient time to consider them properly. That is quite understandable. However, I would be grateful for your assurance that you will call a special meeting of the MCC committee within the next 30 days to consider these amended proposals, which I believe are very much in the interests of cricket and Lord's.'

Instead, the MCC committee decided to reschedule the first phase of the Masterplan – the rebuilding of the Warner Stand – to begin towards the end of the 2015 season, with just 20 minutes allocated to the Morley Plan at their April meeting. This dismissive attitude towards RLP was further underlined at the May 2014 AGM, when president Mike Gatting announced that MCC were proceeding with their Masterplan and that they would not consider the Morley Plan or any other proposal until 2019 at the earliest. The Grace Gates had been shut in Rifkind's face yet again.

The decision sparked another letter to Stocken from Robertson: 'I am writing to express my strong and continued concern about the governance at MCC, both generally and specifically relating to the long-standing saga of the strategy for Lord's and the Morley Plan.

'I understand there was in-depth dialogue between the MCC executive, Sky, ECB and David Morley, out of which came the Morley Plan. I was led to believe the executive felt the plan had ironed out the reported objections of the original Almacantar proposals.

'I am told the Morley Plan was discussed at the April MCC committee meeting, but no papers were distributed before or after the meeting and only 20 minutes were allocated to a presentation of the plan. It was agreed at the meeting that members of the committee could submit their questions about the plan to the executive. However, this process was quickly shut down and no further discussion of the plan was allowed.

'Such a major project, which could have significant operational and financial implications for Lord's and indeed cricket, deserves, in my view – and I suggest in many others' view – a full business review. I assume a detailed cost-benefit analysis was undertaken to compare the Morley Plan and what the committee has now proposed with the Warner Stand?

'This whole process has left me with a sour taste and I do not believe it reflects well on the governance of Lord's. I can only see further negative publicity and damage being done to the club unless there is more transparency as to how and why the MCC committee makes its decisions. The members of MCC deserve no less.'

This was followed by an email to MCC members from another Rifkind ally, Simon Elliot. He wrote: 'All the undersigned have been members of MCC for many years, and what unites us is not only a love of cricket but also the interests and welfare of the home of cricket – MCC.

'For the past few years, a debate has been going on within the main committee as to how to upgrade our current facilities, which have become tired and in bad need of modernisation. Earlier this year, David Morley, who has been resident architect to MCC for many years – indoor school, Lord's shop, ECB offices, the Nursery Pavilion – came forward with a new scheme.

'The scheme was worked up along with our executive, Sky, ECB and the City of Westminster. It addressed all the previously legitimate criticisms of the Vision for Lord's. It reduced the residential development from five blocks to two and, most importantly, it did not impinge on the current cricketing facilities of the Nursery Ground.

'David was recently invited to address the committee and the scheme was met with general applause and enthusiasm. Furthermore, if planning permission was granted and MCC gave its approval, a cheque for £100 million with no strings attached would be received for us to spend as we wished on upgrading the ground.

'You will see from the attached letter by Sir Simon Robertson what happened to the scheme – outright rejection yet again, with no attempt to analyse the pros and cons or seek the opinion of the membership. The result is that we continue to pay £156,000 rent per year for some temporary hospitality tents and are looking at a very laboured and long-term development (probably 20 years) funded from our own inadequate sources.

'The Morley scheme could be the most significant development in the recent history of MCC. It deserves a full hearing and not to be cut off at inception without the membership at large having their say.'

Stocken wrote back to Robertson on 4 June 2014:

'You will be no doubt aware of the statement which the president made at last month's AGM and which has been sent to all members. The statement was, "The club is putting all the resources at present into plans to redevelop the Pavilion End of the ground, including the south-western corner which comprises the Tavern and Allen stands, the Thomas Lord Building, the Middlesex office and the pavilion extensions. Until the club has completed the redevelopment of the Warner Stand and the south-west corner, there is no need to consider any further presentations from RLP. The club must not be distracted from its plans. When the committee begins to give detailed consideration to new facilities at the Nursery End, that will be the time to resume discussions with RLP."

'You continue to make comments regarding the finances of the club. As I have mentioned to you previously, I believe that on our finance committee we have very experienced and responsible individuals, including the vice-chairman of Rothschild, the chief executive of M&G, the chairman of the Treasury select committee and the former chief executive of Barclays. I am confident that with a committee of this standing, nothing will be done to put the club at any risk financially.'

The exchange of letters between the two warring sides continued, with the disaffected group of MCC members writing to all members of the main committee and the sub-committees on 26 June.

'We are all long-standing MCC members with deep concern over the governance processes of MCC – particularly with respect to the

Morley Plan. During the past year, Sir Simon Robertson, who is one of the signatories of this letter, has exchanged views with Oliver Stocken. The key point that is being made by Simon is that there should be a full cost-benefit analysis of the Morley Plan (which is, in effect, the redevelopment of the leasehold land at the Nursery End of Lord's), when compared to the redevelopment of the Pavilion End of the ground.

'We do not believe a one-page slide at the AGM by the treasurer is a credible way to present the financial capacity of the club to complete the development of the stands without any contribution from the cash which would be available as part of the Nursery End development.

'At no time has Simon or anybody else made any assertions which throws into doubt the competence or sincerity of the members of the finance committee. It consists of people of the highest integrity. The point we are making, and have consistently made, is that the membership at large have not had the opportunity to consider the depth of the Morley Plan.

It should be noted that this drawn-out process has so far cost MCC over £3.6 million, as well as an ex-gratia payment to Almacantar of £125,000.'

PS: For the avoidance of doubt, not one of us are involved commercially or economically with RLP.'

On 10 July, Brewer responded in a combative way to Sir Simon Robertson, David Gower, Lord Grabiner, Steve Hollis and Brian McGowan. 'There are a number of inaccuracies in your letter. Rather than go through them, I would like to make two key points.

'First, and for the avoidance of doubt, both the MCC committee and executive are totally aligned in putting all the club's resources into the much-needed redevelopment of the three stands at the Pavilion End of the ground.

'Secondly, the presentation of the Morley Plan to the MCC committee was not at my instigation. David Morley was engaged by RLP and not by MCC.

'Meetings with RLP on the proposed scheme were characterised by pressure from Charles Rifkind to place the scheme before the MCC committee. Indeed, when Robert Ebdon and I met him and Jonathan

Levy on 16 January 2014, he asked that the proposed scheme be presented to the MCC committee on 12 February and insisted the committee decision be communicated to him the next day.

'It is very disappointing and unhelpful that the approach of the MCC executive in listening to the Morley proposal and facilitating the engagement of third parties such as Sky and ECB is being used to portray a division between MCC executives and non-executives which does not exist.'

The same month, MCC were equally dismissive about RLP's demand for their Vision costs to be repaid following the settlement with Almacantar. Brewer wrote to RLP: 'As you know, the letter from Keith Bradshaw dated 18 December 2008 created no legal obligation.

'There was a commitment to work together on the possibility of an agreed masterplan, a planning strategy and a detailed heads of agreement for a development partnership This did not come to fruition and we operated in a spirit of partnership. You have no entitlement to reclaim the costs you are seeking. As to the breach of user clause, you will appreciate that you have suffered no loss and therefore have no claim.'

Brewer's aggressive approach brought a mixed reaction from Rifkind's set of supporters, who included American banker John Botts, chairman of specialist publishers United Business Media. Botts called Brewer's letter 'unprofessional and wrong' and said that it had 'most likely been dictated by the committee'. He recommended that Rifkind 'get an article in a broadsheet comparing MCC's record to the governance, management and strategic success of the All England Club and the RFU in investing in the facilities and the sport. David Yelland [former *Sun* editor] thinks this is worthwhile.'

Simon Robertson thought it was worth replying to Brewer. Simon Elliot suggested widening the reply to all committee members and hoping it was leaked.

Gower emailed: 'I would be against such a letter to Derek. He has been very open to me privately, and helpful on this whole issue. I would not like to jeopardise that relationship, especially as we fully suspect that the letter he sent to you was largely at the behest of Oliver and the committee. He is not our target.'

Brian McGowan agreed with Gower. 'Derek is in an impossible position, as have been previous MCC chief executives. I have gained the impression that he agrees with us but is powerless to say so. I would rather have him as a silent supporter from inside than a real and visible opponent.'

Sir Simon Robertson responded to Gower: 'We will not send it. I take your well-made points.'

Gower wrote back: 'Whatever the consensus, I would not be a signatory to the response for my reasons as stated. The rest is your decision.'

The Rifkind camp's preferred strategy was to keep up the pressure by recruiting influential support to their cause. One of the big names they were chasing was the former MCC chairman Charles Fry.

A draft copy of the letter sent to committee members on 26 June had included Fry's signature, but he was worried about the consequences of making his support public. He told the Rifkind team: 'I have always been totally in favour of looking closely at Nursery End development. However, if I were to put my name to this letter, I would have to resign from the MCC Foundation, and this would leave my CEO (who has worked her socks off) in a very difficult position and could destroy all the work we have done for the last three years.'

The Ashes-winning England captain David Gower was a prize signature for RLP. He said: 'I'm very fond of Lord's. I scored my first first-class hundred there, for Leicestershire against Middlesex. There's a buzz every time you go there, whether the ground is full or not. There are some extraordinary people involved with the club.

'I thought when I had a spell on the main committee that I could help give them a better understanding of the media and bring them closer together, but it wasn't going to happen and I ran out of enthusiasm for committee work. Their attitude is very conservative.

'I'm proud to say that I approached the redevelopment issue with a totally independent mind. I wanted to find out the real situation. I went to see Derek Brewer. I met Charles Rifkind on various occasions. We chatted at dinners and on the pavement outside the Grace Gates. He had boundless enthusiasm.

'I thought the Morley Plan was really impressive. It would have given Lord's a great vista from the Wellington Road, rather than a prison wall shutting out cricket from the outside world. The design would have helped restore Lord's to being the finest cricket ground in the world, which it isn't – the grounds in Melbourne, Sydney and Adelaide show what can be done, albeit with the help of government funding.

'Unfortunately, the conflict with Charles had closed some people's minds in the MCC hierarchy to any involvement with him. I wished they could have calmed down and listened to each other. Instead they kept asking anybody who wanted to look at both sides whether they were in Charles's employ in some way. Chris Cowdrey is my best friend and he was asked: "Is your mate being paid by Charles Rifkind?"'

'When I was in the president's box after I had written to *The Times* in support of the Morley Plan, Mike Brearley came up to me and said: "Are you a property developer now?" There was always this great suspicion within the club.'

Senior civil servant Sir Ian Magee was an unlikely figure in the Reform Action Group. Despite his vocal opposition to the Lord's establishment, he was later fast-tracked onto the MCC committee as chairman of the membership and general purposes committee.

Magee had been befriended by Mark Williams when he started contributing to the MIOLP. This new relationship led to Williams contacting Sir Simon Robertson on Magee's behalf:

'I am writing on behalf of Sir Ian Magee (former Second Permanent Secretary in the Department of Constitutional Affairs) to ask that he include your name in a communication he is about to send to the MCC trustees designed to knock some sense into the present hierarchy of MCC – a difficult task, in all conscience.

'Sir Ian has been in communication with Mike Griffith, appointed by Oliver Stocken and the committee to chair a group to select Oliver's successor as chairman. The group comprises only MCC committee members and trustees. There will be dismay within the membership at such a lack of transparency.

'Sir Ian has now decided that the right way forward is to say to the committee and trustees that if they cannot agree to an open process, it will be necessary to call for an SGM. Members would be asked to pass a vote of no confidence in the club chairman and demand the setting up of an independent selection panel to choose his successor.

'We hope to include 10 to 15 names. I have just completed a three-year term as an elected member. I will be standing again for election over the forthcoming winter. The ballot papers are issued again in December.'

When Ian Magee wrote to the three trustees – Anthony Wreford, Andrew Beeson and Mike Griffith – he quoted the support of Sir Simon Robertson, David Gower, Lord Grabiner, Sir David Metcalf, Jonathan Fry, Brian McGowan, Tom Page, Steve Hollis, Tim Royce, Paddy Briggs, Nick Gandon and Mark Williams.

Magee wrote: 'It's hard not to detect the hand of the present club chairman guiding the process and to conclude that the next club chairman will be carefully selected to ensure the club's present policy towards ground redevelopment will be persisted with, including keeping RLP at arm's length.'

Wreford replied: 'I do not propose to comment on your email at this stage. Clearly this remains confidential until we have met. It would be extremely unfortunate if any aspects of your note were to find their way into the press before we have had a chance to debate the issues.'

Magee replied: 'The sometimes unwelcome publicity that has characterised MCC affairs in recent years has, in my mind, reflected the lack of transparency in the way the committee has gone about much of its business. The critics, some of whom have been associated with the publicity to which I refer and are among my list of supporters, may have acted out of frustration as much as anything.'

Magee was worried that Stocken's closest ally, treasurer Justin Dowley, would be the automatic successor. Magee wanted to put pressure on Beeson and the other trustees to look outside the committee room for the next chairman.

Beeson: 'The development conflict had blown up between my time on the committee and becoming a trustee. Things had become quite controversial, to say the least. The cricketers were very adamant there had to be a Nursery Ground. Their views swayed a lot of us. The Nursery

Ground had to be sacrosanct. Then there was a lot of discussion about the trees, which goes back to when Gubby Allen ruled the roost.

'There was a complete disconnect between Charles Rifkind and MCC, which was not terribly impressive. I became a sort of conduit because Simon Elliot, who was acting as Charles's consigliere, was a friend of mine. I was consulted in the hope of creating some sort of dialogue between the two sides.

'My view all the way through was that if MCC could afford to re-develop the stands, we should do that. We didn't need to do a deal with Rifkind. The vast majority of members remain supportive of the committee. I didn't think the redevelopment proposals would ever get through.

'I was involved in selecting Gerald Corbett as MCC chairman. I think he is a very able chap. He might be a bit upfront, but he attempted to get a discussion going with Charles Rifkind.'

A members' meeting at Lord's at the end of October 2014 indicated that RLP were not building a support base for Morley's plans, apart from their small band of influential MCC members.

John Hegarty wrote on the MIOLP after the meeting: 'There appears to be very little knowledge of the Morley proposals. Mark Williams questioned the lack of inclusion of RLP as a potential funding option for the Tavern and Allen stand development. Mr Leigh's response that the committee had a mandate from the members at the SGM not to build blocks of flats at the Nursery End drew strong applause. So if RLP's tactics are to raise awareness and build critical mass within the membership to press for committee engagement with RLP, then this approach is clearly failing.'

In January 2015, Stocken starred the four candidates, ensuring Williams had no way back onto the committee. His choices included Mike Gatting, whom was guaranteed to support his chairman at every turn. The other three were Chinmay Gupte, Chris Guyver and Graham Monkhouse. The three candidates not starred were Peter Carroll, Julian Vallance and a devastated Mark Williams, who finished fifth in the ballot.

Stocken's covering letter, in which he explained his choices, stated: 'The purpose of starring is to maintain, so far as is possible, the balance and experience of the committee. The four who have been starred would, if elected, best preserve the committee's combination of knowledge and expertise, which is essential for the efficient running of the club.

The online forum went into meltdown. Paddy Briggs called Stocken's starring 'cronyism'. Laurence Dillamore called it 'an insult to MCC's spirit of cricket'. 'John Fingleton said: 'The committee should, in my mind, hang its collective head in shame.'

Nick Gandon: 'I wonder to what extent the committee understands what sort of affront this business is to the proposers of the three unstarred candidates, which, as it happens, include two former England cricket captains, three former club presidents and a former prime minister.'

Oliver Stocken: 'The starring system was helpful to get a balance of abilities on the committee. In retrospect, I made a mistake – I should only have starred two. But you need to get one or two on with the experience you need.

'Gerald decided to go overboard and scrap the starring system, but I don't agree with that. The weaker members of the committee like it scrapped because it makes it easier for them to remain on. If you're an Angus Fraser or a Mike Brearley, you will always get elected because of your name, but you don't want the committee full of ex-cricketers.'

Stocken's quadruple starring took the number of candidates recommended by the committee since 1969 to 53, 51 of whom were elected. The same proportion of international cricketers who stood for election during that period were successful.

Page made his feelings clear in a letter to Stocken that demonstrated a lack of courtesy from the Reform Action Group, which only strengthened MCC's resolve against the ever-courteous Rifkind.

Page wrote about the starring: 'It simply reinforces my views on your arrogance and unwillingness to consider any view other than your own. I first suspected this when you responded to my point from the floor at the SGM in 2013. Your suggestion of a possible future change in property law was a breathtakingly disingenuous statement. How can you possibly have a fair election for four spaces when four of the candidates have a star on the ballot papers and extra validation and campaign support in the covering letter?

'I believe the power of the MCC committee to star candidates has been blatantly abused.

My prejudice has been to regard starring as an abuse of authority, a presumption based on arrogance as who would make the best candidates and a barely disguised contempt for the ability of members to think for themselves.'

However, Stocken did agree to a thorough review of the Morley Plan in March 2015, after the MCC committee had approved the final plans for the Warner Stand and taken the expensive South-Western Project to planning application stage.

Stocken told members in an email: 'It is opportune for the committee to take matters forward by asking RLP for their latest submission, the Morley Plan, and to propose a thorough review of their detailed scheme, which will include an analysis of financial and commercial factors. External advice will be taken. It is recognised there is a significant amount of confusion amongst members on this subject and the committee is keen to clarify the position.'

But confusion only increased with the questioning of treasurer Robert Leigh at the May 2015 AGM over a £35 million black hole in his financial update on the MCC's Masterplan.

Page: 'Leigh put up these figures. After the Warner Stand, they were talking about doing the South-Western Project, involving the Tavern and Allen stands, and then the Compton and Edrich. Leigh's cashflow projection showed that although MCC had dipped into the red, we would be back in the black by 2022. His capital expenditure for revamping the media centre, rebuilding the Warner Stand and then the South-Western Project came to £80 million. He was £35 million out.

'I raised this as a question and he said "Well, it doesn't include all the South-Western Project because if that was unaffordable, we could defer that to a later date." But doing two separate construction works for the South-Western Project three years apart didn't make sense. They were selling it as being ready for the 2019 World Cup.'

Leigh later emailed Page and denied there was a missing £35 million. He insisted he had always said that each building would only be undertaken when the club could afford to do so and that there would have to be incremental revenue and capital raising through new memberships, life memberships and debentures for each project.

Ian Magee commented on the forum: 'Robert Leigh's response reveals a staggering degree of complacency. I was intrigued and puzzled as to why the numbers had to be teased, it appeared reluctantly, out of the treasurer at last week's AGM.'

Hegarty: 'The Morley Plan review agreed by Stocken was meant to happen within a year. But it didn't, partly because Charles did not want to talk to the club while Stocken was still chairman. He wanted to wait for Gerald Corbett to come on board.'

Hegarty had been helping to put together the resolutions that the Reform Group talisman Mark Williams continued to work on from his hospital bed. But the agreement to work with MCC on the parameters for a development review allowed the club to take charge of the process.

Hegarty: 'We had progress meetings with MCC, but what we didn't hear was how they were engaging with Charles. We talked to them about Charles. Derek called him an "awful man" and "hard to get on with", or words to that effect. There was little or no engagement – they just wanted his final offer. And it sort of spiralled out of our control. We thought, in good faith, that they would offer engagement with Charles.'

Andrew Lloyd: 'Unfortunately, the review was subsequently manipulated by the club into a binary choice between Morley and the Masterplan.'

Rifkind: 'They seduced the people who put forward the resolutions to work together with MCC, to the detriment of the resolutions and the members. MCC took charge of the situation and the resolutions trickled away. An independent review became in an in-house review. They took the stuffing out of the process.'

Sir Simon Robertson wrote to the incoming MCC chairman Gerald Corbett: 'The governance of MCC is not fit for purpose in this day and age of transparency. As I have constantly told Oliver, it is at the heart of many of the problems which have faced MCC. It needs a wholly independent person to take a fresh look.

'Derek Brewer is an excellent person, but he is no more a chief executive of MCC than the man on the moon. All power resides with Oliver, and Derek's positions is wholly undermined. I really do believe the chief executive should be more fully empowered than is the case now.'

Williams, who became ill with lymphoma in February 2015, continued working on the redevelopment of Lord's right up to his death in June. Despite the alarming deterioration in his health, he visited his beloved Lord's on 12 April to watch Middlesex's first game of the season. From his hospital bed the following month, he put his thoughts on Lord's development in a long email and sent it to his Reform Action Group colleagues Tom Page, Ian Magee, Nick Gandon, Paddy Briggs, Andrew Lloyd, John Hegarty and Sir David Metcalf on 15 May, after the MCC AGM had voted in favour of the diluted resolution to carry out an MCC-led development review.

Williams wrote: 'It might be helpful if I set down my clear understanding of the current timetable. My source is Robert Ebdon, whom I had half an hour with at Lord's on 12 April. The overriding priority is to have the Tavern and Allen built ready for the World Cup and Ashes year in 2019. Nothing must get in the way of that.

'2019/2020 is about the time that the club, having kicked Morley into the long grass at the 2014 AGM, said we might talk to RLP again. Big of us. I will spare you an account of the Cuban ambassador's house, 12 Grove End Road, as per Charlie Sale's recent accurate report in the *Daily Mail*. It beggars belief.'

Williams was referring to report that MCC were considering switching secretary Derek Brewer at 4 Grove End Road with the Cuban ambassador at 12 Grove End Road, to prevent Rifkind from doing a deal with the Cubans. He added: 'With an incoming chairman Gerald Corbett having an entrepreneurial background (a first for MCC) and a new trustee Adrian Beecroft who has made millions as a corporate finance man, we have some real expertise to advise us on whether or not MCC might take a degree of risk to secure the future of our wonderful ground so we end up with a Wimbledon-like triumph.

'As you know, an undercroft beneath the Nursery Ground was a key feature of the old Vision for Lord's. The costs of this, opposed by Stocken, Dowley et al, was one of the keys to the collapse of The Vision. But the concept of utilising underground space still makes huge sense, and I have come increasingly to realise that we would be mad not to allocate some of our potential £175 million development profit to construct an undercroft.

'I wanted to set down the possibilities open to the club if we were to embrace RLP/Morley and really go to town to transform Lord's. From what I have been told of RLP, there is nothing that would appeal more to Charles Rifkind than to be part of transforming Lord's into a modern jewel of the international sporting landscape, sitting as it does in the heart of Westminster. Since we share that dream too, we can then all die happy.'

On the same day, Williams forwarded his email to Gerald Corbett, Derek Brewer, Robert Ebdon and Colin Maynard, together with another note urging them to form a new relationship with Charles Rifkind and move the process forward. He wrote: 'I have been working with a small team in recent months, seeking a review of development and funding options for the future of Lord's. As you know, I am delighted that the club have embraced the need for a review.

'From my hospital bed, I have attempted to distil some of the elements we will need to factor into the forthcoming review. I urge you all to think very carefully about how to re-engage with Charles Rifkind. I have studied him from a distance via a wide number of people who are close to him or have worked closely with him.

'He seems a remarkable man. I bumped into him once outside Lord's, distributing leaflets in the early morning members' queue. My friends decided there and then that he was not to be trusted. Such can be first impressions.

'He is clearly sufficiently wealthy that making money from the Lord's project is a second or third consideration for him, though no doubt he relishes cutting a hard deal. This is a man who feels deeply aggrieved at his treatment by MCC over the years. No doubt these things cut both ways, but he believes we are sitting on £1 million of his money.

'He had David Morley present to the committee. We then kick him into touch for five years after the 2014 AGM. In the wake of that, we approach him and suggest he/David Morley might like to come and share his ideas for the Pavilion End of the ground – presumably to assist our planning thoughts for the South-Western Project – and then, as quickly as the suggestion is made, it is withdrawn. I could go on.

'Suffice to say that while he may be a tough and resilient man, I understand he carries deep bruises from his dealings with MCC. If there is a future for MCC and Rifkind to work together for the greater good, this will not come about through a couple of friendly lunches to break the ice. I venture to suggest that an initiative from Gerald, with his special skills and absolutely no baggage, might be the key to recreating an atmosphere of trust.'

Corbett's response was brief. 'Thanks, Mark. Simon Robertson made similar points to me last week. We will ponder on your words. Hope you've a TV in your room that gets Sky.'

Williams's memorial service at St John's Wood Church took place on 3 October – three days after the end of Stocken's six-year term as chairman. Stocken was given a retirement dinner in the Long Room at Lord's on 1 October. Mike Gatting was one of the speakers, saying: 'So many people here who I know and respect have turned up for Oliver. It just shows the esteem in which Oliver is held. A man who has done so much for the club.'

Brewer sent Rifkind his tickets for Williams's memorial service in the post, informing him in an accompanying letter that MCC did not want to consider a joint approach for 12 Grove End Road, the Cuban Ambassador's residence whose lease from MCC was shortly to expire.

CHAPTER 13

Simon Says

CHARLES RIFKIND WAS INCREASINGLY RELIANT on the support of his two influential backers, Sir Simon Robertson and Simon Elliot. Relationships with MCC were so fraught that he felt he needed allies in the meetings with them.

Sir Simon Robertson: 'I knew that Simon [Elliot] thought Charles had been treated very badly. I got stuck in with Simon and we became quite a thorn in the side of MCC. We talked a lot about strategy. I spent a lot of my personal time helping Charles and Simon even more.

'Charles is a very decent man. I like dealing with that sort of bloke. I don't like people being run down and maligned because of who they are, ie a North London property developer. I really objected to this.'

Simon Elliot: 'I knew Charles back in the nineties. I was director of a property company, and there was a potential deal we were both working on. In 2008, Sir Simon Robertson was chairing a meeting in his office and two of the participants were myself and Sir Michael Jenkins, whom I had never met before. Before the meeting was over, Jenkins apologised for having to leave early because he had to go to an MCC meeting. He said he was meeting a "rather troublesome developer". I perked up and said: "Do you mean Charles Rifkind?"

'Jenkins was amazed: "Do you know this man?" he asked. "People at MCC say awful things about him." I said: "I've known him for 10 years. He's extremely honourable and very bright."

'Sir Michael was very interested and I told him that I could easily arrange a meeting between them. The meeting took place and Michael was very impressed with Charles and somewhat confused by the way MCC had been treating him. Sir Michael, over the next seven years until his death from cancer in 2015, was extremely supportive. He talked to John Major – they had done Maastricht together – and various other people. He genuinely tried to advance the dialogue between MCC and Charles. After Michael died, I persuaded Simon to take on the mantle.'

Elliot explained that he was paid by Rifkind for his help in the build-up to the members' vote in 2017. He said: 'I was in contact with Charles on a regular basis and was used as a sounding board. I was trying to help form a link between Charles and MCC, which had completely broken down. For two years starting in 2015, Charles paid me a modest retainer. But it was a very modest amount of money.'

MCC's next move left Rifkind so annoyed that it required Elliot and Robertson to stop him venting his anger during the negotiations. The resolution agreed with the Reform Action Group and passed at the 2015 AGM meant that MCC had to properly analyse Rifkind's Morley Plan. The club started that process by wanting him to answer over a hundred questions, some of which Rifkind felt were highly intrusive.

Brewer wrote to Rifkind on 18 May 2015:

'Colin Maynard, Robert Ebdon and I are pleased to be taking forward discussions with you on behalf of the MCC committee to assess RLP's proposal. The committee has pledged to provide members with full details of the scheme you are proposing as part of a consultation process with them.

'In order to take matters forward, a list of questions for RLP has been prepared and this is attached. The message I have received very clearly from members is that there is a real desire for detailed information to enable them to form a view on the proposals. Accordingly, I should be very grateful if you would respond in writing to the questions set out and the more detail you can provide, the better.

'Finally, I believe it would be mutually beneficial for our discussions to be conducted on a confidential basis without recourse to the national media. That, of course, works both ways and we can cover this in more detail when we meet.'

The questions to which Rifkind most objected were listed under 'real estate-related considerations':

'Please provide details of the current ownership structures of RLP and current debt funding or other commitments of RLP.

'Please confirm the beneficial identities of all individuals and entities that currently have or at any time in the past have had an interest of any description in RLP, the current or any past development plans relating to Lord's or the leasehold strip of land itself, or who stand to obtain financial benefit from the invitation or completion of any development relating to Lord's.

'Which entity would provide performance guarantees and/or security for RLP's obligations to MCC, Network Rail, contractors and others? What guarantees of payment will be offered to MCC?

'Please clarify whether RLP (and any backer/founder) intends to sell on its interests in the proposed development at any stage before the completion of the development on site.

'Assuming that RLP does not intend to sell on its interest and that RLP would remain a partner with MCC, what commitment/indemnity would RLP be prepared to offer in support of such an approach?'

A furious Rifkind felt that MCC didn't need to delve so closely into his background when they had hardly engaged with him. His view was that any money he guaranteed MCC would be delivered on time as per the contract – as he had done with every previous property development deal he had done.

Rifkind: 'I have a relationship with Investec that has been in place since the start. Keith Bradshaw, David Batts and Robert Griffiths were aware of the deal, but nobody wanted to believe me. I couldn't answer the questionnaire – it would breach the confidentiality with Investec. It would be inappropriate. I was acting on behalf of a consortium.

'Investec had put in £9 million 20 years ago. They would expect a return of three or four times that amount – they must want to make £30 million. To make £30 million from their option to convert to a third of the ownership, the Nursery End land has to be worth £100 million.

Robertson and Elliot were alongside Rifkind when he next met MCC. This move surprised the Lord's high command, who failed to understand why the two Simons were so supportive of Charles.

Dowley: 'Neither Simon Elliot nor Sir Simon Robertson had got involved in MCC business before. They might have been paid – we don't know.'

We now know that Elliot was on the Rifkind payroll between 2015 and 2017, albeit in a small way. During that period, Robertson and Elliot met with MCC officials on five occasions.

Sir Simon Robertson: 'When we had a meeting with MCC, we told Charles not to open his mouth – we knew he would be in danger of exploding because he was so emotional about it. And Charles, in those meetings, didn't say anything. He was very upset when they started to question his finances.'

Simon Elliot: 'We had meetings at Simon [Robertson's] office in St James's Place, in Charles's flat and in the Long Room at Lord's. Each time I took notes and each time, when we went into the meeting, we were faced with a very different scenario from what we were led to believe.

'Derek Brewer was just a cypher – I think he was out of his depth. He didn't offer anything. They were opposing anything Charles came up with. There was no appetite for doing a deal with Charles, who did absolutely everything he could.'

On 20 July, Rifkind responded to Brewer's questionnaire, hand-delivering two letters to Lord's. He wrote: 'I appreciate that you have been waiting for a response to your letter and questionnaire of 18 May, but since then we have met and there has been text communication between us.

'I was somewhat surprised to read in today's *Daily Mail* that MCC are awaiting a reply from RLP. I can only presume that the reference to the questionnaire came from one of your committee members. This is unhelpful. I believe that we have agreed that our negotiations would remain confidential until such time as you report back to the members at large.

'As a result of this, I feel it is sensible and reasonable, given that that MCC has appointed a new chairman Gerald Corbett, who is taking office on 1 October 2015, that the two principles should first meet and establish the basis for any commercial transaction. To do otherwise is "putting the cart before the horse".

'As you are aware, RLP has been involved in many abortive conversations over the last 15 years with constantly changing faces at MCC. There is now an excellent opportunity to put the past behind us.

'I am available at any time to meet with Gerald Corbett, but it is worth considering that to minimise delay, Populous, MCC's architects, and David Morley, RLP's architects, should be instructed to immediately start a process of adapting the Morley Plan to incorporate the wishes of MCC.

'You will note that this letter is personal to you only and has been copied to Gerald Corbett. I do not wish it to be copied or communicated to anyone else.'

The second letter outlined the basis on which RLP would be willing to proceed once Corbett took over.

'I am delighted that after many years, MCC have now committed to presenting the Morley scheme to members. Since December 1999 I have had a dialogue with three chief executives and many MCC committee members and their representatives, and now I find myself once again negotiating with new faces.

'RLP have spent in the region of £1 million of abortive money on the Vision for Lord's, which was ultimately terminated unilaterally by MCC. I would state for the avoidance of doubt that RLP are not willing to enter into any form of joint venture or partnership with MCC.

'Rather than responding to your questionnaire of 18 May, I would suggest that in order for negotiations to proceed, we initiate the following:

'David Morley Architects (on behalf of RLP) and Populous Architects (on behalf of MCC) are retained to agree a joint masterplan, incorporating both designs and including the Grove End Road properties.

'If approved by the members, this can then form the basis of a planning application which we believe will be favourably received, since Westminster Planning Department have always wished to see an overall masterplan.

'RLP are proposing a total of £130 million for the surrender of MCC's lease at the Nursery End, payable as £100 million in cash with a bank guarantee, plus the provision of £30 million in facilities.

'I can also confirm that Investec have indicated they will finance any transaction, based on the figures as proposed by RLP. I also confirm that should MCC wish to reopen negotiations with Almacantar, they would be willing to do so.'

David Morley: 'When I told MCC we were doing some work for Charles, I received a very frosty response. There was a lot of animosity at that time. They even intimated that a lot of architects had turned down the opportunity to work for Charles – not true, if you see all the architectural models he has commissioned.

'I had presented to the committee in April 2014. There was applause at the end – it was great. That scheme was not very different from what we proposed in 2017. The crazy thing is that there's all that space underground and the broadcaster compound clutter above it. It was a no-brainer. We were just using the area of the tunnels, so it meant that the corner mess could all go underneath.

'Our plan was to put a building there that married up with the stylish mansion blocks in St John's Wood. It would have created a frame with St John's Wood Church. It all made good architectural sense. And there would have been 97 apartments to provide the funding.

The Morley Plan's Nursery Ground

'After the April presentation, we thought there would be a process, with the plans being circulated more widely. I can't recall being informed by MCC that they had rejected the Wellington Road proposal. We found out things had happened rather than being told directly.'

'We wanted to strike up a dialogue with Populous to jointly fit in with their Masterplan, but MCC would not allow us to talk to Populous. We had to come up with our own vision at what the Compton and Edrich stands might be like, so we did a scheme. They gave us a brief that they wanted it expanded by 3,000. We said, "You would end up with something taller than the media centre, and it's going to block the view of the trees."

'The eventual chosen design is taller than the media centre and encroaches on the Nursery Ground, which we didn't think was necessary and nor does it makes sense. MCC will have to live with that smaller Nursery Ground for six years at least.'

Rifkind was frustrated enough with MCC's attitude to write again to Brewer on 18 August:

'What gave me great concern over the letter is the implied criticism that I am impeding progress. Given the history between MCC and RLP over the past 15 years, I find any suggestion of delay on my part unacceptable.

'I also take exception to your paragraph about "openness, transparency and partnership working". I feel there is an implied criticism in sending you a confidential letter. I thought that the reasons for doing this were very clear to you.'

Rifkind also wrote to Oliver Stocken, following his invitation to lunch shortly before his six-year term ended. He turned down Stocken's proposal, writing: 'I can't help feeling that after six years of trying to arrange such a meeting/meal, there is an irony in the fact that it has only been offered In the last couple of weeks of your tenure, when it is essentially too late to have any meaningful discussions about the future of MCC.

'Only you know your reasons for resisting the possibility of a partnership with RLP. From our stance, it has caused confusion, since our wish has always been to enhance the standing of Lord's. RLP have consistently been open to negotiations in order to reach this goal.

'I am sure you will neither be surprised nor offended by me declining your invitation. I feel at this late stage, it would be more beneficial for both MCC and RLP to start fresh discussions with the new chairman Gerald Corbett when he takes office from 1 October 2015.

'I wish you well in your retirement from the chairman's position and hope that should talks between MCC and RLP prove to be productive, you will be supportive and offer the benefit of your knowledge. However, if you would like to meet up after the new chairman takes up office, perhaps in the autumn, do let me know.'

Stocken had forthright views about the way Corbett handled the development issue after taking over as chairman:

'Gerald, in typical Gerald fashion, said he would do things differently when he took over. I think Derek [Brewer] found it very difficult. Gerald was having conversations with Charles when he should have left it to the chief executive. The chairman should be the fallback person. The chief executive should do all the grunt work.

'It took Gerald about a year to realise the problem wasn't an easy one. I like Charles as an individual, but he is very pushy and he has this amazing ability of appearing around the corner, bumping into people.

'I was in my seat at Twickenham and suddenly there was Charles, saying "Hello Oliver, how are you?"

"What brings you here? I've never seen you here before", I replied. He claimed he had seats.

'He said "We must have lunch." I was quite happy to have lunch, so I went to have lunch with Charles. We spent the first 45 minutes not talking about MCC. Then he made the most amazing comment. He never knew I had a knowledge of property. When I joined Rothschild in 1968, we made six property acquisitions in two years and set up a property company. I've spent half my life in property. I chaired the Stanhope property company.

'I said, "Charles, where do you think I'm making these comments from?" He does all his homework, so for him to say that was remarkable.

"We never knew how much money Charles actually had. He had £9 million from Investec. I was at the Oval and I sat next to the chief executive of Investec, a tough South African. We had a nice chat and I asked him how he got involved with Charles. He said his bank managed about £2 billion in property and one of his chaps told him about an interesting situation that, for a £9 million investment, they had the chance of making a lot more. His attitude was "What's £9 million out of £2 billion?" So he let them have their head.

'Investec invited me to their box at Lord's and, within ten minutes of my arrival, Charles was there. He asked who was taking over as chairman. I told him it was not my decision. He thought it would be Justin Dowley. Then Charles said: "The rate at which you are going, you will have to be dealing with my son." I replied, "Charles, at the rate we're going with a 120-year lease, they might be dealing with your grandson."

'I've always liked Charles, but I always kept my distance, whilst Keith Bradshaw didn't. You daren't get too close. And then Gerald realised that the numbers didn't add up.'

A new chairman had given Rifkind a fresh opportunity – Corbett claimed to have arrived at Lord's with an open mind over the development saga.

Rifkind: 'Gerald decided it was a good idea for us to meet. We met in my Pavilion Apartments flat and I gave him a two-hour introduction to the story. When I gave him a lift, he said: "I must phone my wife to tell her I've got in a car with you." His attempt to be humorous really demeaned the relationship, but he did come in to the chairmanship wanting an independent review of the whole story, which I was naturally pleased about. But he hugely let me down. His position changed and it became an in-house review, which is entirely different.

'We had a meeting in the Tavern Stand with David Brooks Wilson, the new estates chairman, Gerald Corbett, Derek Brewer and Robert Ebdon. It was very convivial. The mood was "There are same new faces around here, so can we have a serious look at this again?"

'I thought they were positively on board with the view that this should definitely go to the membership as on option, moving forward. I took a lot of encouragement from this.

'David Morley prepared a professional brochure of his plan. I wanted it circulated to the membership, but Corbett stalled on that, for whatever reason. Instead MCC produced its own Lord's updated Masterplan.

'I then felt that between the texting, the phone calls and the emails, the position seemed to change. Corbett withdrew in terms of his personal involvement and brought in others. And Robert Leigh, Robert Ebdon, David Brooks Wilson and Derek Brewer were all pretty negative in their approach.'

Brewer still wanted an answer to that questionnaire. He wrote to Rifkind on 23 October 2015:

'When I wrote to you on 18 May with the list of questions, it was with the objective of eliciting sufficient information from RLP to facilitate a detailed review to share with members of your latest proposal for development on the leasehold strip of land and to enable comparison with the club's plan.

'At our last three meetings, which have also involved Colin Maynard and Robert Ebdon, you made it clear that you would not be responding in writing to the questions until after 1 October 2015. It would be extremely helpful to now receive your written responses to the questions. As you have outlined at meetings between us, there may be questions you believe that RLP cannot answer or are not prepared to answer. In your response, you will, I am sure, make this clear.

'The committee very much looks forward to receiving the information, to enable the club to undertake the review stipulated. As the committee believes it is committed to updating members in early December, a response by Monday 23 November would be extremely helpful. This letter has been written after consultation with and agreement of the MCC committee.'

Sir Simon Robertson, acting on Rifkind's behalf, had a meeting with Brewer and Corbett to see if he could help bring the sides together. His notes suggest that MCC would not back down over the questionnaire demands:

'They acknowledge that Oliver did not treat Charles at all appropriately, and Gerald in particular says he has told Charles that he is apologetic on behalf of MCC.

'They do want the questionnaire answered. I said it was offensive in some parts. They said they want to sit down with Charles and discuss his answers in detail.

'I told them Charles has nothing to hide. They accept that completely, but believe a refusal to answer questions does not look that good to suspicious members.'

Brewer's letter to Robertson on 27 October confirms that they either want the questions answered or the reasons why they can't be:

'It was a pleasure to meet you yesterday and to discuss some very difficult issues in such a professional way. The purpose of this letter is just to reiterate the point made by both Gerald and myself at the meeting. Before further meetings are held with RLP, the club does need to receive a written proposal, including answers to as many of the questions as possible.

'Whilst noting the depth of feeling held by Charles, there is a thirst for information on the subject from our members, who have mandated the committee to undertake a detailed financial review of the latest proposal from RLP.

'Indeed, having reread your letter of 30 May 2014 which we discussed yesterday, I believe that you and MCC are closely aligned. You commented on the need for a "detailed cost-benefit analysis" to be undertaken to compare the Morley Plan and the committee proposal. If we are to do this, it is essential that RLP provide us with the relevant information.

'As far as the questions are concerned, my letter of 23 October, written on behalf of the committee, made it very clear to Charles that there may be questions that RLP cannot answer or are not prepared to answer.

'The suggestion I have articulated, both orally and in writing, is that he makes this clear in his written response. Charles may find it helpful to explain which questions he has difficulty with and why he feels so strongly about them.

'At the end of the meeting, you undertook to have a further word with Charles and, as mentioned at the outset, both Gerald and I appreciated your candour openness and interest.'

Simon Elliot had lunch with trustee Andrew Beeson to put Rifkind's case, as he and Robertson continued to do their best to combat the MCC juggernaut. His note afterwards read:

'Understood and accepted by RLP that MCC require him to answer the 18 May questionnaire. But Charles considers some of the questions under "real estate-related considerations" "inappropriate and irrelevant". Charles's view is they can be addressed at such time as the members have given a positive response to the proposed development.

'The proposed Morley Plan is an illustrative example of how a development might look yet still meet MCC requirements and bring acceptable returns to both parties.

'It makes sense for MCC architects Populous to engage with Morley and for RLP to be given the opportunity to present to committee and members at roadshows.

'Meeting between Charles and new MCC chairman to clearly mark the beginning of a fresh relationship.'

Elliot: 'I saw quite a lot of Andrew, who was nothing but helpful, but I don't think there was much he felt he could do.'

The first signs that MCC were tiring of Charles being represented by Simon Robertson and Simon Elliot appeared in November. Corbett wrote to Robertson: 'We need to get Charles on board with tabling as full a proposal as possible. His instinct will be to do nothing and let us make the running. That won't work and there will be many our end who will say "I told you so" etc.'

Brewer wrote to Rifkind, copying Robertson and Elliot:

'There have been discussions recently with third parties on the club's letter of 18 May in particular and the Morley scheme at a very general level. The new club chairman and I believe it more appropriate to engage in dialogue with you direct.

'It is positive to read that RLP accept the requirement for the questions which accompanied the club's letter of 18 May surrounding all matters relating to the Morley Plan to be answered. The club had made it clear on a number of occasions that a detailed written response is required on the latest RLP proposal, known as the Morley Plan.

'There is no appetite on behalf of the club to involve Populous, as this will only add to the confusion. You will, I am sure, recall that the MCC secretariat spent several weeks in dialogue with David Morley and his team in the first four months of 2014.

'In this connection, I was surprised to see Simon Elliot describe the Morley Plan as an "illustrative example", given the depth of the discussions with David Morley. Moreover, it is the Morley Plan you have circulated to 4,000 MCC members, and it is that which the committee wishes to have reviewed.

'For the avoidance of doubt, there is no merit in discussing variations to the Morley Plan. The new club chairman and I both sense that you would like to open a process which would end in you retabling the Vision for Lord's. I repeat that it is the Morley Plan that we wish to review, not that.

'There is no need or rationale to appoint an independent valuer, as suggested by Simon Elliot. The resolution approved by MCC members at the AGM has already determined there would be an independent valuation of the figures and the details submitted by RLP.

'The new club chairman and I are prepared to discuss this letter at any time. We await your written proposal and answers to our questions to enable the review finally to commence.

'In conclusion, by way of reiteration, the situation is complex enough without the further confusion which is caused by third parties acting on behalf of RLP. Accordingly, I look forward to resurrecting more conventional lines of communication between you at RLP and the officers of the club.'

Despite Brewer's desire to deal directly with Rifkind, the next talks were between Sir Simon Robertson and Gerald Corbett. Afterwards Robertson wrote a briefing note to Elliot and Rifkind:

'Stocken acolytes are still alive and kicking in MCC but, as Gerald said, happily they will be fading out over time. He felt that if Charles was not at a meeting, it would play into the hands of the Stocken brigade, who are pretending Charles is not for real.

'I really think Gerald is trying to help here, so I think we must go along with him and his request until he lets us down. There is no doubt there are still Stocken elements and Derek, while in favour of the

Morley Plan, is somewhat hemmed in. It only goes to show that the governance of MCC is still a shambles.

'I definitely think we have to seize this moment, because if we do nothing then it will play into the hands of the Stocken brigade who are still painting you, Charles, in a black light.'

The engagement between Sir Simon Robertson and Corbett resulted in the first development summit with the MCC chairman and Rifkind at Robertson's Mayfair office on 13 November 2015. Also in attendance were Derek Brewer and Simon Elliot.

Corbett: 'I remember going down with Derek Brewer to see Charles at Sir Simon Robertson's office. I have the photograph of Derek clutching a big envelope of Charles's documents. That was Charles's initial proposal which we started analysing.'

The MCC side were, once more, adamant that Rifkind must answer the questions about his finances. Following the meeting, Elliot sent an email to Brewer. 'It was good to meet. I thought it was very successful and I am hopeful that it signals the start of a new dialogue between MCC and RLP.

'In respect to the financial questions, it requires a conversation between Charles and Gerald to establish the framework of how the aspirations of both parties can be met. However, as was made clear, there are some questions which we felt were intrusive and irrelevant. But assurances can and will be given which will give comfort for MCC over RLP's ability to be able to meet any financial commitments in the event of an agreement being successfully negotiated.'

Another meeting between the two sides took place in January 2016 at Sir Simon Robertson's office. MCC's aggressive position is clear from the minutes that were taken.

MCC treasurer Robert Leigh: 'We intend to carry out a development review that will take between six and nine months. The offer on the table of £100 million plus £30 million towards MCC facilities is regarded as totally inadequate. And MCC feel they do not have control of the process.'

Simon Elliot: 'What is the logic behind such a combative approach?'

Brewer: 'The nature of cricket attendances is changing, and there is uncertainty about Lord's being granted two Test matches.'

Elliot: 'Having this eureka moment over the need for a review staggers belief. Have MCC's property advisers valued the site at more than RLP?'

Brewer: 'No.'

Ebdon: 'Stephen Hubbard of CBRE has been appointed as an adviser, and his view is that MCC should receive a larger share than 50/50.'

Rifkind: 'Due to what has happened in the past, Stephen Hubbard is not acceptable to me.'

Leigh: 'We know about this, but we only discovered what happened after the appointment had been made.'

Rifkind: 'Who has sanctioned MCC spending £5 million on building up the Vision for Lord's?'

Leigh: 'I am unaware of this expenditure being agreed by the finance committee.'

Elliot: 'The discussion is not about what might be built, but the value of the land.'

Leigh: 'I agree.'

Rifkind: 'If you include the Pavilion End and the south-west perimeter, which is 100 per cent owned by MCC, the total value could be in the region of £650 million, producing £275 million for RLP and £375 million for MCC.'

Leigh: 'MCC are not prepared to take any development risk. I don't feel many members want to see the club turned into Wimbledon.'

It was Simon Elliot who wrote to Brewer on 21 January 2016, following the acrimonious summit that had ended in an impasse. The long email was also copied to Gerald Corbett, Robert Leigh and Andrew Beeson:

'Charles and I have had time to reflect on what Robert Leigh and yourself put to us. We were both taken aback by the three opening statements by Robert, which in essence were:

1. To put consideration of the Morley Plan back six to nine months, as MCC were now waiting to do a further review 'of all their options'.

2. That it was felt that the offer on the table of £100 million cash plus £30 million of facilities was totally inadequate.

3. That the members were wanting more protection, in the form of restrictive covenants on any development that was ultimately agreed.

'This took us by surprise, as we thought that you had asked for the meeting to raise questions over the Morley Plan, of which there must have been some. It could not have been a surprise to you when we expressed astonishment that yet more strategic views were to be embarked upon.

'I believe at last year's AGM you made a commitment to the members to report back to them by last October on the Morley Plan. This was then put back to next month, as per your latest letter to members. We are now being told it can't happen until the autumn at the earliest. I cannot believe members will find that easy to swallow, but maybe you have your good reasons.

'All negotiations since the beginning of the Vision for Lord's are based on a 50/50 split. I accept you were not CEO at that time, but I presume you have had sight of the 11 draft documents and the 29 reports that were prepared by Alistair Parker of Cushman & Wakefield, Keith Bradshaw and David Batts which confirms the basis of the agreed split.

'Robert Ebdon went on to say that Stephen Hubbard of CBRE had been retained and you were acting on his advice. You also acknowledged at our meeting that it was only subsequent to his appointment you realised that he had past history involving the Wellington Road land and he was not a choice that RLP would be likely to accept.

'I can confirm RLP would not be prepared to negotiate with Stephen Hubbard/CBRE. We should not be discussing designs, as RLP are open to what is built as long as it produces the expected returns for both parties.

'RLP have always made clear that is not necessarily about the Morley Plan. That plan has evolved as a result of the members' reaction to the Vision for Lord's scheme. RLP employed David Morley Architects to look again at the Wellington Road/Nursery End. After much consulting with MCC, Sky and others, Morley came up with the current proposal. It has been produced so that the members could see what could be done, taking into account their comments and not impeding on the cricketing facilities.

'It is understood the members might vote for no change, but they at least deserve to be given all the facts, so they can make their own judgement. In conclusion, your chairman has confirmed that the past is behind us, but I am not optimistic about the future, unless some enthusiastic co-operation is now shown by MCC.'

Elliot also wrote to his friend the MCC trustee Andrew Beeson, expressing delight that Corbett had reached out to Rifkind with an invitation to a Lord's Test match against Pakistan that summer. It was the first proper invitation Rifkind had received from MCC since he became their landlord at the Nursery End.

'I feel it is an extremely generous and shrewd move, as for the first time Charles feels that he is not only being treated with respect, but that there is genuinely a new approach to see if common ground can be found. I think both parties (including me) owe you for the role that you have played in making all this possible.'

At the same time, MCC continued to look at their own development plans. There was increasing doubt about spending £85 million on the South-Western Project, for which planning permission was in place. There was also controversy inside MCC about Rifkind being invited into the chairman's box during a Test match. It was even debated at MCC committee as to whether he should be on the guest list at all, with Peter Leaver threatening to resign over the issue.

Rifkind: 'I think Gerald was embarrassed about all the invitations I had offered to him, none of which he had accepted.'

Corbett: 'I thought it would be nice to have him up in the box. He's our landlord, we pay him rent – we must be seen to treat him as a normal person. Otherwise we would never settle this, and people would think we regarded Charles as a pariah.

'We had to treat Charles properly and to be seen to negotiate and get the best out of him. Peter Leaver did not like that. When I said we were inviting him to the box, he called it "the worst decision he had ever seen in the committee room".'

'I said: "Peter, we have got to be seen to be talking to Charles." Everybody supported me. Mike Gatting said: "Just don't sign anything, chairman."

Peter Leaver: 'I thought it was wrong at that stage. We were still deciding whether to go along with Charles. You don't invite someone who you might be doing business with to your box and offer him hospitality. If we had decided to go with him, that would have been the time to invite him. I don't think you do it before.

'I was so pissed off with the way Gerald was running things, I may well have offered my resignation. But the problem with resignation is that I'd been elected by the members. I take the view that once members had elected you, you get on with it – it's only for three years.

'Gerald was making so many wrong decisions at the time – it was just not right. It was a hospitality occasion, not a business occasion. By that stage, everyone knew there was no chance of going ahead with Charles. We were spending a fortune on reports. What were we doing this for?'

When Rifkind went to the Lord's Test, he was placed at lunch two seats away from David Brooks Wilson, chairman of the estates committee. On the pitch, Pakistan's 42-year-old Misbah-ul-Haq scored a memorable hundred and famously celebrated with ten press-ups. But in his chairman's box, Corbett seemed more intent in watching how Rifkind was faring with some of his committee arch opponents. He had arranged for Justin Dowley, Tony Alt and Nigel Peters to come and talk to Rifkind between lunch and tea.

Rifkind: 'Gerald Corbett watched from afar and smiled. He told me I was doing very well. He looked like a supporter and ally.'

The same cannot be said about Alt.

'It was very fractious,' said Rifkind. 'Alt had decided that I should have no interest in Lord's. He was not a believer in what I was doing and would not be swayed. He retained the same stance as he had done for the last ten years. His body language was fairly aggressive.

'Alt basically didn't want me around and thought it best not to deal with me. As far as he was concerned, MCC had been forced into talks because I owned the land, and The Vision was my idea. He didn't like it.'

Corbett: 'I like Charles. I think he was much misunderstood. We had some fun together in the box.'

However, the day out at Lord's did nothing to change MCC's

stance. The day after the Test ended in a Pakistan victory, Rifkind met with Corbett and Leigh. As ever, he had the two Simons alongside him.

Corbett said there would be no dialogue until after the feedback from a membership survey. It was part of the review into development opportunities that resulted from the resolution at the 2015 AGM. Rifkind, in turn, continued not to answer the questionnaire sent to him by MCC on 18 May 2015, shortly after that AGM. The compromise agreed was that he would not supply any further answers until such time as MCC formally engaged in negotiations.

A new entrance for Lord's to replace the 'prison wall'

Rifkind outlined his position in a letter to Brewer two days later: 'MCC have confirmed they do not wish to enter into a dialogue with me until after they have had feedback from members. Whilst I wish it was otherwise, we have agreed that given that constraint, it has put RLP in a position that makes it impossible for RLP to respond to the questions that you have raised. I raised concerns over MCC presenting the "Morley Plan" to the committee and the membership at large and asked that David Morley architects should be allowed to do this.'

However, despite the outlined differences, Rifkind and David Morley were given the opportunity to showcase their latest proposals inside Lord's. Brewer wrote: 'I am pleased to extend an invitation to you and David Morley to give a presentation to the members of the principal committees of MCC at Lord's on Wednesday 14 December at 4.30.

'Once you have confirmed your availability for the presentation, an invitation will be extended to members of the MCC committee, arts & library, cricket, estates, finance and membership and general purposes. In total, an hour and a half has been allocated for the session, to include a Q&A. It will be chaired by the club chairman. I suggest your presentation lasts no more than 45 minutes.'

David Morley: 'The presentation was in the banqueting rooms and there was a completely different atmosphere from the one in April 2014, when our plans were well received by the MCC committee.

'MCC laid out a formal setting. The presentation went OK, but there was no applause. Then there were some very hostile questions, including from Sir John Stevens, head of the Metropolitan Police, who went on about security.

'We asked for a transcript from that meeting, because Charles and I were busy answering questions so couldn't take notes. MCC insisted we couldn't have a copy. They had a recording but we couldn't have a copy – we were allowed only to read a copy in the library. So any sense of co-operation just wasn't there.'

Leaver: 'I remember saying to Charles after his presentation to the principal committee members in the banqueting suite, "Where is the £100 million coming from?" He said: "There's going to be a bank guarantee." I replied: "Banks don't give £100 million guarantees without security, and who's going to be providing the security for the guarantee?"

'It was financial nonsense. Investec wouldn't have provided the money without a guarantee. We were supposed to do a deal with someone who needed to sell all the flats to recoup his money.'

After the lukewarm Lord's reception, Corbett, who was now firmly against the RLP proposal, wanted a lot of amendments to their proposal.

Corbett: 'I wanted a proper review done, once and for all. I don't mind confrontation. Sometimes that approach, grasping the nettle, has got me into trouble, but that's my style.

'I was open to Charles. The club weren't talking to him when I took over. We had embarked on the 2013 Masterplan, building the new Warner Stand followed by the South-Western Project – that was our programme. It was clearly a funding challenge – we either ploughed on with it and financed it out of our own coffers, or we did the thing with Charles that would have given us a big one-off cash injection in return for flats at Lord's.

'At that particular time, the club had closed off the Charles option, but had rarely debated it at the main committee, let alone the membership or negotiated with Charles. The issue was tearing the club apart. There was a minority of highly articulate members who thought the club should not close the door on Charles; on the other hand, there were people in the club who said they would have flats at Lord's over their dead bodies. Both sides had taken positions and were chucking rocks at each other. Sir John Major had resigned. That was the problem I inherited.

'We agreed at the AGM in 2015 to review the options. We invited Charles to come up with a proposal. He didn't come up with a proposal that summer. I understand why he didn't, because Oliver was still there.

'It did take a long time to get into it. We eventually got the proposal in November 2015 and the SGM was in September 2017. So the whole process and the review took nearly two years. It was a difficult time because as the chairman I was the grit in the oyster. I had all the people who didn't want the flats believing I was supporting flats. "The chairman had Rifkind in his box" etc – I got grief from all of them. Plus I got grief from those who wanted the flats, saying: "The new chairman has gone native." It was an interesting period.

'The projected cost of the South-Western Project had gone up from £55 million to £90 million. We had to have the debate about whether that was the right project and what were the alternatives. The club had never done that.

'The problem with the South-Western Project was that not only did it cost £90 million, but that it would not have added many seats, whereas the Compton and Edrich was £40 million and an extra 2,500 seats. So if you built the Compton and Edrich first, it would transform the cash flow – that was pretty fundamental in my thinking. There was a difference of £50 million. And if we had stayed with the South-Western Project, we would have had to do flats to afford it.

'I said that to Colin Maber. He went bonkers and said: "The chairman wants to do flats." Eventually we wrestled that to the ground and Colin retired to Nottingham. So Colin going, getting the estates committee under control and doing the cash flows through to 2035 and getting the right plan was pretty fundamental. If you start off with a £90 million project with no return, you'd have to have had the flats.

'We then had to get the best deal out of Rifkind. It was obvious that if we didn't engage with Rifkind and didn't talk to him, and didn't treat him properly and didn't negotiate with him, this would not go away. I was very strong on this – we had to be seen publicly to go to him and get his best offer. We ran that process. I was very unpopular doing that, because they were petrified I was going to do a deal with him. They thought Charles was going to give me one of his flats.

'Charles had a fundamental problem. Back in 2008, he'd agreed with the club a joint venture with a 50/50 split. He felt he had agreed that. And he had put his own money into that venture. But that had all been torn up and stopped. Although it had been through 12 drafts, it had not been signed. Charles had a bee in his bonnet about that.

'Yet our advisers CBRE and Knight Frank said that because we had around 120 years left on the lease, 50/50 wasn't right and it should be 70/30 in MCC's favour – they couldn't support us. That would have meant that if we had done the deal that Charles wanted us to do at 50/50 and put it to the membership, our advisers wouldn't have recommended it. I couldn't get Charles off the 50/50 – he just had a block about it. We had a lot of discussions about that, and Charles got emotional.'

Corbett's attempts to improve the RLP offer were laid out in a letter on 22 February 2017. It stressed MCC control of every aspect of a leasehold land development, including the return of the head lease.

The demands were explained to Rifkind in more detail at a meeting to discuss MCC's development review held in the committee room on 6 March 2017. He faced the MCC trio of Robert Leigh, David Brooks Wilson and Robert Ebdon. The minutes went as follows:

Brooks Wilson: 'The letter sent by the club chairman followed advice from both the estates and finance committees that MCC should control any transaction with RLP over the leasehold land.

Rifkind: 'If that's the case, I need to work with a small group of mandated MCC personnel.'

Leigh: 'It will ultimately be up to the members' vote whether there will be residential development.'

Rifkind: 'I do have a problem with MCC pursuing a 70/30 split in land value. I have an agreement with MCC that the split should be 50/50, dating back to 2008. Also I don't understand how MCC property advisers DP9 could give such different advice over the granting of planning permission at the Nursery End compared to their favourable forecast in 2008.'

Ebdon: 'DP9 are advising on different schemes. Their advice now is based on a scheme that is cricket-led, without enormous volumes of cricket facilities being placed underground. Also, the MCC Masterplan took into account the views of an eminent heritage and townscape consultant, which had not been the case with the Vision for Lord's in 2008.'

Rifkind: 'I have got a letter here dated 26 April 2011, confirming DP9's fees for their 2008 advice had been £100,000. I will not agree to MCC releasing their development review in its present form, as it devalues RLP's asset and misrepresents the Morley Plan.

'We are soon to publish our Morley scheme brochure. We believe we can quickly complete 97 sales, based on £3,000 per square foot. The maths are simple. 266,000 square feet times £3,000 equals £798 million. Less construction costs of £400 million equals £398 million. A 50/50 split gives MCC £199 million.

'The development review document would hang, draw and quarter me in public if published – I could not let this happen to the Morley scheme. I still believe Oliver Stocken is very much manipulating MCC's approach to ground development.'

Leigh: 'Oliver has had nothing to do whatsoever with the club's ground development plans since he retired as club chairman.'

Brooks Wilson: 'I agree with that.'

Ebdon: 'So do I.'

Leigh: 'It seems MCC should delay sending out the development review to members, as Charles has made it clear the Morley scheme is being effectively withdrawn from the review.'

Brooks Wilson: 'It is MCC not RLP that creates value at Lord's, and this opinion is shared by CBRE, our advisers.'

Rifkind: 'Sir Michael Jenkins agreed in 2007 that this was a 50/50 marriage value, confirmed by a David Batts letter on 11 April 2008. This principle is not negotiable. David Morley and MCC architects Populous should meet and work through the issues at the Nursery End for MCC to consider. The review needs to be a friendly document. If it's not, I will not give MCC permission to describe the Morley Plan in the way they have done. Instead I will distribute my brochure to MCC members.'

Brooks Wilson: 'Can you respond to the club chairman's letter of 22 February 2017?'

Rifkind: 'Could MCC draft this for me?'

Brooks Wilson: 'That would be inappropriate.'

Rifkind: 'OK, I will reply in writing.'

It was agreed to meet back at Lord's in three days' time. This time Rifkind would have Simon Elliot and David Morley alongside him, whilst the MCC trio remained the same. It turned out to be the frankest debate in the 20-year story. RLP were furious with the way the Morley Plan had been portrayed in extracts sent to them from the initial draft of the development review.

Leigh: 'There are two possible ways forward. MCC proceed with the review document, or RLP and MCC discuss Gerald Corbett's 22 February 2017 letter and agree on changing the control structure. This would enable MCC to remove many of the negatives currently in the review.'

Elliot: 'We're not here to discuss the chairman's letter. We want to focus on the review report, which was very disappointing in our opinion and far from impartial. I have shared MCC's extract on the Morley scheme from the review with three members. They all thought it was biased.

'The review also reports that 35 questions sent to RLP remain unanswered. That is inappropriate. I also think it is astonishing MCC could write such a document, when there had been no negotiation with RLP on any commercial terms.'

Brooks Wilson: 'There is no mandate from members to negotiate commercial terms, only to compare the Morley scheme with MCC proposals. MCC had been looking for clarification from RLP on numerous occasions. The club had also spent many hours in discussion with David Morley.'

Elliot: 'Since January 2016, RLP has kept to its word and not leaked anything to the press. Any leaks going on are of MCC's making and the gloves will come off if the review contents get into the public domain.'

Rifkind: 'I can give three recent examples of MCC's principal committee members leaking material.'

Elliot: 'It is unacceptable now for MCC to advise its members that the split should be 70/30. This seriously devalues RLP's value of the land. The way it is addressed in the review document could became a legal issue.

'MCC confirmed a 50/50 split in David Batts' letter of 11 April 2008. We made it very clear a year ago there was no deal at 70/30. At no stage since have MCC indicated they would be maintaining this stance.'

Leigh: 'I disagree. The 70/30 split is a fundamental issue for MCC, and has to go in the review.'

Rifkind: 'Who at MCC should I be dealing with?'

Brooks Wilson: 'It should be myself, Robert Leigh and Robert Ebdon.'

Elliot: 'There has been huge disrespect shown to Charles for 17 years. There have been so many changes in personnel, and now it is disrespectful of MCC to ask Charles to respond to MCC's 22 February letter by 20 March. It is putting him under duress.'

Rifkind: 'MCC are still ignoring the £1 million which RLP spent on the Vision for Lord's in 2008 and 2009. I must remind you of the club's own legal advice from Slaughter & May that until the members voted on the Vision for Lord's, the club was in breach of its agreement with RLP and liable to pay the £1 million.'

Brooks Wilson: 'The legal advice was not one-sided at all. No terms or co-operation agreement has ever been signed regarding the Vision for Lord's.'

Rifkind: 'I considered RLP and MCC were acting in good faith. There was intent for both parties and fees were being paid by both parties. I refer to an MCC document dated 27 May 2009, a report written for the MCC committee on The Vision. It was intelligent, powerful and lucid. Its findings were that MCC needed RLP's windfall cash. After a new Warner Stand, MCC would not have sufficient cash to pay for its ground redevelopments.'

Leigh: 'That may have been the opinion of a report written in 2009. But in 2016 and 2017, a significant amount of detailed financial analysis has been undertaken by the club. MCC can afford to fund its ground development without the need for residential development on the leasehold land.'

Rifkind: 'In that case, RLP cannot go forward.'

Leigh: 'The land value split followed professional advice. It is backed up by a second opinion from Knight Frank, proposing 75/25. So the chances of MCC not including this opinion in the review is remote.'

Elliot: 'We have had professional advice to say the land value split should be a marriage at 50/50 and MCC should acknowledge that in the review.'

Ebdon: 'The review does state that RLP's view of the split is 50/50, and we will make it clear that this is backed by professional advice.'

Rifkind: 'What is the process for getting any negotiated agreement between MCC and RLP passed by the MCC committee structure?'

Brooks Wilson: 'If a deal were to be agreed between us, it would be reviewed by the estates and finance committees, who would make a recommendation to the MCC committee. The timetable of getting to an SGM by the end of September is important, as the MCC committee changes in October 2017 and Robert will no longer be treasurer.'

Elliot: 'We shouldn't be talking about percentage land value splits. No deal has been negotiated, which is why it is so wrong for the review to be so dismissive of RLP's propositions.'

Leigh: 'You must remember the wording of the resolution to which the review is responding – that is why the club chairman's letter of 22 February is important. MCC will find it much easier if they are in control of the process.'

Brooks Wilson: 'My understanding from the discussion with Charles on 6 March is that RLP are now offering MCC £199 million, based on the sale of 266,000 square feet at £3,000 per square feet, less construction costs of £400 million, giving a profit of £398 million divided 50/50 by MCC and RLP.'

Elliot: 'That is right.'

Rifkind: 'Precisely.'

Leigh: 'Our responsibility to members is to not undersell the asset value with 120 years remaining on the lease. Debate will return to an appropriate split in land value and whether MCC should receive 70 per cent of the £398 million.'

Elliot: 'The key issue is whether 266,000 square feet of residential is realistic. We believe it is, and anything less would render the deal null and void. The other issues are the control of the process as addressed in the club chairman's letter and the land value split.'

Leigh: 'I agree that these are the key points.'

Elliot: 'Rome is burning, the ground is deteriorating. There is one final opportunity to accept RLP's proposal and move forward together.'

Leigh: 'Rome is not burning. The ground is in fine form and is benefiting from a splendid new stand, a refurbished media centre, a new scorer's box and record levels of investment in infrastructure and maintenance. We also have the financial ability to fund our own ground development.'

Rifkind: 'Do MCC want to accept the £135 million or not? The review document should be thrown in the bin.'

Ebdon: 'Is RLP's position that they are withdrawing permission for MCC to report on the Morley Scheme in the way it has been drafted? That would mean it would have to be published with all references to the Morley scheme detail being redacted?'

Elliot: 'Yes.'

Rifkind: 'Absolutely.'

Leigh: 'We cannot bin our review, but we could accept that issues of land value split and the acceptable density of development would be possible sticking points.'

Elliot: 'The facilities at Lord's are very second-rate. My son plays real tennis here, so he knows. The RLP windfall would be the fastest way of MCC realising its ground development plans.'

Leigh: 'There is not much difference in timing. And it is incorrect to imply, as the RLP brochure does, that the ground development can be carried out in five years if the RLP windfall money is taken. Lord's has to remain open and fully operational. We would never have partially completed stands in an Ashes year.'

Rifkind: 'I've heard enough.'

Elliot: 'Both sides should try and work towards common ground.'

Leigh: 'We don't believe 266,000 square feet is realistic.'

Morley: 'Westminster City Council have said it is. Have MCC heard differently?

Ebdon: 'Westminster have advised us informally that 266,000 would be unlikely to receive consent without reducing the amount of residential square feet. We've asked for David Morley to share with MCC the written response from Westminster to RLP's pre-application consultation, but it hasn't happened.'

Elliot: 'Stumps should be drawn now if there is not a willingness to keep an open mind on development volume and land value split.'

Leigh: 'MCC is open-minded, but the deal has to be fair and realistic.'

Elliot: 'The cake is big enough for us all to enjoy. The MCC stance is hurting its own members. They would be livid if they knew the club had wasted £7 million in getting nowhere.'

Brooks Wilson: 'The review explains that the leasehold rent due to RLP has been factored into the financial outlook and the Nursery Pavilion could be moved off the leasehold land.'

Rifkind: 'Too many of MCC's principal committee members had no expertise but were all passing comment in the review.'

Brooks Wilson: 'If MCC are to negotiate possible control of a development, we can't have legal threats.'

Elliot: 'If we do negotiate, then MCC cannot proceed with the review document.

Can David Morley tell us about the design aspects of his scheme?'

Morley: 'New Compton and Edrich stands could accommodate an

extra 2,000 people and fit onto the site. It would ensure a larger nursery playing area and still provide space for the Morley residential scheme.'

Leigh: 'MCC will want to maximise the capacity of the Compton and Edrich stands and not merely accept 2,000 extra seats.'

Ebdon: 'Our architect Populous advises that given planning, heritage, sighting limitations and shadowing effect on the Nursery Ground, it will not be possible to accommodate more than an extra 2,000 people. Populous doesn't consider the David Morley solution for the stands workable.'

It was agreed that further discussion on the design detail would not be productive.

Elliot: 'We don't want to talk about the chairman's letter today, but if MCC are prepared to discuss matters openly, then a meeting next week would be worthwhile.'

Leigh: 'How widely has RLP's prospectus of the sale of 97 apartments been circulated?'

Rifkind: 'It hasn't been issued yet. It's been discussed amongst our supporters, and close to 25 per cent of the apartments are near to signing contracts.'

Rifkind later emailed Ebdon to clarify that 50 prospectus documents had already been issued.

Leigh: 'MCC could issue a letter to MCC members, updating them with progress on the review and advising they were in discussions with RLP which remained confidential between both parties.'

Elliot and Rifkind: 'That would be appropriate.'

Rifkind: 'RLP have pulled back on the Cuban ambassador's house and are no longer supporting the enfranchisement claim. It is MCC's house if MCC want it.'

It was agreed to meet again on 20 March. The next day, Elliot emailed David Brooks Wilson:

'I hope our frank discussion yesterday will lead the way into opening a new chapter in this long-running saga. But I must reiterate. There is no question of us withdrawing the Morley Plan. We cannot accept that it can be presented to the membership in the format of your latest draft. To be absolutely clear, this is non-negotiable.'

Brooks Wilson emailed back: 'We fully intend to interact in a collaborative way, by endeavouring to describe the Morley Plan in a manner that is factual. But you must appreciate MCC have a legal duty to communicate all material facts. Contentious issues such as planning, square footage approval level, asset split, security and heritage will have to be addressed – unless the Morley Plan as drafted is formally withdrawn. We look forward to the meeting on 20 March in a positive frame of mind. In that context, it would be helpful to have a formal reply to our chairman's letter of 22 February before we meet.'

Elliot replies: 'We are unable to accommodate the presentation of your consultants' opinions without any reference to ours. I am sure you would agree to present only one side of the advice being given hardly presents a neutral tone.

'Going back as far as 2010 and the Vision for Lord's, there was considerably more square footage envisaged than in the Morley Plan. Your current professional opinions basically voids any development scheme before it is even tested through a planning submission.

'While we understand your legal obligations to report "material facts" to the membership, all you have received is opinions. With reference to Gerald's letter, I can only repeat that whilst we are very open to have a discussion on the points raised, we must first resolve the difficulties over your fourth draft as presented to us.'

Ebdon replied for MCC in a letter to David Morley that demonstrated MCC were in no mood to compromise. They had seized on Elliot's admission of showing the draft report findings to three MCC members and of Rifkind having to clarify how many residential sales prospectuses RLP had sent out.

Ebdon wrote: 'Given the club's long relationship with David Morley Architects, we are disappointed with the tone of your emails of 1, 6 and 13 March. The club has not seen any formal comments from Westminster City Council on the RLP pre-application consultations, despite having requested this of you. We therefore remain very concerned about assuming the Morley proposals would receive planning permission without important amendments.

'It is indeed Populous's advice to MCC that in order to best meet MCC's cricketing priorities, it is not possible to satisfactorily expand the Compton and Edrich stands by 2,000 extra seats and build your residential development on the leasehold land without reducing the playing area of the Nursery Ground.

'MCC is fully aware of the collaboration between Populous and David Morley Architects over one of the venues at the London 2012 Olympics. But it has been David Morley Architects that has not been prepared to allow MCC to show its drawings and solutions for the Compton and Edrich stands to Populous. You wanted to preserve your intellectual property. Populous have reciprocated and do not consider there would be much to be gained by a shared workshop.

'It has been very clearly stated informally to MCC by Westminster City Council that 266,000 square feet would be unlikely to receive planning permission.

'The club have deemed that an earlier version of the draft document should be sent to the 140 members of the club's principal committees. All are bound by confidentially agreements. This is MCC's procedure and, with respect, it is not for you to question the club's procedure.

'MCC is very concerned to have learnt from Mr Elliot at the meeting on 9 March that he breached the confidentiality discipline by sharing the club's draft review with three MCC members. The club considers this to be a very serious matter. Can the club please be assured this will not happen again and that you and others have not circulated it further?

'MCC is further concerned that despite the assurance given at the meeting on 9 March that no prospectus documents had been issued, it has now been admitted that 50 such documents have been issued to members of the public offering the sale of residential units, without the agreement of MCC. Apart from being misleading, this somewhat pre-judges, in the most biased manner, the consultation process the club is planning to hold with its membership.

'With regard to the brochure titled "Delivering the World-Leading Home of Cricket", MCC notes from your email of 8 February that your client has circulated 250 copies of this document already. You have sent 150 of these to MCC to issue to our principal committee members on 14 December 2016. So please would you advise to whom the other 100 copies have been sent?

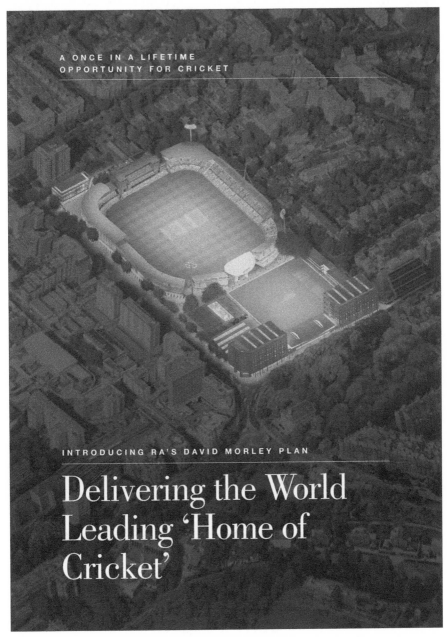

A ONCE IN A LIFETIME
OPPORTUNITY FOR CRICKET

INTRODUCING RA'S DAVID MORLEY PLAN

Delivering the World
Leading 'Home of
Cricket'

The front cover of the Morley Plan brochure

'The club requires your assurances that the document will not be issued to anyone else. This brochure passes off and misleads the reader in a number of ways – not least inferring the brochure somehow represents MCC's proposals to its members. You do not have MCC's permission or agreement to publish this document, either in hard copy or electronically, and please desist.'

Meanwhile, the City heavyweight Malcolm Le May had proposed to finance the Morley Plan through his company Opus, in a joint venture between RLP and MCC called Project Wellington. Le May put forward the initiative in an email to Corbett and Ebdon on 10 March 2017.

'I would recommend that we restrict any initial discussion to those copied on this email, so as to focus on the key aspects of the proposal without being deflected by other emotions attached to this long-running discussion.

Robert Leigh responded: 'We must include the MCC executive in the process.'

Le May wrote back: 'I note your comment that you are obliged to share the Opus proposal with other members of the MCC executive. In due course this is obviously appropriate. But I feel that prior to doing this, it would be advisable to secure at least conceptual agreement between RLP and yourself and Gerald.'

Corbett immediately shot down the plan, as he returned from a trip to the United States:

'Malcolm, I have literally just got off the red eye, so please excuse fruitiness of my reply. The idea that Robert and I should seek to evaluate your proposal without executive support until we have reached "conceptual agreement" is not on. We are not capable of doing so. We have a committee we must bring with us. They will be bemused in the extreme if we sought to come to a view without involving the executive. We cannot expect the executive to be accountable if we don't share such things with them and it is potentially divisive. Your proposal is doomed from the word go if that is how you expect us to operate.'

Le May: 'Your note is fully understood, and I apologise if my comment regarding the executive was misconstrued. I was in no way suggesting the executive – whom I don't know – should not be involved. I was trying to see if in principle the idea of a joint venture company made sense.'

The 20 March summit between RLP and MCC ended in predictable stalemate. Leigh emailed Le May the next day to reject the short-lived Opus blueprint:' As you know we met yesterday, four from RLP and four from MCC. We felt that it would not be worth having further discussions with you at this stage. The issue of control of the process is very important to MCC.'

Another Ebdon letter to Rifkind on 31 March made it clear once more that MCC was unhappy with the Morley plan brochure:

'The club's lawyers have advised MCC that your document "Delivering the World-Leading Home of Cricket", with its www.lords-masterplan.com address and lack of any reference to RLP, is misleading and passes off as something that it is not. In its current state, MCC does not consent to your brochure being issued, whether in hard copy or in any other medium.'

Relationships were at an all-time low in the build-up to the members' vote scheduled for September 2017.

CHAPTER 14

A Recommended Vote

THE DEVELOPMENT CONFLICT REACHED BOILING point at the AGM on 13 May 2017 and at the annual MCC dinner afterwards. MCC president Matthew Fleming opened up the AGM by raising the issue of Colin Maber's resignation as chairman of estates.

Fleming: 'The committee received news of Colin's decision with considerable regret. The Warner Stand, in particular, was a project that he led superbly. I think in these circumstances it is always preferable for a member who has resigned to explain the rationale, if he is prepared to, and Colin has indicated that he might be prepared to. Colin are you still here?'

Maber: 'Thank you very much for your kind words and for the opportunity to explain the background to my decision to resign from the role of MCC chairman of estates. This was a decision that I came to after a great deal of heart-searching. My departure did not result from bad health or a single dramatic event – far from it.

'My presence has been required at Lord's often on two or three days a week. I live in Nottingham, which is three hours from door to door, with six hours' commuting time to be added to a full day's work. From what I have just told you, you will appreciate that one can only sustain a lifestyle like this for so long and I reckon that, all things considered, six years was a pretty good innings.

'The second major influence on my decision was Gerald Corbett's appointment as chairman of MCC in October 2015. Right from the word go, he and I failed to establish a working rapport. I recognise that these things do happen and I am pragmatic about such matters, but it certainly does not lead to a rewarding working relationship and that is no way to live one's life.

'In the prevailing circumstances, I decided that it was both in my interests and those of MCC that I step aside. I did so at this time last year, giving the club six months to identify and appoint an appropriate replacement.'

The new Warner Stand was officially opened by the Duke of Edinburgh, a former president of MCC, before the start of the AGM. It was the first new stand at Lord's since the completion of the Grandstand renovation in 1998. The new structure marked the first major phase of development in the Masterplan for Lord's, MCC's answer to the aborted Vision for Lord's. It was not without its critics even at the very top of MCC, some of whom noted that 50 seats had a seriously restricted view of the cricket.

Robert Leigh: 'We knew about these seats without a view. There was nothing you could do about it because of the overhang from the Grandstand. We shouldn't have sold them as seats.'

Oliver Stocken: 'If you go to the top right-hand corner, you can't see half the pitch. How the hell did we get ourselves into this position? I said to Robert Ebdon: "What on earth do you think you're doing? Surely someone has modelled this."

'When I raised it with Colin Maynard. He said: "We're all right with the Ashes, people will still sit up there." I replied: "This is not the way to do this." I said to Justin: 'This is close to home [Ascot, where Dowley sat on the ruling body, had major viewing problems with their new grandstand]. How can you spend all this money and have seats with no proper view?"

Peter Leaver: 'This is a nonsense. I love Colin Maynard dearly, but I said to him before it was built and since it was built that you are getting money out of some spectators under false pretences. The seats should be taken out. The view in committee was that as long as the members knew that there was a problem with a restricted view, this was their decision.'

Sir Simon Robertson: 'It is utter incompetence. I was on the board at the Royal Opera House, and the most important discussions were over the sightlines.'

At the annual dinner after the AGM, Tony Alt, who had consistently opposed RLP's plans, was responding for MCC to guest speaker Chris Cowdrey. Alt went through a litany of how long he had been on various committees. He then shocked the room by saying: 'We do not want flats at Lord's.' This was ahead of the members' vote over development options, when Alt should have remained strictly impartial as a main committee member. The remark brought howls of protest from the usual suspects on the Members Independent Online Pavilion.

Nick Gandon: 'It seems to me that Mr Alt, who in addition to his membership of the main committee serves as an unelected member of the finance committee and estates committee, has forgotten that he has fiduciary responsibilities that require him to ensure a fair, honest and unbiased review of ground redevelopments. I hope he now tenders his resignation from the various committees to which he has never been properly elected.'

Tom Page: 'I think it was unwise of Tony Alt to air dirty laundry in public. If there were personality clashes or differences of opinion, these are private matters between the individuals involved and should have been kept as such.'

Paddy Briggs: 'An early resignation by Mr Alt from the MCC committee would be in order.'

John Fingleton: 'Tony Alt made the wrong speech to the wrong people in the wrong place and at the wrong time. His performance was so inappropriate and outrageous that perhaps the committee should formally disown it.'

James Mitchell: 'On the basis of the committee's assurance that the process would be objective and unbiased, RLP would probably have a claim for breach of contract/good faith.'

Paul Graber: 'Given that we have been told that the committee are adopting a policy of neutrality until all options have been considered and a recommendation made, this seems extremely unfortunate. Indeed, it seems to me behaviour incompatible with his position on the committee.'

MCC committee member Robert Griffiths, chairman of the development committee disbanded in 2011, emailed Gerald Corbett:

'If I had made comments such as Tony's at the anniversary dinner, I believe the club would have been down on me like a ton of bricks. It seems there is one rule here for those opposed to any relationship with RLP and in favour of piecemeal development and another for everyone else.'

Corbett replied: 'We were all very disappointed by Tony's remarks. He has apologised twice to me and we are considering the matter.'

There was no disciplinary process; Alt merely agreed to exclude himself from future discussions over the development of flats.

RLP had been told by Gerald Corbett in February that their offer wasn't good enough. But it wasn't until 12 May, shortly before the June deadline for the development review document, that RLP revised their bid.

Simon Elliot wanted the fact that MCC were not returning the £1 million for the work done on the Vision for Lord's to be mentioned in the letter sent by RLP's lawyers. He also suggested that Macfarlanes detail that a minority group of members had been determined to stop any transaction with RLP over 15 years, and that Robert Ebdon's fierce letter to David Morley had done nothing to dispel RLP's fears that the MCC commentary in the review document would be misleading.

Charles Martin, senior partner of Macfarlanes, lawyers for the newly renamed Rifkind Associates, wrote to Corbett with the new terms. The offer was for £150 million, comprising a £100 million letter of credit, £35 million for the provision of MCC facilities and a further £15 million as an estimated compensation payment in lieu of Lord's membership subscriptions. It was based on a 50/50 split of the land value.

Martin wrote: 'We are aware that different views have been expressed about the likelihood of obtaining planning permission for the size of the scheme set out in the David Morley Plan. Our client's view remains that it is very much achievable, based on professional advice and consultation with Westminster Council.

'We understand this is consistent with the advice of the planning adviser to MCC (DP9) in 2008, when the Vision for Lord's was contemplated and whom still remains MCC's adviser.

'The letter of credit will be provided by a reputable regulated bank approved by MCC. The provision of the letter of credit cannot be specifically contracted for now or at exchange of the agreement because there would be a significant commitment fee and cost in doing so. However, the form of letter will be carefully prescribed in the agreement and MCC cannot be forced to proceed without an acceptable letter being provided.'

The letter was delivered just in time to be included in MCC's review of development plans. The review had been drafted by MCC executives and an editing group including Sir Ian Magee, chairman of membership & general purposes, Angus Fraser and trustee Adrian Beecroft.

The review had had 13 drafts, during which Rifkind Associates had been sent the commentary on the sections involving their bid. They made suggestions but only some of them were incorporated. And the Morley plan brochure was not sent out as the same time as the development review, as Rifkind had requested.

The MCC committee deemed the Morley literature 'inappropriate', arguing that it was a campaigning document and that delivering it at the same time as MCC's development review of the two options would cause 'confusion to members'. It was eventually posted to members in early August, two months after the development review.

MCC didn't even provide Rifkind a copy of their review. He emailed Corbett: 'Gerald, I am somewhat surprised that MCC did not send the review documents to me, although the request has been made on numerous occasions. I even understand the review was shown to the press some days before MCC's 18,000 members received the documents in the post.

'As of today, I still have not been sent one. On visiting Lord's yesterday to request the review document, I was informed there was no executive staff available and Janet Fisher [Derek Brewer's PA] was without authority to release one. I fear the David Morley plans are being presented with every negative exaggerated and not one positive.'

MCC were no doubt annoyed that their review findings had once again been pre-empted by an article in *The Times* by Ivo Tennant promoting the Morley plan. It called the Morley option 'A once-in-a-lifetime opportunity to build on the Wellington Road frontage and generate £135 million plus a £15 million sweetener to members'.

The article continued: 'David Morley claims his plans will deliver a win, win, win. A hat-trick of spectacular funding, more space for cricket-related uses and a transformation of how Lord's is integrated into the community.'

RLP knew about the piece in advance, as Sir Simon Robertson had sent it to John Major before it appeared in the newspaper. He wrote:

'I thought you would like to see this article by Ivo Tennant, which is due to appear in *The Times* on Thursday. It has been a long haul since you and Sir Michael Jenkins were looking at this. As you have told me before, I don't expect you will want to comment on the plans.'

Major wrote back: 'Many thanks for sending me Ivo Tennant's article, which reads well. It leads me to hope that MCC members (and the committee) will drop their over-conservative caution and embrace a comprehensive development that is long overdue and will enhance Lord's. History has made Lord's The Home of Cricket. it desperately needs the very best facilities to justify that title in the future. This development, if agreed, appears to be an enormous step forward.'

It remains the only comment Major has made on the development issue since his letter to president Phillip Hodson in 2012 complaining about the way MCC had presented his resignation from the main committee. As for their own review of development plans, the MCC press release trumpeted:

'The review is the largest piece of analysis ever produced in the club's 230-year history. It was undertaken as a result of a vote by MCC members at the 2015 annual general meeting. A detailed study of two different development options has been put before MCC's members, with a survey and wide-ranging consultation to take place in the coming weeks.

'The review, which does not contain a recommendation, includes a comparative analysis of the MCC committee's updated Masterplan and the latest revised Morley Plan, as submitted by Rifkind Associates. The choice facing MCC is effectively whether members are content to accept large-scale residential development within the Lord's boundary in return for a cash injection, or pay for the development of the entire ground from club resources but without accepting residential development.'

MCC chairman Gerald Corbett encouraged members to participate in the process: 'MCC would like Lord's to continue to position itself to be the best ground in the world to play and watch cricket. The review is already the result of much consultation and is intended to be as fair as possible. What MCC could or should do – and when – has been subject of much debate within and outside the club for nearly twenty years. It is hoped that this review, followed by an open and thorough consultation process, will produce a resolution to be voted on at an SGM that will forge a clear way forward for the development of Lord's for the next ten years and beyond.'

'When it meets in late July 2017, the MCC committee will receive a report from the five consultation evenings, together with the results of the members' survey. The committee will then call a special general meeting, which will be held towards the end of September 2017. At the SGM, members will consider a resolution, proposed by the committee, regarding the next stages in the development of the ground.'

Corbett had stated the review was intended to be 'as fair as possible'. But the executive summary effectively wrote off the Morley Plan, starting by casting doubts as to why Rifkind Levy Partners had changed names to Rifkind Associates and once again saying their advisers suggested a 70/30 split.

'Shortly before going to print with the review, MCC received notice from Mr Rifkind's lawyers Macfarlanes to the effect that the proposed Morley Plan for the development of the Nursery End up to now put forward by Rifkind Levy Partners was henceforth being put forward by Rifkind Associates. In light of the change in entity making the offer, MCC sought explanation as to the relationship between Mr Rifkind and Mr Levy, RLP and RA and also the legal status, structure and capitalisation of RA, so as to understand how it would meet its obligations.

'The club had wanted to include recent exchanges of correspondence on these subjects between the club and Macfarlanes in this review, but Macfarlanes declined to give MCC permission to include them. In any event the club will continue to seek clarification on the above and other matters, including as regards who owns what assets.

'RA's offer is set out in a letter from Macfarlanes. They value the land at £300 million and their offer is £150 million in cash and kind. Of this amount, approximately £100 million would be available to MCC to spend on the development of new stands and facilities at Lord's.

'The club's advisers state that MCC should receive at least 70 per cent of the land value and significant issues are unresolved concerning control of the development process, the effect of residential accommodation within the ground on security and operations and whether the plans provide adequate space for the cricket needs of Lord's.'

The review also made reference to the head lease having been bought in 1999 by RLS, standing, they assumed, for Rifkind, Levy, Sandelson. It did, but the name was only ever used for the auction purchase and was never registered as a limited company.

'Although MCC was invited to make a pre-auction offer, negotiations proved unsuccessful and at auction the head lease of the land was sold to Rifkind, Levy, Sandelson Ltd, which at some point subsequently assigned it to Charles Rifkind and Jonathan Levy.'

The review was also far from neutral over RA's financial offering, the percentage split in development value, design, planning permission and security:

'Rifkind Associates has not provided information about the identity of its financial backers or developers for this scheme, and neither have they explained the terms and conditions of the letter of credit, other than to advise that a reputable regulated bank approved by MCC would provide it. MCC understands that the £100 million would have to be drawn down against the construction costs of other developments at Lord's.

'The letter offers to make a £15 million disturbance payment, which MCC must pass on in full to cover the cost of all full members' subscriptions for two years. The £15 million is of direct benefit to members, but does not improve the financial position of the club itself and has no relevance to the value of the land.

'CBRE has advised MCC that an equitable split of land value should be closer to 70:30 in the club's favour. A second opinion was sought from Knight Frank, who advised it should be 75:25 in MCC's favour. Both advisers consider those figures more fairly reflect the strength of MCC's position in terms of the length of time remaining on the lease.

'Because the Nursery Ground is not being moved towards the Wellington Road, the stands will cast greater shadows over it than would be the case in the updated Masterplan. The lower tiers appear to have a shallow rake, which means sightlines are unlikely to be significantly improved.

'Gardiner & Theobald advise that the construction of the residential blocks is likely to be completed in the first quarter of 2023. The scheme incorporates 97 flats in two ten-storey blocks, the total net internal area is 266,000 square feet.

'DP9 and Ettwein Bridges, MCC planning and heritage consultants think it will be challenging to secure planning permission. MCC understands there is likely to be significant local opposition to the establishment of residential blocks.

'The residential accommodation blocks within the boundaries of the estate increases Lord's vulnerability to security breaches, according to Metropolitan Police counter-terrorism advice.'

Rifkind responded to MCC's partisan development review by encouraging RLP supporter David Gower to write a letter to *The Times*.

Gower wrote: 'I have a huge love of Lord's and what it stands for. But the "Home of Cricket" is in danger of losing its lustre unless improvements are made to the fabric. I respect the choices being offered to the membership. I personally have a yen for David Morley's plan, which would drastically improve the image of the ground on the Wellington Road side, offering a much more attractive vista than the "prison wall" effect that greets members and the public alike as they walk past now.'

Gower: 'The way the development review vote was so blatantly skewered in favour of MCC was pathetic. Why couldn't they just have played fair, especially as they are set up with the postal vote that practically guarantees they win any ballot. I would say 16,000 out of the 18,000 membership tick the box in favour of the committee recommendations without even reading them, but they came up with every excuse going in trying to write off the Morley Plan – it was one-eyed and quite ridiculous. I'm surprised they didn't mention the residential flats affecting the habitat of great crested newts or a Roman villa underneath the tunnels.'

The Reform Action Group, who had brought about the resolution for an independent review, put their thoughts on the MIOLP forum.

Tom Page: 'The review could have been and nearly was an awful lot more biased than what we ended up with. The three of us made a great number of very detailed comments on the one draft we saw, in order to go some way in addressing the clear bias of the document we saw. Some of our comments managed to get into the final report, but not all of them. The biggest concern was that it was presented as a binary choice.'

Andrew Lloyd: 'My view is that a review that is drafted by the executive with considerable pressures from the various committees is likely to reflect those pressures. We strongly advocated that the independent review of the facts should be carried out by a specialist consultancy, but this option was rejected. This is regrettable, as it leaves the club open to the understandable criticism that the review was crafted to justify the Masterplan and to criticise Morley.'

John Hegarty: 'For two years we had tried to eliminate the risk of bias. However, it is hard to read the review without feeling that this is the club's defence to an outsider's challenge rather than a balanced consideration of what might be best for the club.'

One of the features of the first draft was that it included the comments of the various MCC principal committees – even the arts & library group – which were all heavily against residential flats at Lord's.

The Reform Group representatives managed to have the committee views toned down, yet their damning opinions were still included when MCC sent out their literature ahead of the SGM vote in September. However, even those MCC members who were open to the Morley Plan were unimpressed with the RA offer of two years' worth of subscriptions.

Andrew Lloyd: 'What is disappointing is the £15 million offer to give members a two-year subscription holiday. I am sure that many members will not need this nor be swayed by it.'

Robin Knight: 'Rifkind offering to pay members' subscriptions was a big mistake. It went down very badly. It came over as a bribe. A lot of the members are in their sixties and seventies and are not poor. They don't need to be offered money in such a way. It was a bad move.'

John Hegarty: 'I am disappointed, moreover affronted, by the offer of a subscription holiday, both being offered and it would seem forced upon us.'

The next 'level playing field' was the five consultation evenings held in front of 519 members between 19 June and 26 June at Lord's (twice), Old Trafford, Trent Bridge and Bristol. Robert Ebdon, MCC's assistant secretary (estates), who had switched from being an enthusiastic project manager for the Vision for Lord's into an MCC loyalist once he joined the Lord's executive, presented both options – Rifkind Associates had argued without success that David Morley should be allowed to present his plan at the five meetings.

At the first roadshow at Lord's, MCC member and former Middlesex bowler Rob Titchener-Barrett jumped up to exclaim: 'We don't want these people here. Once they get their feet under the table, anything can happen.' When he sat down, the person sitting next to him introduced himself. It was Charles Rifkind.

Titchener-Barrett's son Dominic insisted his father was not making an anti-Semitic statement, but merely saying what he thought about property developers invading Lord's. Others were not so sure, and said so on the MIOLP forum:

MCC member Philip Banham: 'I was appalled by the remark. The vitriol which I heard expressed against Mr Rifkind, both before and during the meeting, I found offensive.'

James Mitchell: 'I did feel a bit sorry for Charles Rifkind. He was sitting in the front row, next to the member who made the most vitriolic (and somewhat personal) attack on him and his scheme. I thought the presentation was generally even handed, although I might have expected the Morley Plan to have been presented by David Morley. It's a pity that there may be any suggestion at all of bias. From the mood of the meeting – and judging by the speeches delivered and the applause which followed them – I suspect that it would not make any difference in the long run had Rifkind Associates and David Morley been allowed to present their scheme themselves and been permitted to distribute the Morley Plan brochure.

'Doing this would have removed any suggestion of a stitch-up. As it is, if the Morley Plan is rejected (as I strongly suspect it will be), it's hard to imagine that everyone will judge the process to have been entirely fair.'

Philip Banham, who had been dismayed by the comments aimed at Rifkind in the first Lord's consultation evening, attended the second one determined to say something. He said: 'I came up early and by chance met Charles Rifkind in the street. I told him he had been treated appallingly. He called it "the worst week of his life".

'The first speaker, who I think had been planted, was a Mr D. E. Sherman: He said: "The residential development at Lord's. Never, never, never. When the first bulldozer comes down Wellington Road, I will lie in front of it. I really think we should acquire the freehold of this wretched strip of land, which has been such a thorn in our sides, whatever the cost. In 1999, the cost would have been about £50 per member – I would cheerfully have stumped up that cost. This year I don't know what the price of the freehold is, but every man has his price."

'Corbett said: "That was a strong view well expressed." Then I had a chance to speak. I said: "I like the Morley Plan. It may not be perfect, but it looks good, both aesthetically and financially. Mr Rifkind appears to me to have been vilified for having had the temerity to buy the lease. The committee of the day were the real culprits, but we are where we are. Mr Rifkind, having obtained the rights, could turn out to be a blessing in disguise. Are we going to give up the opportunity to work with Mr Rifkind out of spite? Have the committee authorised genuine negotiations with Mr Rifkind or just asked for his best and final offer? Shouldn't Mr Rifkind be allowed to speak if he wishes?"'

Banham had been one of the few people during the five meetings who had spoken out in favour of the Morley Plan. The general mood was against any residential development. Stocken came to the second Lord's roadshow and talked about the complications involving blocks of flats, referencing his own experience from being on the committee of the residential development where he lives.

Rifkind: 'Stocken's hand was very much in play. A lot of the questions that came out at the roadshows were his questions being asked by his old friends or previous committee members. His influence was still very much strong in terms of steering opinion.'

The three members who had proposed the original resolution that had led to the development review, Hegarty, Lloyd and Page, recognised the unfairness in the process. The trio were also unhappy with the binary choice of either the Masterplan or the Morley Plan being offered to the members. In a letter sent to the MCC committee on 12 July, they asked them not to make a recommendation to members as to how they should vote at the SGM in September:

'We believe it would be a lost opportunity if, having put in all this work, the end result was to rush into a hasty binary decision between two options, both of which have significant risks and flaws. We therefore urge the committee not to make a final decision at their meeting on 24 July and request that any final decision is deferred until the club has had an opportunity to consider the key flaws in both options.

'Throughout the two-year process since the 2015 AGM, we have urged the club to have a proper dialogue and, more importantly, negotiation with Charles Rifkind in relation to his Morley Plan. The decision to simply request information and demand a "best and final offer" has resulted in an offer that doesn't meet some of the club's requirements.'

MCC ignored the letter and took more notice of their own survey. There were 4,710 responses, of which 3,780 were sent in by post and 930 online. The online ones were not included in the analysis, as it was considered non-members could have contributed. Either way, the results were ten to one against residential.

So after the MCC committee meeting on 24 July, a statement went out announcing that the club were recommending their own Masterplan. The committee decision had been 15 in favour, with just one vote from Sir Ian Magee to hold further discussions with RLP. Former England and Middlesex cricketers Angus Fraser and Mike Gatting had been particularly vocal against residential at Lord's.

A press release read: 'The MCC committee has today issued a recommendation to proceed with a development of the Lord's Cricket Ground by adapting the updated MCC Masterplan funded from the club's own resources. As a result, the club's members will be asked to approve a resolution at a special general meeting on 27 September, effectively ruling out the building of residential flats at the Nursery End.

'The committee has assessed the results of thousands of hours of analysis, involving advice from nine independent specialist consultants, two sets of lawyers, five principal committees and an editorial board.

'Corbett said: "Today's decision by the MCC committee provides clarity on the extremely important and often controversial subject of ground development. Put simply, the club can afford to develop the ground using its own resources, and it will do so in the coming years without the need for enabling residential development.

'The Morley scheme, with flats at its heart, was considered by the committee to detract from the ambience and special feel of Lord's, as well as containing a number of operational, security, execution and planning risks. Moreover the club's advisers were unable to recommend the proposed commercial terms. All members have been consulted, many have spoken, the committee have decided, the club will now vote and we will then move on.'

Corbett: 'We had to draw a line in the sand. We had given Charles enough chances. It was a crappy deal – no one wanted the flats. I think it was fair enough for the committee to make a recommendation. We had consulted widely with the membership, we had the roadshows, everybody had had their say. I don't think another glossy brochure from Charles would have made any difference. There was a febrile atmosphere on the MCC committee at that time. Being any more positive towards Charles's proposals in the development review would have been very difficult to get through the committee.'

Peter Leaver: 'What do modern public companies do with a contentious issue? The board makes a recommendation to members.'

The opinions of MCC's five principal committees, which Hegarty, Page and Lloyd had at least managed to temper in the development review, were now made public by MCC. Sent out with the SGM notice papers, they were wholly negative about the Morley Plan.

Finance committee: 'The club's financial position is sound, and space should only be sacrificed if the financial position and outlook is so bad that it makes such a sacrifice unavoidable. That would not be the case even if Lord's were to lose its second Test match.

'The demand for high-level residential is uncertain. Locking into a long-term project with Rifkind Associates, who don't appear to have the financial resources or expertise to deliver it, would be unwise.

'The finance committee would be unable to support proceeding with RA's Morley Plan and would recommend that the development of the ground be financed from the club's own resources.'

Estates committee: 'The economic and long-term interests of MCC mandated as the premier cricket club in the world far outweigh those of Rifkind Associates. Should MCC wish to promote a major residential scheme on the Nursery Ground to finance the ground redevelopment, the estates committee believes the club should partner with an organisation that has the track record, equity and resources to deliver such a project. There are only a handful of companies that would be able to do that, and these do not include Rifkind Associates.'

Cricket committee: 'It is important to maintain the quality and size of the Nursery Ground. There is a need for sufficient sunlight on both grounds. Having two building sites on the go at one time, residential plus Compton and Edrich, will be catastrophic for cricket at the Nursery End. Flats at Lord's would destroy the iconic image. We believe the RA Morley Plan, complete with its residential development, would present a significant risk and threat to Lord's as both the Home of Cricket and the world's finest cricket ground.'

Membership and general purposes committee: 'No overt support for Morley Plan from anyone, but a minority view is there is scope for further negotiation. There is substantial concern about preserving the atmosphere, setting and history of the ground. The M&GP recommendation is by a clear majority in favour of the club's updated Masterplan.'

Arts & library committee: 'The special character and feel of the ground would be destroyed by residential flats and cause harm to the heritage as well as the overall setting of Lord's, including its relationship with St John's Wood Church and its churchyard. The ground had been extremely well developed since the 1980s, and residential would be a retrograde step. Under the Morley Plan, the club would be required to take out a lease and pay rent to a third party for leasing space for a museum. This would not be the best way of providing long-term security for the artwork and memorabilia.'

MCC followed their SGM mailout with an online posting that included Mike Gatting saying on camera: 'I am a great advocate for the updated Masterplan because it gives us what I say is a proper ground, a little village green with nothing other than grass, and it will have a lovely feel about it.'

The bias of the MCC approach prompted another former England captain, David Gower, to write a second letter to *The Times*. It was published on 4 September 2017, just three weeks before the SGM members ballot:

'MCC thinks it has been fair to all members in giving them a say in the plans. But the club has sent out in an email to members a video which presents only the case for the committee's preferred Masterplan. Every speaker on the video, including my former England captain Mike Brearley and another in Mike Gatting, are in favour of the Masterplan. Although questions are asked about the concerns of those who favour the Rifkind-Morley plan, which would have a completely different effect on the Nursery End, not one speaker is featured to endorse the possible aesthetic and financial benefits of that scheme.

'They urge members to vote as a matter of supreme importance, but have shown those members a very one-sided view of the options. I for one will not be voting in favour of the Masterplan – but it will make, I suspect, little difference, as the great body of membership normally prefers to be led like red-and-yellow tie, blazer and cap-wearing sheep.'

Gower: 'I was offered the chance by the chairman Gerald Corbett to apologise for using the word "sheep". I declined. If any member merely accepted what the committee recommended without any further consideration, then I am not embarrassed to call that man a sheep.'

David Morley, who had kept a low profile in the months leading up to the vote, went on the attack in a long email to MIOLP founder James Mitchell, which he posted on the forum. The architect was damning about almost every aspect of the club's approach over the previous year.

Morley wrote: 'Although the last 12 months were intended to be an unbiased consultation of its members by MCC, it feels that much has been done to convince members there is no value in the Wellington Road frontage.

'The main difference between MCC's vision and ours is in the treatment of the Wellington Road frontage. Our vision is to create a 365-days-a-year frontage of cricket-related activity. And, by including some residential development, generate £150 million worth of benefits for members, cricket and the public. MCC's vision is to grass over part of the disued railway tunnels and retain the other part for a car park and broadcast compound, leaving the tunnels empty and leaving the prison wall intact. I remain convinced there are huge potential benefits which would come from a collaborative process between MCC and Rifkind Associates which has not yet been adequately explored.

'Neither David Morley Architects nor RA were involved in the preparation of the MCC development review report, nor did we approve of the way our proposals had been presented. We were only shown a draft of a section of the review in advance, and the majority of comments we made were not accepted by MCC.

'Extraordinarily, many of the benefits of the Morley Plan were either omitted from the report entirely or significantly understated. The report stresses Gardiner & Theobald's credentials by referring to their 20-year involvement at Lord's, but does not mention David Morley's 24-year involvement across 15 projects.

'There appears to be no mention of any of the following benefits: expansion of the existing underground space to relieve congestion, increased size of the Nursery Pavilion, increased size of the broadcast compound, potential for a street-facing Lord's shop and/or museum, underground car parking – benefits amounting to £150 million. No acknowledgment that the Nursery Pavilion provided will save on the necessary future cost of developing the East Gate building, so significantly understating the financial position of the David Morley Plan.

'On the roadshows, we were not allowed to present our proposals. At every presentation apart from Old Trafford, ex-committee members, including a former chairman and two former chairman of estates, delivered pre-prepared speeches objecting to the Morley Plan.

'What took me back was Brian Thornton, a former chairman of estates who ran the Warner Stand design competition that we won, although another company was later commissioned to do the work. He was allowed to speak at Bristol because he was no longer on the committee. He gave this incredibly negative speech about "any development over his dead body". I thought he was going to speak in our favour.

'I was flabbergasted that our plan should have been spurned because of historic ill-feeling at losing out at the auction. But I was also staggered at how unprofessionally we have been treated. It did not uphold the way you would expect MCC to be run. It was the pettiness. They had a report from a heritage adviser saying it would be harmful and we had a report from a heritage adviser saying it wouldn't be harmful. They didn't mention ours.

'There was a long list of items – each one doesn't sound particularly significant, but they added up into an incredibly negative impression.

'If we had had the opportunity to sit down with MCC's architects Populous, I think we could have come up with a joint proposal. We worked with them for the water polo venue at the London Olympics.

'The issue of affordable housing was raised as a risk to MCC. We had only limited opportunity to reassure members the risk lay entirely with RA. Negotiations with Westminster can only take place once members have indicated their support to progress the scheme.

'There were 25,000 copies of our brochure printed to explain the benefits of the Morley Plan. However, MCC elected not to circulate the brochure to all members until after the MCC committee had met to decide on their preferred way forward. The majority of members were unaware of the full range of benefits when they completed the MCC survey.

'We were advised our brochure would be issued with the SGM papers. It was, in fact, issued by MCC separately beforehand, without our knowledge. And with an accompanying letter from the chairman, which implied the committee had rejected the plans.

'In October 2016, in an introductory meeting with your new chairman and new chairman of estates, it appears that our proposals were of genuine interest. A process was established for presenting them to MCC's principal committees before consulting with members. Our client, in good faith, proceeded to invest considerably in further design work, consultancy and explanatory brochures in the run-up to a meeting on 14 December 2016 to present proposals to MCC's principal committees.

'MCC requested a lot of detail about how the Morley Plan would impact on their Masterplan. We proposed the most effective way would be workshops with Populous, MCC's Masterplan architect, but the request was declined. It therefore fell on us to demonstrate that our proposals were compatible with other components of MCC's Masterplan (which we had not seen). The initial premise of the Morley Plan was that it would generate a cash injection to fully fund the south-west corner development, which had detailed planning approval and was scheduled to be the next phase of MCC's Masterplan.

'MCC advised us in the autumn of 2016 they were now considering renewing the Compton and Edrich stands before the South-Western Project, for commercial reasons. That decision appears to have taken no account of the fact that the South-Western Project could have been made affordable by the proceeds of the Morley Plan.

'The presentation of 14 December 2016 was recorded, but we were not allowed a copy of the recording nor a copy of the transcript. We were only permitted to read a transcript in the Library under supervision.

'MCC engaged a number of consultants to analyse our proposals, but on no occasion were we contacted by any of them to assist in their understanding of the proposals. We were shown in advance one report prepared by Gardiner & Theobald on the construction programme, which we commented on, but our comments were ignored.

'MCC's cost consultants claimed they had insufficient information about how the David Morley Plan would affect the costs of the other projects. Had the review document been produced in a collaborative way, these anomalies could have been resolved before publication, removing the risk that members might possibly get misled.

'MCC's planning consultant, DP9, during a period of collaboration in 2008–9 were supportive of a much larger-scale redevelopment. However, in the review process, without having made any contact with the RA David Morley team, they were quite negative about a much more modest scheme.

'In return for agreeing to let MCC use our images in the review document, we requested to see a draft before they were published. We were told that if we did not give permission, they would proceed to publication without them and that MCC's invitation to attend the road-shows would be withdrawn. We requested that the brochures could be circulated by MCC at the roadshows. The request was denied, but it was accepted that RA could hand them out to people arriving and leaving.'

Morley's complaints over MCC's conduct was followed by a letter to the committee from Lloyd, Page and Hegarty:

'We are not intending to challenge the committee's recommendation to the SGM. We recognise such action would raise the hackles, invite allegations of sour grapes and, in any case, fail to achieve much, on account of the tendency within the membership to do the committee's bidding and because the outdated and undemocratic postal voting system allows members to vote prior to debate. In some instances, by omission and misrepresentation, the review is simply misleading, including in its presentation of finances – as if it were drafted to a predetermined preference.'

Hegarty: 'I had been to two of the roadshow meetings. We could see how the great and the good were being wheeled out to offer their views. We knew the SGM will be the same, stage-managed just as the roadshows had been. The club's political engine really revs itself up to manage these events – this is what they're very good at. They painted Charles as a rapacious property developer, stealing our ground and making a profit out of us. They completely played down that he was the landlord. If they had been serious about Charles proposals, they would have re-educated the membership, but they never attempted to do that.'

The SGM on 28 September 2017 took place in Westminster's Emmanuel Centre – a sizeable venue was needed and Lord's had long-standing bookings. Despite being held away from their headquarters, it was still very much an MCC production. Rifkind wasn't even allowed to attend because he wasn't a member of the club.

Hegarty: 'We thought we might carry the room; we didn't. We were faced with this procession of people coming up with this concern, that concern. Tom Page spoke at length, I gave my view that I couldn't vote for either of the options because they didn't give us a proper choice. What we wanted was a proper negotiation and then to bring it back to the members. What Charles proposed wasn't something I wanted to vote for anyway. We hadn't got the best possible deal on the table.'

Tom Page: 'People had made up their mind before the meeting and wouldn't be persuaded by rhetoric.'

MCC communications director Neil Priscott: 'I don't think the speakers on the Rifkind side did themselves any favours. I had no idea where Tom Page was coming from – he never came across at any point that he liked cricket, which presumably he must, but it's not all about dollars and bills. Nick Gandon came across with a particular arrogance, which didn't play well with members. Then you hear from someone like Robert Ebdon, with solid principled values – there was no competition. A lot of preparation went into it from the MCC side. Gerald spoke brilliantly.'

The committee's recommended resolution was approved by a 90.5 per cent majority. A total of 7,163 were in favour and 748 against, including postal votes.

Corbett said afterwards: 'This is a landmark day for MCC and for the future of Lord's. MCC members have made their feelings abundantly clear – they do not want blocks of flats to be built at their ground. This is an unequivocal outcome that closes the door on the residential debate.'

Corbett: 'We did the consultation, we got the feedback from members. At the end of the day, we were able to say that the membership didn't want flats. And we didn't need the money because we had our own programme. They were always going to say it was unfair. Charles should have put his best foot forward. This was his chance with a new chairman.

'It should have been 75/25 in MCC's favour over the land value. Our advisers would have considered this an acceptable deal that we should think very carefully about. Charles's mistake was offering us such a crappy deal. I think the reason that he made that mistake is because it's his own business. He's a sole trader, while a company with a board of directors would have had varying opinions. Charles had a bee in his bonnet about 50/50.'

Sir Simon Robertson: 'It was all fixed very elegantly. Charles had no chance. But to be fair to them, they might have been right about the membership not wanting a developer to be involved even though they were getting £100 million. But they didn't have the balls to offer the membership a proper vote – they were scared. The whole build-up to the SGM was a farce. Charles was not allowed to put his case – he was thwarted every time. They've made life difficult for him in a wholly inappropriate way.'

Keith Hague: 'It was rigged, it was awful – it was a travesty of justice. Charles should have had his opportunity to put his cards on the table and present to as many members who wanted to come. I felt for him – I saw him go from elation to the depths of despair. When it was boiled down and everybody took their spoils, I don't think he would have made much at all. We would have made money out of it, MCC would have made money out of it and the patients would have benefited. Charles would have delivered on any financial package, I can promise you that. It's an obsession. It still is.'

Simon Elliot: 'I basically gave up after the vote. They completely shut the door. It was an open-and-shut case before the vote, and they rigged the roadshow meetings.'

Rifkind: 'There was no form of acknowledgement, no thank you. MCC just carried on their way. It forced me to present an alternative plan.'

CHAPTER 15

No Light at the End of the Tunnel

RIFKIND'S PLAN B TURNED OUT to be a rash move. On 25 April 2018, six months after the heavy defeat at the SGM, cricket fans around the globe were offered the chance to buy shares in the 200-metre-long, 38-metre-wide strip of tunnels under the Nursery End.

The shares would cost £500 each and would come in the form of Lord's Tokens, printed by the Royal Mint and listed on the London Block Exchange – a market for online cryptocurrencies such as bitcoin. The investment would be handled through the property consortium New Commonwealth, chaired by David Gower and run by Rifkind's former business partner Johnny Sandelson.

Sandelson had established New Commonwealth in January 2018, with the aim of giving the public the chance to own shares in lucrative central London property. He was reappearing in the saga two decades after he'd first seen the development potential of the Wellington Road site.

Brian Kirby of Railtrack: 'During our discussions after Charles had brought the lease, he said to me: "If I can't do a deal with Lord's, I'm going to cut it up a square foot at a time, auction it off around the world and give everyone a certificate." We might even have joked about it the day before the auction.'

The launch took place in Rifkind's flat in Pavilion Apartments, across the road from Lord's. The backers included former West Indies captains Sir Clive Lloyd and Sir Viv Richards, as well as former England players Allan Lamb and Chris Cowdrey.

Former MCC chief executive Keith Bradshaw flew over from Australia for the launch, having written an updated foreword to the Vision for Lord's publication he had signed eight years previously:

'Let us hope that the expected groundswell of opinion that accompanies the launch of this new 'common wealth' will inspire the guardians of this great club to act rather than witness another fallow and frustrating decade. But those participating in the purchase of land at the Nursery End should not be under any illusion: the long-term development rights are possible, but negotiation with MCC is challenging and might well prove fruitless.'

Gower said: 'Although I supported redevelopment at the Nursery End, this is not a protest or reaction to the members voting against it. I should like to have a friendly association with MCC. I want Lord's to regain its status as the finest in the world. If I receive any flak, it cannot be as bad as when we lost the Ashes in 1989.'

MCC were distinctly nonplussed by the initiative. Chief executive Guy Lavender said: 'It is not for us to speculate on whether this will be a workable solution. It is an investment vehicle, and we have no concerns about the involvement of Keith Bradshaw and David Gower.'

Gower had become involved through Johnny Sandelson. 'I was offered the position by Johnny,' he said. 'Charles was removed from the process. I had done some work for Johnny before as an ambassador for his company Thomas Goode. There was no salary, and any return I receive is based on the take-up.'

The minutes of the May 2018 AGM record MCC's scepticism about the sales pitch:

'Mr Natali asked what was known about Mr Rifkind's strange new plan. The secretary said that the club took the establishment of New Commonwealth seriously, but it would be inappropriate for him to make observations on its potential success or the strategy behind it. Members would have to make up their own mind about it. The scheme appeared to use a digital currency to sell tokens that might or might not have a future return. The plan did not affect the club's ability to proceed with ground development as planned.'

The same month saw an attempt to drum up more publicity, with reports that the South Australia state government were interested in buying some of the £500 parcels of land. The claim came in a letter from Bill Muirhead, who happened to be the government's London-based PR agent. As Gower admitted: 'There may be an element of timing in when the letter has been made public.'

Then, in August, the scheme was mothballed, after it emerged that the blockchain technology was not properly regulated to enable cricket fans abroad to participate.

Gerald Corbett: 'They would have never got this scheme through the regulator, and rich Indians do not part easily with their money.'

In July 2020, Sandelson put forward his own new proposal for a Nursery End development to Lavender and Corbett. It involved a tie-up with the Oberoi hotel group, who are building 23 serviced apartments in the Thomas Goode building on South Audley Street in Mayfair. MCC's response was non-committal.

Just as Rifkind had used the sale of shares to hit back at MCC, Lord's have shored up their own defence against the property developer with the design of the new Compton and Edrich stands. Following the members' overwhelming support to update the ground using their own resources, MCC appointed the architects WilkinsonEyre shortly before Christmas 2017. The Eyre involvement brought MCC full circle, the firm's founding director Jim Eyre being a descendant of the Eyre family, from whom Thomas Lord had first rented Dorset Fields in 1787.

MCC Chief Executive Guy Lavender sent out their plans for members' approval at the May 2019 AGM. He said: 'There is no doubt in my mind that the project will be transformational. It will be the largest, most complex and, at £52 million, the most expensive project undertaken by MCC.'

An aerial view of the new Compton and Edrich stands

How the new Compton and Edrich stands will look from the Pavilion End

The concept design for the new stands was developed by the end of May 2018 and was exhibited at Lord's that summer. It was well received by MCC members, though the vast majority of those looking at the models might not have realised the Machiavellian tactics at play. The footprint of the new stands, housing an extra 2,600 spectators and taking the ground's capacity to 31,100, meant the Nursery Ground would be reduced in width by around 20 yards, making it too small for competitive cricket and leaving only enough room for net practice and big-match activation for spectators.

The plan is for the grass area to be reclaimed from the leasehold land at the Wellington Road end of the ground in six years' time, when MCC plan to knock down the Nursery Pavilion. The Morley Plan – rejected by over 90 per cent of the membership – had been heavily criticised by MCC for simply creating shadows on the Nursery End playing area; now MCC themselves were encroaching onto that supposedly 'sacrosanct' surface through increasing the size of the new Compton and Edrich stands.

As Robert Ebdon, assistant secretary (estates and ground development), said on an MCC video: 'You can see from the footprints, the new stands are significantly larger.'

The Compton and Edrich design also greatly hinders Rifkind's chances of developing his leasehold land. The boundary rope for the Nursery Ground when, or if, it returns for match cricket, will be just in front of the 'prison wall' on the Wellington Road.

An MCC chairman, a treasurer and a chairman of estates don't try to hide the fact that enlarging the footprint of the Compton and Edrich stands was part of a plan to block Rifkind.

Oliver Stocken: 'Charles must have spotted that the way the Compton and Edrich has been designed greatly impacts on the Nursery Ground and the advantages of a Wellington Road development. Of course it stymies further development if you want to retain a cricket ground at the Nursery End. Of course it was a tactical move by the club. Property development is a long-term game.'

Robert Leigh: 'It was tactical to build the new Compton and Edrich the way it is – it means the Nursery End boundary rope has to go right to the wall.'

Blake Gorst: 'There's no denying that the extra width of the new Compton and Edrich impacting onto the Nursery Ground is a blocking tactic against Rifkind. It means that to keep the Nursery End as a cricket pitch, we will have to put the boundary at the edge of the leasehold land. That will put an end to any development on that end of the ground.'

Charles Rifkind: 'They could have gone slightly forward, by ten to twelve feet. There's plenty of surface to do that. David Morley showed it was not necessary to encroach onto the Nursery Ground. In one word, what MCC have done is down to spite.'

By the time of the topping out ceremony to herald the construction of the new Compton and Edrich stands in September 2019, the 12 London plane trees behind them had already been removed. MCC president Anthony Wreford told committee members there had been no complaints about the trees disappearing, though Gubby Allen's view of those trees and the tree line in St John's Wood Church Grounds from his chair looking out of the committee room window had reputedly been a major reason why the original Compton and Edrich stands had such a shallow build.

After work started, the builders discovered the previous concrete foundations to be more extensive than expected. In addition, there was historical damage to the Victorian sewer running underneath the entire length of the building site.

These setbacks, plus bad weather at the start of 2020, meant the main contractor ISG had to spend most of the £2 million contingency putting the building project back on track. Westminster City Council co-operated, allowing building work at weekends over a four-month period.

The club's decision to prioritise the Compton and Edrich stands also led to the loss of the £4 million spent working up the South-Western Project. A five-year planning consent granted in February 2016 to redevelop the Tavern and Allen Stands and the surrounding area meant that construction had to start by February 2021. With this not happening, the costs incurred on working up the South-Western Project were written off.

Their development decisions, or the lack of them, had now by cost MCC nearly £20 million. This included losses on the Vision for Lord's (£5.6 million) and the South-Western Project (£4 million), the drop in value of 6 Grove End Road (£4 million), loss of rent for 12 Grove End Road (£1.2 million), loss of repair value at 12 Grove End Road (£400,000), Nursery End leasehold rent since 1999 (£2.7 million) and legal costs (estimated at £2 million). These were considerable sums even before Covid-19 struck, devastating the finances of all English sport, MCC included. But ironically, the coronavirus pandemic could have been the light at the end of the tunnel for Rifkind; Lord's suffering serious unforeseen financial problems was looking the only possible scenario in which a residential development at Lord's would come back to the table.

A buoyant MCC enjoyed one of their best years in 2019. They had a turnover of £59.4 million from a golden summer that saw a World Cup victory and a Lord's Ashes Test. Rifkind's development hopes looked virtually non-existent. There had been the members' vote, which by a massive majority had rejected residential development in favour of the club's stand-by-stand plan. In addition, there was £20 million in the MCC bank. But the coronavirus pandemic in the spring of 2020 changed everything, especially as MCC had embarked on their costliest building project, the £52 million Compton and Edrich stands. From being able to comfortably finance the construction from their own resources, suddenly MCC needed £15 million to keep the building work on track through to the scheduled opening of the stands in May 2021.

MCC were open about the dire financial situation brought on by the pandemic in the literature that was sent out to members ahead of the 2020 AGM – to be held on 24 June via Zoom video conferencing technology.

Chairman Gerald Corbett wrote: 'It will be the club's first wholly virtual AGM and, let us hope, the last. These are not easy times for many people nor many businesses, but we will endure. Throughout the period of Lord's closure, we have been able to maintain progress with the new Compton and Edrich stands. This £52 million project was planned, with works to pause for the 2020 season then resume the following winter, ready for the official opening in the summer of 2021.

'We are faced with a big decision this summer before we continue in the autumn. Extending the pause further, with a view to completing the building programme in calmer times, would preserve our cash position, but the financial and operational cost we would suffer in the years to come makes this option very much the last resort. Instead, the committee is recommending a proposal for raising £15 million through life membership, which will enable us to finish the stands and emerge from these dark days strongly financed and well positioned.

'The proposals are similar to those the club has implemented before, most recently in 1996, and are priced to be attractive to members. The other alternative – debt finance – would also provide funds for continuing the project as planned. However, with the redevelopment project still to be completed, the committee will not take on the additional financial risk, cost and burden this approach would bring.

'This has not always been the club's approach. In the run-up to the 1999 World Cup, one of the big projects overran. It was at this time that an area of land on the Lord's estate – the only area not already in the club's ownership – came up for auction. The debt option had already been exhausted, the club was cash-constrained and the land was purchased by a third party. We are still living with the effects of those decisions today. Taking on debt would weaken our club, but the committee's proposal will strengthen it.'

Corbett had referred to the two-decade development conflict. But what was astonishing in the light of MCC's dire financial circumstances was that Rifkind's latest offer was not mentioned as an option, having been dismissed by the MCC committee in rapid fashion.

The pandemic had prompted Rifkind to bring his plan C to the attention of MCC, following the encouragement of two MCC committee members. It involved building a state-of-the-art sports clinic on the Nursery End strip rather than residential development, allowing Wellington Hospital to take advantage of the tunnels they had long coveted.

Rifkind had formed a strong bond over the years with Keith Hague, former chief executive of the Wellington Hospital. Talks started in 2006 and had reached an advanced stage in December 2010 – just before the Vision for Lords collapsed – when Hague wrote to Rifkind:

'The last four years of negotiations between RLP and ourselves has now developed the real concept of the Wellington Hospital becoming one of the largest medical centres in Europe. We envision a major 14-floor, 200-bed acute care facility, connected underground to the existing Wellington Hospital and also with access and communication to the underground tunnels.

'The tunnels themselves are significant to the long-term success, involving the connectivity of the whole campus. The development of the hospital is expected to take over about one third of the land controlled by RLP, and will be designed to fit harmoniously alongside the plans for residential development.

'Such a development, when completed, will mean that the Wellington can then be considered for teaching hospital status, something which will greatly support medical teaching and training for the NHS within the capital. I am due to meet Andrew Langley, health secretary, to take this forward. I envisage that such an application and the movement towards teaching status will take about two years.

'The Vision for Lords designed by Herzog & de Meuron is outstanding, and I congratulate you. I have watched your determination and commitment for the eight years that I have been at the Wellington Hospital. I only hope that we are successful in concluding terms in this exciting venture. I look forward to more detailed discussions at the start of 2011. I hope you enjoy your Christmas trip to Kenya.'

However, shortly after Rifkind returned from his safari, the Vision for Lord's was effectively killed off, with the development committee disbanded.

Keith Hague: 'We were using Lord's for meeting rooms and for social events. We had a box at the Test matches – we got to know them very well. I was on the Lord's community group. But we were starting to get a lot of polite resistance – it was getting annoying and bureaucratic. I couldn't see the issue. We were willing to pay a lot. They would have done well. There was talk of sports injury clinics above ground.

'What did it for me was when I was looking around and I passed a groundsman sat on a tractor eating his sandwich in one of the equipment huts. I told a member that this type of scene wouldn't be part of a global stadium. He said to me: "That's the problem. We don't want to see an end to that – we're happy for the guy to sit on the mower with his sandwich and pot of coffee." That's how the members wanted it. They wanted to keep this homely village cricket atmosphere inside Lord's. We were taking the lead from Charles. We got the feeling that although they were polite, MCC never wanted it.

'It went on strong until 2010. We were talking with Herzog up to the point that they were asking how much space we needed. That Vision for Lord's was incredible – it was a great open-plan design.

'I had many false starts, false dawns. There were issues over Arab money coming in and whether that was the right thing. It was the Qataris – they're easy to work with, but it was like a red rag to a bull to MCC. The Qataris were talking about funding for Charles, and we were speaking to them as well.

'We put a lot of effort into the tunnels. As we developed our thoughts, there was an opportunity to punch through the tunnels into a tower block. We would have had to share a few floors, but we could have offered patients suites that overlooked Lord's or Regents Park. Can you imagine what they would have paid? It was any hospital developer's dream solution.

'Wellington would have put in £200 million at one stage, for our development. Planning permission would have been easy to achieve – there's no planning consent below ground. The Wellington would still be very keen – all other expansion possibilities have been utilised. I could attract anyone from around the world to build a facility there. Raising the money from the Wellington's owners HCA, the largest private hospital group in the world, would not be a problem – it turns over billions of dollars. I feel that the boundary between ourselves and Lord's is a wall of politics.'

Rifkind's plan C was the third time a hospital element had been included in the proposal. But this time it was centre stage, in the hope that MCC members would be more receptive to a development based around sports medicine instead of residential.

London Health and Sports Hospital proposal

Gower: 'The tie-up with Wellington Hospital had a certain synergy, while the Nursery Ground being retained for first-class cricket is madness. What's the point of spending all that money so that extra cover and mid-wicket can go five yards deeper? It's a practice ground, pure and simple.'

A planning document titled 'London Health and Sports Institute designed by David Morley' was sent to Westminster City Council, but kept under wraps from MCC until Rifkind was ready to release it. The upper levels of the two blocks at either end of the Wellington Road leasehold would be eight-storey-high wings with medical facilities. The proposed medical uses were a sports clinic and a research institute specialising in diabetes, mental health and obesity. Shared diagnostic and treatment facilities would link the two wings together at basement level. At the centre of the lower levels would be a new entrance from Wellington Road, instead of the prison wall. This would have a two-storey-high enlarged Nursery Pavilion, giving space for hospitality and banqueting for 1,000 people, with related exhibition space and cloakrooms.

Rifkind: 'I have had a relationship with the Wellington Hospital for the duration of this project. I have known five of their chief executives, and each one has seen the possibilities of expanding into the tunnels. The only access point is from Wellington Hospital's South Building.'

Even MCC members who were set against residential were more receptive. The trustee Andrew Beeson said: 'A sports injury clinic above and hospital operating theatre underground makes quite a lot of sense.' But MCC chairman Gerald Corbett said: 'We haven't see a proposal from Charles, and I don't think it will get very far.'

Rifkind revealed his hand on 20 April 2020 in a letter sent by his friend Baroness Scotland, a Labour Party peer and secretary-general of the Commonwealth, to MCC president Kumar Sangakkara. This was a surprising move by Rifkind, as Baroness Scotland was at the time embroiled in controversy over her Commonwealth role and attracting plenty of negative publicity over alleged cronyism. She had been widely criticised for awarding a lucrative consultancy contract to a friend – Baron Patel, coincidentally a director of the England and Wales Cricket Board – and for extravagantly redecorating her grace-and-favour apartment in Mayfair. Both deny any wrongdoing.

In addition, Rifkind would inevitably raise hackles inside Lord's by introducing his latest scheme through a third party. He knew that MCC had disapproved when he brought in his allies Sir Simon Robertson and Simon Elliot to represent him at meetings and write letters on his behalf.

Baroness Scotland's letter to Sangakkara read: 'I hope you are keeping safe and well in these uncertain times. It seems a lot has happened since we met at the Wolseley restaurant in the summer of 2019.

'It is an undeniably a difficult time for all, but particularly for participation in the future of cricket going forward. As the daughter of a true West Indian, cricket has always been close to my heart, and Viv Richards and the others have never allowed me to forget it.

'I am aware that there has been some tension between Charles Rifkind and MCC in respect of the land at the Nursery End on Wellington Road, perhaps complicated by committee structures, over the development proposals and more recently the settlement of the outstanding review of the rent payable by MCC. From my conversation with Charles, I believe that he is still hoping to open a dialogue with MCC to explore whether something can be done with the leasehold land which would find the support of MCC members and provide some much-needed funds to help alleviate the financial challenges no doubt facing MCC as a result of the Covid-19 crisis.

'One interesting possibility which Charles mentioned to me is the potential construction of a hospital focusing on such things as diabetes, obesity, mental health and sports injury recovery. Such a development would be unlikely to provide windfall profits of anything like the amount potentially generated by residential development, but it would produce a facility of which MCC could rightly be proud.

'I did not go into any details with Charles, but my understanding is that such a development might produce a profit for MCC and the developer of around £30 million each. I wonder if a development of this nature might address most of the concerns expressed by members when the residential development was put to them?

'Charles told me that although this would be his preferred option, he would be happy to explore other proposals, including revisiting the possibility of a residential scheme that would deliver a more significant revenue receipt. I understand this would be in the region of £200 million to MCC, based on the original Vision for Lord's at both the Nursery End and Grove End Road. I am sure that there are many other schemes which could be considered.

'Although day-to-day management would need to be discussed and agreed, Charles has told me that he would give MCC full control, including the choice and scale of any project. All sides have helped me and I would like to help, if I possibly can, to ease the tension. I would be thrilled if you and I, working together, could help to bring about a rapprochement between the different sides. Neither you nor I have been part of this historical battle, but we both love cricket and, speaking for myself, respect and like all the parties involved. Do you think it might help?

'May I ask you to put this to the committee in your capacity of MCC president, to establish whether there is any appetite for future constructive negotiations? If there is, I would be happy to approach Charles and see whether he would agree to put forward some outlined heads of terms as a basis for further discussion.

'I would also be happy to meet with any of the other parties or to engage with you in a meeting, with Charles or otherwise. I have also attached a copy of the Hospital Sports Centre brochure, which I would ask you to view in complete confidence.'

Rifkind followed this up by persuading James Mitchell to send his 'non-negotiable terms' to Lord's. Mitchell also posted them on the Members' Independent Online Pavilion:

1. If some sort of development can be agreed, Rifkind says he is prepared to give the club complete control of its nature and scope. The amount of any profits generated is not relevant. If the club decided that a hospital development was something MCC could support – albeit with a far lower profit – that would be fine. If the club needed to generate a bit more income, there would be a range of options. It would be the club's choice alone.

2. There would have to be a 50/50 relationship in all aspects between MCC and Rifkind Associates, on all developments on the Nursery End and on Grove End Road.

3. The club must agree to pay £1 million to Rifkind Associates, representing the amount provided to MCC for the aborted Vision for Lord's.'

Mitchell added: 'I am not batting here for either Rifkind or the club. I am a disinterested party. I have no interest in persuading the club to accept Rifkind's terms and nor am I interested in encouraging Rifkind to back off. Any involvement I have had to date has been as a go-between and I am now stepping away.'

It didn't take long for MCC to deliver their answer, despite the financial predicament brought on by the pandemic. The MCC committee took less than hour to reject the proposal. They would not deal with Charles Rifkind, even in these unprecedented times.

Some of the committee felt the timing of the proposal was linked to the coronavirus pandemic, although Rifkind had been in talks with the Wellington Hospital since buying the leasehold strip in 1999.

Chief executive Guy Lavender wrote in an email to members: 'We recently received a further outline proposal for development on the leasehold land, which was relayed to the club through a third party, Baroness Scotland. The proposal centred on facilities for the nearby Wellington Hospital and was followed by a communication setting out non-negotiable terms, which was sent to the club separately through an MCC member.

'The committee reviewed both the proposal and the stated terms, alongside advice and commentary received from our professional property advisers, CBRE. Having debated the issues, the committee agreed that the terms proposed are not acceptable and the proposed development does not address many of the critical issues that were pivotal in the club's rejection of the previous scheme. I accordingly wrote to Mr Rifkind to politely decline his proposal.'

Rifkind: 'They threw Baroness Scotland's letter in the bin – I don't think they even read it. Until Robert Leigh and his merry men go, it's not going to happen. I was giving them the opportunity to do whatever development they wanted, whether it brought in £30 million or £200 million, but they didn't seem to understand that.

'It's never been about the money. From the start, I've been trying to enhance Lord's for the good of London. Knock down that prison wall and open up the ground to the community. I wanted to make MCC more than just about cricket. That was what my various initiatives had all been about. Keith Bradshaw got what I was trying to do, but I was never given the opportunity to fully explain it to the MCC membership.'

However, Rifkind's vision of utilising the tunnels for operating theatres will have a significant legacy elsewhere in London. The talks with the Wellington, which included plans for other hospitals to use the proposed medical facilities in the Lord's tunnels, provided the impetus for the building of Cleveland Clinic London in Grosvenor Place, Belgravia. The American banker John Botts, an adviser to Rifkind whom he first met during talks about developing Queen's Club, has helped arrange the finance for the 200-patient hospital. It is strikingly similar to Hague's grand ambitions for transforming the Danubius Hotel in 2010. Hague and others in his Wellington Hospital team have also been closely involved in delivering the state-of-the-art facility before its planned opening in 2022.

Meanwhile, the MCC committee decision not to engage with Rifkind or Baroness Scotland enraged some MCC members on the MIOLP.

Philip Banham: 'To turn down the offer without even a face-to-face meeting seems utter madness.'

Edward Collier: 'Having read Baroness Scotland's letter and our committee's apparent summary dismissal of it, I find I am almost ashamed of our club.'

Gower said: 'The whole thing has got out of hand, although involving Baroness Scotland wasn't the best move.'

MCC chairman Gerald Corbett had his say about Rifkind and Baroness Scotland on an MCC webinar for members in May 2020:

'I had two years of speaking to Charles. I liked him. We had umpteen meetings with Sir Simon Robertson. Charles came to our Lord's box, our wives went to art galleries together, we met up with him in Australia, but we could not get him to table a better offer in 2017. It was not a good offer – it was a lousy deal. Our advisers would not recommend it, and very few members wanted flats. We came up with our own plan to develop the ground and received over 90 per cent support.

'Since then, we've had the New Commonwealth with David Gower to attract rich Indians that didn't get anywhere. Then we've had Baroness Scotland. It would be utterly bizarre to support something rejected by 90 per cent of the membership. When you talk to Charles, he doesn't drop his price.'

Corbett, speaking before the coronavirus pandemic, was determined never to go back to Rifkind. He put forward other ways of raising money:

'We have a mortgage on the houses in Grove End Road. That gives us a facility of £15 million for the next five years that we can draw upon. It costs us £150,000 a year. If we hit trouble with the Compton and Edrich, we fund it. We could do accelerated memberships. We could raise £30 million through that, but we don't want to. It smells a bit, but in an emergency we could do it. As long as I'm chairman, there will be no debt.'

Despite the 'smell' of accelerated memberships, Corbett's MCC committee recommended the sale of memberships to raise £15 million. MCC justified it as a 'frequent method by which the club has raised money when required'. It had been offered on six previous occasions. The first time was in 1864, and the £780 raised helped fund the purchase of James Dark's house on St John's Wood Road, MCC's first property purchase.

MCC utilised their well-honed campaign strategy in the run-up to the AGM vote and brought out tried and trusted committee men to promote the life membership scheme. Angus Fraser and Kumar Sangakkara backed the cause online and broadcaster Mark Nicholas conducted a friendly interview with Gerald Corbett. The vote was another predictably large majority in favour of whatever the MCC committee recommended. It was carried by 5,144 votes to 1,330.

Having been approved in June, MCC were able to report in September 2020 that their scheme had been 'wholly successful'. It enabled them to bank £26 million from the sale of 339 life memberships.

After raising nearly double their target, MCC decided not to sell the remaining 11 life memberships permitted by the resolution.

Lavender wrote in an email to members: 'The revenue generated has safeguarded MCC's position, as we approach the completion of the redevelopment of the Compton and Edrich stands. MCC remains debt-free and we have built important cash reserves to create much-needed security.'

The life membership money has also made the annual rent MCC pay RA for the leasehold strip less of an issue, although both sides will want to reduce the costs of going to arbitration every five years – the latest review brought legal bills of over £300,000 to each party. The arbitrator increased the rent from £156,650 to £189,773 a year, which MCC say is in line with their long-term financial plan. Another review is due in January 2022, which will likely take the annual rent well above £200,000. And if match cricket is to be played on the Nursery Ground, the Nursery Pavilion will have to come down.

Corbett: 'The direction of travel is clear. We have another 116 years to sort out the lease, whether Charles sells it, or his sons or grandchildren. We have a much stronger team now that Colonel Lavender is definitely in charge. I am delighted with the Compton and Edrich stands – they give Lord's even more of a sense of grandeur.'

The two previous chairmen also agree that Lavender has strengthened the MCC secretariat.

Stocken: 'The problem with Keith [Bradshaw] is that he always said yes to the last person he spoke to. Derek [Brewer] was a bit better. He spent a lot of time weighing up the pros and cons, yet wouldn't necessarily take a decision. But I think Guy does take decisions. He has got the balance right on what he can do himself.

'I was responsible for changing the title from secretary to chief executive, and there's a big distinction. Secretaries do what they're told. Chief executives run the show, and Guy is a chief executive.'

Charles Fry: 'I think MCC is changing and Guy Lavender is beginning to exert his authority. Until his arrival, MCC was very much run by the chairman and treasurer, plus their like-minded colleagues on the committees. The secretary basically did what he was told. Oliver was dictatorial, and I probably was as well. It was probably not the best way to run things, looking back.'

Looking into the future, Stocken said: 'There will be a big shoot-out eventually, but until then MCC will let the lease run. Charles will eventually sell. He'll want £75 million, MCC will say "Go away" and they'll settle for £25 million, but maybe that's ten years away.'

But the outspoken Lord Grabiner fears the old guard will keep their power base. He says: 'It can only change if, at some stage, the fiefdom passes into the hands of a fair-minded person anxious to achieve some sensible governance. But they'll make sure they only hand on the baton to like-minded people. You will always find like-minded people in that environment. Basically, it's a nasty, little Englander, fascist little world.

'I'm sure there are loads of decent fair-minded people within the membership, but there's an old boys members' club atmosphere. I think it is very, very difficult to shift it. Nobody has really bothered to do anything about it. That's how it is, and that's how it has always been. As for the presidents, they're not in office long enough to do anything about it. By the time they get to grips with the situation, it's somebody else's turn.'

David Morley: 'Where does it end up? I don't see that wall staying. The best case is that the people who are politically motivated to oppose this begin to fall away. Then there could be a resurgence of enthusiasm. The worst case is that it lingers until the lease expires.'

Peter Leaver: 'I won't be alive when the leasehold problem is sorted – that's for future generations. We're talking about 2137; a lot of water is going to flow under the bridge before then. Are Rifkind's successors going to be that interested? He should do a deal with the club.'

Colin Maynard: 'I think it's game over. The Nursery End will have its boundary ropes on the Wellington Road wall.'

Blake Gorst: 'We never want to sell our birthright. We have debentures to fall back on and accelerated membership.'

Gerald Corbett: 'We have a perfectly good plan, and Charles has had his chance. We would be exactly in the same space banging on about 50/50. We don't want anything on the Nursery Ground, that is clear.

'I think it's finished – I don't think any chairman will want to go through all that again. We received over 90 per cent of the vote. If another proposal comes up, it won't get anywhere. I think there's a moment when Investec will have to write down their investment with Charles. He has to keep things afloat. The rent brings in a certain amount, but it was the development potential that attracted Investec. And when it comes to valuation time, Charles will be telling a story. It was the bitcoins and then the hospitals.'

Alistair Parker: 'I don't think it's all over. Charles is an extraordinary character, and I don't think he was ever in it for the money. He has two very able sons who will carry on the fight.'

Rifkind: 'We wanted to increase the share ownership of the piece of land, so it's not represented by one person's sole interest but many people's interest – cricket benefiting Lord's and depersonalising the relationship. However, many people want to participate in that story. That is the way forward now and for the next generation.

'The asset will never be sold until such time as the development will occur. That development will occur at some point in time – it is only a question of when. Naturally, the longest vision for this to occur is the length of the lease, but cricket has to make decisions well before those 116 years. And the further we approach that date, the value of the asset naturally improves.

'I want to keep the relationship going, knowing that personalities change at MCC. I wanted to keep the door open and hope that at some point in time, MCC will realise the benefits of my offer. My two sons are well briefed about the whole saga. They've grown up with it being the main talking point around the dinner table for the last 20 years, and they will keep my dreams alive for many years to come.'

MCC intend to 'pause and reflect' as to their next step, following the completion of the Compton and Edrich stands in May 2021. Twenty years ago, in March 2001, Rifkind prepared a draft copy of a letter to Roger Knight, when the frustrations with dealing with MCC had already become apparent. He ended it by saying: 'We feel that one day our attempts will be viewed positively, although we recognise that we may well have to wait a long time to fulfil our dreams.'

The wait goes on.

CHAPTER 16

The Blame Game

THE DATE IS 19 MAY 2020, the event an MCC members' webinar during the first coronavirus lockdown. The question to MCC assistant secretary (estates) Robert Ebdon: 'Did you buy 6 Grove End Road to stop Charles Rifkind?' The one-word answer: 'Yes.'

Nothing could have been more unequivocal than the answer given by Ebdon to explain why MCC spent £8.5 million on a house that is now valued at £4 million. This moment of openness was remarkable for an organisation famed for its lack of transparency. Even more so when you consider that at the time of the purchase in 2014, MCC and Rifkind had an agreement in place to work together in acquiring property on Grove End Road.

So, in proportioning blame for what has gone wrong during the development saga over the last 20 years, nothing is as straightforward as Ebdon's admission of MCC's strategy on Grove End Road. Anti-Semitism, which is mentioned as a possible reason for MCC snubbing Rifkind, is a grey area.

Lord Grabiner: 'I'm sure MCC were very determined to protect their original bad decision, and to make sure that the Jew would not make any money out of this, to be perfectly blunt. That is a very serious allegation, but you are dealing with the establishment here. It's subtle, it's not out-and-out. It's there – there's just a whiff of it, to encourage people in a certain direction. It wouldn't be a difficult thing to slip into the conversation. "You don't want any of these Jews making any money" would be the kind of approach.'

Peter Leaver: 'I have never ever heard anyone say anything anti-Semitic. It's too easy. Why would anyone think "anti-Semitism"? You can find it anywhere you want – I've never experienced it.'

Andrew Donn: 'I know there's a general perception of us as a money-

308 | The Covers Are Off

grabbing race. It's a real stereotype, so I wasn't surprised by MCC's negativity when they found out it was Charles who bought the tunnels. But I never felt that. It was just a clear-cut commercial deal and I felt bad for Lord's. As much as I was elated that we had got a good price, I felt a bit sad for Lord's.'

Sir Simon Robertson: 'I would go as far as saying there was a whiff of anti-Semitism. No question.'

Simon Elliot: 'The MCC hierarchy regarded Charles as a North London property developer, and all that entails.'

Sir David Metcalf: 'It is quite plausible that some of the opposition was down to anti-Semitism and "This guy, who outbid us, is not going to profit."'

Nick Gandon: 'After the first development roadshow at Lord's in 2017, I had the misfortune afterwards to find myself in the Tavern in the company of some ignorant member who launched a disgusting anti-Semitic tirade. When he refused to apologise, I and another member promptly left.'

John Fingleton: 'I'm absolutely sure there was anti-Semitism. No question.'

Andrew Lloyd: 'In any WASP organisation, there's an element of anti-Semitism.'

Dominic Titchener-Barrett: 'What my father said at the Lord's roadshow – "We don't want that type of people" – was entirely in support of the committee. He didn't want property developers just interested in making money involved in any way. It is preposterous and totally untrue to suggest there was anything anti-Semitic about it. I have Jewish heritage on my mother's side.'

James Mitchell: 'There was an element of anti-Semitism – I really do think that. I've heard members say they don't want to deal with a Jew. We do have members like that. I raised it on the forum and I was backed up. I am sure it played a part.'

The question of whether Rifkind was ever given a level playing field by MCC to present his proposals also splits opinion.

Colin Maynard: 'I think Charles was given every chance. He had never dealt with an MCC committee. He was used to making quick-fire decisions himself, and that was not the MCC way. For a lot of members, money didn't come into it. At the end of the day, MCC is a cricket club, first and foremost. None of Charles's supporters seemed to grasp that.'

Robert Leigh: 'It's bollocks to say Charles wasn't given an opportunity – he was given every reasonable opportunity. He could call us whenever he liked. He was at all the roadshows with his architect David Morley and had the chance to speak. The committee couldn't support Charles, as our consultants would not have backed the deal. There was also the problem of affordable housing.'

Gerald Corbett: 'We gave Charles every chance to come up with a decent quote, but he didn't.'

John Fingleton: 'Charles has been treated very badly, unquestionably. I'm no great fan of his, but he's been treated like shit. He was never given a chance.'

Simon Elliot: 'MCC is run by a cabal of those who have networked in the City all their lives. They know they have the postal vote behind every resolution in their pocket, so they control it. They were almost dishonest in the way they treated Charles.'

Peter Leaver: 'I don't think Charles was treated particularly badly. He was very successful in making life uncomfortable for MCC. He leaked a lot of inaccurate stuff, which created a degree of hostility.'

Sir Ian Magee: 'Charles is 25 per cent to blame, the club 75 per cent. Charles was pushy and not understanding of how the club worked, but how the club treated him was scandalous.'

James Mitchell: 'I voted against the Morley Plan, but I am angry that MCC never treated Charles with openness, transparency and communication. He should have been allowed to present at the roadshows. It was appalling that Robert Ebdon did that role for both sides.'

Andrew Beeson: 'I've never changed my views about residential at Lord's, but there should have been a friendlier approach with Rifkind. Derek Brewer was very good with dealing with the ECB, but when it came to negotiating over a property development, he wasn't the right person. It was difficult because there was no communication between the two sides. It should have been handled better.'

Those involved in the conflict are also divided on the question of whether Rifkind or his chief opponents Oliver Stocken and Justin Dowley should shoulder most of the responsibility for the impasse.

Brian McGowan: 'I think Stocken is the man to blame. He could have stood up and said: "This is a load of rubbish, there's no way it's going to get through the committee." But he agreed with everything and then did something completely different. Dowley was more honest, but I think he genuinely got scared of the finances. It was a lot of money.

'Charles is his own worst bloody enemy. He can't keep quiet, and he goes on and on. He kept on prodding away. There's no doubt he made a number of enemies because of his style – he ruffled quite a few people's feathers unnecessarily.'

Stephen Musgrave: 'Stocken and Dowley didn't want the Vision for Lord's from the start, and they did their best to ensure it didn't happen. They were the two most powerful people at Lord's, and they made that count.'

Blake Gorst: 'Charles is an arrogant chap and rubbed up people the wrong way. He didn't know how to play MCC and they didn't know how to play him. He was too pushy. I don't think the membership ever wanted residential and they would never vote for it.'

Lord Grabiner: 'I think Stocken and Dowley are absolutely at the heart of it. I think they were in a position to manipulate the whole of the organisation and they did so, no question about it. The MCC governance arrangements are so decrepit that they got away with it – it was an absolute disgrace. I wanted Stocken and Dowley in on the meetings, otherwise it was a waste of time. They did come, and Stocken in particular agreed with what we were doing, and yet it was completely turned around and reversed the next day or next week.'

Julian Vallance: 'Charles tried to buy the membership with his £15 million offer to pay subscriptions for two years, an astonishingly bad move. It should never have been a 50/50 deal, more like 85/15. Ask any financier – it's ludicrous to suggest that the value is 50/50. MCC's value doesn't diminish for another 100 years. Talk about 50/50 is absolute rubbish.'

Peter Leaver: 'Charles never had a plan B. If he'd suggested developing the Grove End Road of the ground, putting our properties together, that could have been an attractive proposition, but the finances never got within a million miles of stacking up. It all depended on getting enough planning permission for enough flats to raise the money, and that would never have happened. Westminster Council would never have allowed it.

'Robert Griffiths was too much in Charles's pocket. He said the leasehold contract was worth £80 million. It might be worth £8 million to £10 million, which the club would have paid and which would have given Charles a nice £6 million profit, but £80 million was ridiculous.'

Keith Bradshaw: 'It was quite amazing to see Stocken and Dowley speak out against something they had already agreed – and this happened over and over again. They were absolutely hell-bent on Rifkind not making any money out of any deal.'

Others thought that both sides could be blamed.

Robert Leigh: 'The issue caused horrendous aggro inside the club. The relationship between the two sides was always fraught. Neither side understood each other and neither should be proud of their behaviour. There had been a lot of talk about what percentage each side should receive, but that was irrelevant if you couldn't agree a partnership.

'Charles got greedy. He could have done a deal, but he thought he could encourage people inside the club. There were a lot of leaks, and nobody knew who to trust during committee meetings. Also, Charles didn't really have anyone on his side who had Lord's in their blood.'

John Hegarty: 'Charles didn't understand MCC, and MCC didn't understand Charles.'

Roger Knight: 'Mistakes were made by both sides. The talking should have continued, but instead relationships became acrimonious.'

Simon Elliot: 'It's a terrible wasted opportunity on both sides, and cricket is the loser.'

Neil Priscott: 'Part of the problem for Charles was that his supporters were hugely successful people in their own right, but did they know cricket? I don't think the case was ever made in a cricket-led way or was compelling enough for the average cricket-playing member of MCC to get their head around.

'MCC's redevelopment reports were viewed by Charles's side as ridiculously over-the-top in their bias, while those not wanting change saw the same findings as far too concessionary. It was laughable at the time – you just couldn't win.'

Nigel Peters: 'I think rather like so many issues – Covid-19, Brexit, Heathrow's third runway, and Crossrail – matters could have been handled better by both sides, and blame can always be attributed in hindsight, of course.'

Steve England: 'I think Charles is too much of a problem for MCC. The two of them are now insurmountable objects, whatever the right or wrong. Charles should step aside and fresh blood should come in, but it's his baby. It was the Nursery End, not even the Main Ground. They should have worked together, but it become too personal.'

There is a consensus that MCC governance, which is slowly being reformed, played a negative role from the start. An SGM on 15 October 2020 brought an MCC majority in support of their resolution to move to a smaller, skills-based MCC committee by 2023, but the Lord's old guard will still control the nominations committee who make the appointments. For instance, the selection of Bruce Carnegie-Brown as the new MCC chairman from October 2021 was managed by a working group led by trustee Robert Leigh, MCC's longest-serving main committee member.

Justin Dowley: 'The fault was with the governance structure of MCC. A committee of 22 people doesn't work. It's too big and unwieldy and not possible for everybody to make a proper contribution. It produced a lot of confusion. You need a smaller, more organised board, and one in which the members feel their voice counts. The club are trying to change things, and not before time.

'Keith Bradshaw was a very nice chap, but he tried to please everybody and he became too close to Charles Rifkind. I don't blame

Charles – he was looking after Charles. He was full of bright ideas and also played the media far better than MCC did, which meant that a one-sided version of events kept appearing in the press. It gave the impression that everyone was in favour of the residential redevelopment apart from just a few obstructive opponents. That wasn't the case, as the votes both in committee and at the SGM showed.'

Robert Griffiths: 'Part of the problem for the MCC executive is that once you get a reputation for being shits as an institution, no one really wants to deal with you anymore. There has to be a major revamp of their image – they are self-congratulatory and potentially self-destructive. There are 17 acres at Lord's, and it takes a special kind of genius not to make real money from 17 acres of land in central London.'

Gerald Corbett: 'If we'd had a proper board set-up, I don't think the Rifkind thing would have got as far as it got. A proper board would have said: "We've got to close this down now. Are we going to do this, or aren't we?" We should have had the development review five years earlier.'

Alistair Parker: 'I would struggle to work for MCC again. No one likes wasting time on an organisation that can change its mind that erratically.'

Robin Knight: 'The whole history of MCC over the last 50 years is one error of bad judgement after another, but they don't see it that way – they just try and clear up the mess afterwards. There's a pattern of behaviour that is essentially undemocratic. It is buttressed by this gigantic waiting list, and all attempts to change are thwarted. The club is stuck in a pre-Second World War era. The last thing they want to be is accountable and democratic.'

Keith Hague: 'MCC are reluctant to change, reluctant to move away from what they've always had. It's very sad – Charles should have been allowed in to see the senior people. MCC would come in my office and we'd have a cup of coffee. I always had the feeling they were, in Yorkshire vernacular, "pissing up my back". MCC is like a ball with a very hard shell. If you try and pierce it, it just bounces off.'

Keith Bradshaw: 'MCC is not run as a modern business should be run. Our business partners constantly complained that we were slow to make decisions or act on initiatives. I'd frequently field calls from commercial partners asking me to cut through the red tape that was preventing the club from making decisions and acting in a timely manner. Mostly this was owing to the committee structure and the strangling of the executive's powers to make decisions without approval from the relevant sub-committee, main committee or both. For a business with a £40 million annual turnover – now £50 million – this was exhausting, and it escalated over the years.

'I remember attending one particular sub-committee meeting when it was decided to form a group to address a particular issue. I mentioned three or four names. Afterwards, I was taken aside and asked to explain why I had gone for three Etonians and no one from Harrow.'

Peter Leaver: 'It is completely deplorable the way the MCC committee system acts like a revolving door. It is a very poor show. It is wrong. It is a self-perpetuating oligarchy. What do the trustees do? What are their responsibilities? What are their duties? Why does anyone listen to them? It just keeps the same people inside the tent.'

Colin Philips: 'The old-fashioned membership process meant Oliver Stocken always knew he had control. Look at those postal votes – most of them tick what the committee recommend. If MCC recommended a sheep's head should be president, they would vote for it.'

Phillip Hodson: 'I have always thought that the committee system is unwieldy. The main committee is far too big. The organisation should be run by the CEO, treasurer and chairman.'

Lord Grabiner: 'I don't think anyone, least of all Charles Rifkind, understood how difficult it is to deal with MCC. How do you deal with a committee of 22, some of whom turn up at meetings having not read the briefing papers. Some had no experience apart from a bit of cricket, and they were being asked to make these fundamental decisions. It was ridiculous.'

MCC's failure to buy the Wellington Road strip in 1999 is seen as another crucial element in the blame game.

Peter Leaver: 'If MCC had been a better-run organisation, it would have raised the money to buy the tunnels.'

Robert Griffiths: 'The main problem was that MCC didn't buy that strip of land. It all flowed from that. It was the most catastrophic mistake that MCC has made in its history. The Wellington Road frontage was a natural fit for a major development – there's a natural building line from the Wellington Hospital to the Danubius Hotel.'

Lord Grabiner: 'Everything stems from that bit of the story. It was an exceedingly naïve piece of nonsense, a terrible mistake. Since then, MCC have put their heads in the sand to protect their own position from the failings of that committee in not making a proper bid, and to ensure that the person who got it doesn't make any money out of it.'

Andrew Lloyd: 'MCC are going to have to live with the fruits of their short-termism. They made their own bed when they failed to buy the lease.'

The author's view is that everything goes back to 11 December 1999. Allowing Charles Rifkind to buy the lease paved the way for the 20 years of turmoil that followed. All along, it was MCC's defence to a challenge from outsiders rather than a balanced consideration of what might be best for the club.

When the most suitable development scheme – the revised Morley Plan – eventually evolved, the split was too acrimonious and positions too entrenched for that impressive design to be given a proper appraisal. There should have been collaboration between the two sides from the start, but it didn't happen. When it did flicker on brief occasions, it was quickly extinguished by those who were fiercely against any proper relationship being formed.

Rifkind was never given the opportunity to properly present his grand blueprint to the membership – the plan to knock down the prison wall on the Wellington Road and open up the world's most famous cricket ground, enhancing London and associating MCC's iconic brand with more than cricket. For him, it was never just about the money, whatever MCC might have insinuated.

Any hope of an early alliance was killed at birth by the all-powerful MCC estates chairman Maurice de Rohan's opposition to Rifkind and the club's humiliation at losing out at the auction. De Rohan's immovable stance was fuelled by his mistaken belief that senior MCC figure Lord Alexander had tipped off his son-in-law Johnny Sandelson, Rifkind's then business partner, about MCC's maximum bid ahead of the auction. There is no evidence whatsoever to that effect, and nor does it ring true that Lord Alexander would break committee confidence in such a way, but there's no doubt that Alexander's familial links with Sandelson helped create the initial tension between the two sides that never eased over the next 20 years.

Ever since his talks with Roger Knight in Cape Town in January 2001, Charles wanted everything done at top speed, which is the way he conducts his business life. This contrasts with MCC bureaucracy, which has the turning speed of an ocean liner. Knight informed Rifkind on the phone in November 2001 that things would progress at a 'slow pace'. That is their way of working, with any major decision needing to go through the committee labyrinth. MCC also like to manage the information coming out of Lord's and are paranoid about leaks, yet Rifkind played the media so adroitly that favourable articles backing his proposals regularly appeared in the press at the most opportune times – ahead of big matches at Lord's or crucial main committee meetings.

When MCC kept asking Rifkind for a detailed explanation of his own financial set-up, he refused to provide it. He also didn't help his cause by using Baroness Scotland to introduce his 2020 Nursery End development proposal. The club, although they employ plenty of outside consultants themselves, had already told Rifkind they wanted to deal with him directly rather than through third parties. On the other hand, there are numerous instances of questionable behaviour by MCC that only a private members' club could get away with. Rifkind was treated with suspicion from the start, and the MCC hierarchy frequently suggested that those who backed his proposals were being paid or had received favours.

Rifkind was consistently kept in the dark by MCC when they were supposedly working together on a joint venture, on which the property developer had spent around £1 million – yet to be paid back. During this period, MCC even sent Rifkind a bill for work done building up the club's own alternative development plan on their freehold land. And MCC did not tell him until the deal was completed that they were buying Lionel Frumkin's Grove End Road house in 2014, when an agreement of sorts was still in place to jointly purchase properties bordering Lord's.

Finally, there was never a level playing field in the way the development review vote was handled in 2017. This was unnecessary, especially considering that MCC know in advance that postal votes virtually guarantee them success in any ballot. They were in a position to be even-handed to Rifkind and give him no reason to complain about the process; instead, they didn't allow Rifkind Associates to present their own proposals at the roadshows, nor to send their brochure to members until it was too late to have any influence.

The MCC plaque in St John's Wood Church Gardens

MCC produced a one-sided development review report that was almost wholly negative about the Morley Plan. And the MCC committee recommended members support their Masterplan ahead of the vote, despite requests from some members to remain neutral. The final irony is that Rifkind, whose proposal had included a £15 million sweetener to members to pay their subscriptions during two years of building upheaval at Lord's, wasn't allowed into the SGM vote because he wasn't an MCC member.

Of course, MCC set their own rules. And whatever the incentives, their conservative, elderly membership were highly unlikely ever to vote in support of residential development at Lord's. But at the very least, MCC should have worked with Rifkind to develop plans on which he had invested 20 years, to see if there was enough common ground to satisfy all parties. Instead, he was forced to produce scheme after scheme, without ever knowing what MCC wanted or who in the club supported him. Such a passionate commitment for two decades deserved a balanced hearing.

To the question posed at the beginning of this book, 'Was Charles Rifkind "slit up a treat" by MCC?', my answer is yes.

But maybe a tulip tree planted by MCC in September 2020 across the road from Lord's in St John's Wood Church Gardens is a portent to a more collaborative future. The planting of the tree, whose leaves turn red and yellow in autumn, is part of MCC's increasing community engagement, something that has always been at the core of Rifkind's ambitions for Lord's.

The plaque reads, 'This tree forms part of a donation by the Marylebone Cricket Club to the St John's Wood community. A partnership to last centuries.'

Cast List

LORD ALEXANDER

Acknowledged as one of the best barristers of his generation, Alexander acted for Kerry Packer against the Test and County Cricket Board and for Ian Botham and Jeffrey Archer. He was the first independent chairman of NatWest, president of MCC in 2000/01 and chairman from 2001 to 2004. He was chairman of the MCC arts & library committee when he introduced his property developer son-in-law Johnny Sandelson to Lord's.

GUBBY ALLEN

The most influential figure in the history of MCC, Allen died in 1989 but still epitomises MCC and its traditions. He ruled the roost at Lord's for 30 years, and chose to sell houses rather than put up membership fees when the annual subscription was around £20.

TONY ALT

Vice-chairman of Rothschild Bank and another long-term MCC committee figure, Alt's poor video presentation in the MCC committee election in 2019 saw him fail to gain enough votes to return to the top table.

MIKE ATHERTON

Former England opening batsman and captain and now an acclaimed broadcaster and *Times* cricket correspondent. Atherton was persuaded to sit on the MCC development committee, but once it was disbanded had no wish to get further involved in MCC politics.

PENNY BARNARD

The girlfriend of MCC committee member Mark Williams, it was at Barnard's home in St Lucia that Williams worked on the resolutions in advance of the 2015 AGM.

DAVID BATTS

Managing director of Radisson Edwardian Hotels before becoming MCC deputy chief executive, Batts delayed his retirement to become project director of the Lord's Masterplan.

KEITH BRADSHAW

A Tasmanian cricketer who was MCC's innovative chief executive between 2006 and 2011. Bradshaw returned to Australia because of family problems, before becoming chief executive of the South Australian Cricket Association and helping complete the acclaimed redevelopment of the Adelaide Oval.

MIKE BREARLEY

Ashes-winning England captain in 1981 and a psychotherapist following his retirement from cricket, Brearley surprised many when he became an MCC establishment figure, serving as president and trustee.

DEREK BREWER

MCC secretary and chief executive between 2012 and 2017, following seven years in the same post at Trent Bridge and 24 years in banking.

TCHAIK CHASSAY AND MALCOM LAST

The co-founders and partners at the Chassay & Last practice, who alerted Charles Rifkind and Johnny Sandelson to the possibility of buying the tunnels at the 1999 auction.

GERALD CORBETT

A top businessman who has been director of 13 public companies and chair of seven, Gerald Corbett became MCC chairman in 2015, at the height of the acrimony over the redevelopment. He had been chief executive of Railtrack at the time of the auction of the Wellington Road strip in 1999, but played no part in the negotiations.

MAURICE DE ROHAN

Australian chairman of the MCC estates committee, he oversaw the building of the media centre and the major refurbishment of the pavilion. Prior to his death in 2006, aged 70, de Rohan was in line to be appointed governor of South Australia.

ANDREW DONN

The senior sales surveyor at Railtrack when they were selling off their property assets that included the Nursery End head leasehold above the tunnels, Donn negotiated with MCC and their agents Knight Frank from the start of discussions in March 1999.

JUSTIN DOWLEY

A distinguished international investment banker, MCC treasurer from 2006 to 2012 and a steward of the Jockey Club, Dowley was also a director of the Ascot Authority during the controversial development of the course's new Grandstand. He is seen as a chairman-in-waiting by the MCC hierarchy, but his role with Melrose Industries meant that he didn't want to be considered to succeed Gerald Corbett in October 2021.

ROBERT EBDON

A partner at Synergy Construction & Property Consultants when appointed project manager for the Vision for Lord's. He aligned himself to the Lord's establishment when he became MCC assistant secretary (estates).

SIMON ELLIOT
Discreet businessman and ally of Charles Rifkind. Married to Annabel, the sister of Camilla, Duchess of Cornwall.

JOHN FINGLETON
An auctioneer and PR man who retired in 1993 to watch cricket at Lord's, Fingleton spent four months on the MCC committee in 2005, before losing his place over selling tickets for the Henley Stewards' Enclosure.

ANGUS FRASER
Alongside Mike Brearley and Mike Gatting, Fraser completes a triumvirate of celebrated former Middlesex and England cricketers who enjoy positions on the MCC committee and are loyal to the institution.

LIONEL FRUMKIN
A wine merchant and Lord's tour guide, Frumkin owned 6 Grove End Road, a pivotal location in the development battle. He turned down various approaches from MCC and Charles Rifkind to sell, before accepting an £8.5 million offer from MCC in 2014.

CHARLES FRY
Grandson of the great all-round sportsman C. B. Fry, Charles Fry was chairman of MCC between 2004 and 2009 – critical years in the Lord's redevelopment battle. Fry was receptive to change, including residential flats at the Nursery End, but deferred to chairman of estates Maurice de Rohan on all matters to do with the ground.

NICK GANDON
A schoolteacher who moved into the charity sector and ran cricket's Chance to Shine, Gandon was elected to the MCC main committee in October 2019, despite being the most vocal of reform activists.

MIKE GATTING

Ashes-winning England and Middlesex captain who became president of MCC and a strong supporter of the Lord's hierarchy.

BLAKE GORST

Chartered surveyor with a number of property business-related directorships, Gorst was another long-term MCC committee figure who succeeded Maurice de Rohan as chairman of estates. Like his predecessor, he was against residential development.

DAVID GOWER

Former England cricket captain who became Sky Sports' lead cricket presenter, Gower was loved as a graceful batsman by the MCC membership to the extent that an SGM was called in 1993 over his omission from an England tour of India. He stood out as a former England cricketer who was supportive of development plans at Lord's.

LORD GRABINER

Leading QC with a stellar reputation across a variety of areas of commercial law. Made a life peer in 1999, Grabiner resigned the Labour whip in 2015 over Jeremy Corbyn's leadership of the party and now sits in the Lords as a cross-bencher. In July 2011, at the height of the Lord's conflict, he was appointed by News Corporation as chairman of a management and standards committee, following the company's phone hacking scandal.

ROBERT GRIFFITHS

Property specialist QC who negotiated MCC's first staging agreement for Lord's Tests. The disbanding of the development committee in 2011 cost him his place on the main committee. He returned in 2012 but withdrew in 2019, following financial problems brought on by losing a six-year court battle over the £3.6 million purchase of Laughton Manor in Sussex.

KEITH HAGUE

Former chief executive of the Wellington Hospital, MCC's neighbours on the Wellington Road, Hague worked on various plans with Charles Rifkind.

PHILLIP HODSON

Yorkshire businessman who was chief executive of the Oval Group, the biggest privately owned corporate insurance brokers in the UK. His troubled MCC presidency in 2011/12 was dominated by the battle over the tunnels.

STEPHEN HUBBARD

A senior executive at property services giant CBRE, Hubbard was brought in as a consultant by MCC at the start of the Vision for Lord's process in 2008. After being replaced by Alistair Parker, he returned as an MCC adviser in 2011.

MIKE HUSSEY

Founder and chief executive of property developers Almacantar, who made the only compliant bid in the Vision for Lord's tender. When MCC ditched the proposed agreement, Hussey took legal action that was settled out of court 18 months later.

SIR MICHAEL JENKINS

A senior diplomat before switching to a successful City career, Jenkins was MCC chairman in 2000/01 and led the development working party in 2007 that recommended a joint venture with Rifkind Levy Partnership to develop the Vision for Lord's. He died in 2013, having been keen on MCC building a new cricket stadium away from Lord's, but reluctant to go public over such a revolutionary proposal.

ROGER KNIGHT

Former Surrey captain who was headmaster of Worksop College before serving as MCC secretary from 1994 to 2006 and later as president. Knight had early knowledge of the possibilities at the Nursery End after talking to Johnny Sandelson, who first came up with the idea of a development.

NIGEL KNOTT

A consultant dentist who has been the biggest critic of MCC governance for four decades, Knott was alone in warning MCC about the problems ahead when they let an outsider outbid them for the Nursery End strip head lease.

GUY LAVENDER

Lavender spent 18 years in the Parachute Regiment and British special forces, before retiring as a 39-year-old lieutenant colonel in 2006. He was appointed MCC chief executive in 2017, having been in charge at Somerset and led the successful completion of the London 2012 sailing venue at Weymouth.

PETER LEAVER

A QC and former chief executive of the Premier League who was forced out after agreeing a TV rights contract without the clubs' knowledge, Leaver chaired the Lord's working party that obtained a royal charter for MCC.

ROBERT LEIGH

The longest-serving MCC committee member, having joined in 1967 at the age of 24. A school friend of Mike Griffith, son of MCC secretary Billy Griffith, Leigh has been around MCC's high table ever since, including as treasurer, while Mike Griffith became president.

COLIN MABER

A Nottingham architect who worked with Derek Brewer on renovating Trent Bridge before becoming MCC chairman of estates for six years, Maber was responsible for producing the long-term MCC Masterplan. He resigned in 2016, having failed to establish a working relationship with Gerald Corbett.

SIR IAN MAGEE

A senior civil servant who became chairman of MCC's membership and general purposes committee, Magee was appointed despite having been critical of Lord's governance. Yet his own elevation was typical of the way MCC worked, with him gifted the M&GP chairmanship by Gerald Corbett.

SIR JOHN MAJOR

The former prime minister and passionate cricket fan who served on both the MCC committee and the development committee, as well as being president of his beloved Surrey. When Major became prime minister, MCC called to bring forward his membership, but his private secretary thought it was one of his friends playing a prank and put the phone down on MCC secretary John Stephenson.

CHRISTOPHER MARTIN-JENKINS

Esteemed BBC broadcaster, journalist and author who became MCC president in 2010, at the height of the civil war over redevelopment. Diagnosed with terminal lymphoma in March 2012, he died in January 2013 at the age of 67.

COLIN MAYNARD

Maynard joined MCC straight from school in October 1975 and remained at Lord's throughout his working life. He served as acting secretary on two occasions and knew more than anyone about MCC and its workings, strongly opposing any threat to its traditions.

BRIAN McGOWAN

Co-founder of Williams Holdings, one of the UK's largest conglomerates, and a chairman of House of Fraser, McGowan was one of the most vocal members of the 11-strong development committee.

JAMES MITCHELL

A Slaughter & May lawyer who retired aged 53, Mitchell founded the Members' Independent Online Pavilion forum, which has been the main vehicle for holding MCC to account since 2012.

DAVID MORLEY

The architect responsible for designing the Nursery Pavilion, the Indoor School, the Lord's shop and ECB offices. He won a design competition for the new Warner Stand, but MCC subsequently chose another company. The Morley Plan for the Nursery End evolved when he began working for Charles Rifkind after meeting him at a clay pigeon shoot organised by Robert Ebdon.

STEPHEN MUSGRAVE

The chief executive of Grosvenor Estates in UK and Ireland when MCC chose the firm as their proposed partner in redeveloping Lord's in 2003 – a project that never materialised – Musgrave returned in 2010 as MCC's property adviser.

ALISTAIR PARKER

A leading property consultant with Cushman & Wakefield, Parker was employed by MCC on three occasions during the development saga. He wrote 11 draft documents and 29 different reports for the Vision for Lord's.

NIGEL PETERS
A High Court judge and long-time MCC committee member, Peters put himself up for election for a fourth time in 2019 and returned to the committee in October 2020.

CHARLES RIFKIND
A qualified barrister turned property developer who rode the eighties housing boom in central London with remarkable success, Charles Rifkind is also responsible for the 500-home Matlock Spa development in Derbyshire's Peak District. He has raised several million pounds for numerous charitable causes, most notably diabetes, successfully campaigning for the Freestyle Libre monitor to be made available on the NHS. He is also the mystery man who paid for fish and chips for everybody in the Oxfordshire village of Denchworth where he has his country home every Friday for 12 weeks during the first wave of the coronavirus pandemic.

JAMIE RITBLAT
Heavyweight property developer who founded Delancey in 1995, having learnt the ropes at his tycoon father Sir John Ritblat's British Land. A donor to the Tory party, he built an extraordinary Neoclassical-style mansion on his 3,000-acre Cotswolds estate near Winchcombe.

SIR SIMON ROBERTSON
Knighted for services to business in 2010, Robertson's chairmanships included Rolls Royce and Kleinwort Benson, plus presidency of Goldman Sachs Europe. Awarded France's highest honorary decoration, the Legion D'Honneur, in 2014, his personal wealth is estimated to be in excess of £100 million.

JOHNNY SANDELSON

Serial entrepreneur, whose artist cousin Simone married his business partner Charles Rifkind. Together they acquired the head lease for the Nursery End strip at auction in 1999, before going their separate ways. Sandelson's business ventures include regenerating London's Queensway, co-founding high-end care business Auriens and Mayfair tableware store Thomas Goode.

OLIVER STOCKEN

A City merchant banker with multiple chairmanships and directorships, Stocken is often described as one of the most powerful non-executives in the country. Passionate about sport, he witnessed English World Cup victories in football (Wembley in 1966), rugby union (Sydney in 2003) and cricket (Lord's in 2019). He made a last-minute dash to Tokyo for the Rugby World Cup final in 2019, only for England to lose to South Africa.

IVO TENNANT

Cricket writer for *The Times* who first revealed the existence of the Lord's tunnels and their outside ownership to a wider public in 2008, Tennant has written more than anyone about the development saga.

MARK WILLIAMS

A cricket fanatic who was in the Royal Navy before becoming a diplomat and working for MI6, Mark Williams accompanied the Soviet defector Oleg Gordievsky on a world tour and later became chief executive of Lord's Taverners. He was obsessed with MCC and was working around the clock on resolutions for the 2015 AGM when diagnosed with lymphoma in February 2015. He died four months later, aged 70.

ANTHONY WREFORD

A senior figure in PR and one of the central MCC committee figures throughout the saga. He chose Sri Lankan cricket great Kumar
Sangakkara to succeed him as MCC's first international president.

List of Illustrations

A map of St John's Wood in 1827

The Lord's surroundings in 1890

The details of Lot 11 from the auction in 1999

How Lord's looked in 1999 (*Herzog & de Meuron Vision for Lord's*)

Builders speculate on the wait for the development of Lord's (*Courtesy of Nick Newman*)

The houses on Grove End Road that back onto Lord's (*Herzog & de Meuron Vision for Lord's*)

RLP's redevelopment proposal for MCC (*Cartoon courtesy of Charles Rifkind*)

MCC members' John McEnroe-style reaction to tennis at Lord's (*Courtesy of Nick Newman*)

The Herzog & de Meuron design for Lord's (*Vision for Lord's*)

The details of the Herzog & de Meuron scheme (*Vision for Lord's*)

How Herzog & de Meuron envisaged Lord's behind the pavilion (*Vision for Lord's*)

The Lord's tower at the Nursery End (*Herzog & de Meuron Vision for Lord's*)

A comparison showing the plans for either five blocks of residential development or a single tower (*Herzog & de Meuron Vision for Lord's*)

Sir John Major is upset at the 'conservative' MCC (*Cartoon courtesy of Nick Newman*)

The Morley Plan's Nursery Ground (*Courtesy of David Morley Architects*)

A new entrance for Lord's to replace the 'prison wall' (*Courtesy of David Morley Architects*)

The front cover of the Morley Plan brochure (*Courtesy of David Morley Architects*)

MCC members *Scream* in response to Lord's redevelopment (*Cartoon courtesy of The Cricketer and Nick Newman*)

An aerial view of the new Compton and Edrich stands (*Courtesy of WilkinsonEyre Architects*)

How the new Compton and Edrich stands will look from the Pavilion End (*Courtesy of WilkinsonEyre Architects*)

London Health and Sports Hospital proposal (*Courtesy of David Morley Architects*)

Light at the end of the tunnel cartoon (*Courtesy of Russel Herneman and Charles Rifkind*)

The MCC plaque in St John's Wood Church Gardens

Acknowledgements

THIS BOOK WOULDN'T EXIST WITHOUT Mensch Books publisher Richard Charkin, editor Nick Humphrey and my agent Jonathan Lloyd at Curtis Brown. A special thank you also to cartoonist Nick Newman and Matthew Engel for his peerless Foreword.

Grateful thanks to the following people who agreed to be interviewed, many of whom granted me a generous amount of time. But even the shortest of chats was much appreciated.

Lord Archer, Mike Atherton, Chris Atkinson, Richard Auterac, Philip Banham, Andrew Beeson, Paul Bennett, Penny Bernard, Keith Bradshaw, Paddy Briggs, Paul Brooks, Tchaik Chassay, Robert Gordon Clark, Gerald Corbett, Peter Cunliffe, Andrew Donn, Justin Dowley, Simon Elliot, Matthew Engel, Steve England, Jill Facer, Jim Field, John Fingleton, Lionel Frumkin, Charles Fry, Nick Gandon, Blake Gorst, David Gower, Paul Graber, Lord Grabiner, Robert Griffiths, Keith Hague, John Hegarty, Phillip Hodson, Brian Kirby, Robin Knight, Roger Knight, Nigel Knott, Malcolm Last, Peter Leaver, Robert Leigh, Andrew Lloyd, Sir Ian Magee, Malcolm Le May, Colin Maynard, Brian McGowan, Sir David Metcalf, James Mitchell, David Morley, Stephen Musgrave, Tom Page, Alistair Parker, Neil Priscott, Charles Rifkind, Simone Rifkind, Sir Simon Robertson, Johnny Sandelson, Baroness Scotland, Oliver Stocken, Ivo Tennant, Dominic Titchener-Barrett, Chris Waterman, Julian Vallance.

Those who declined to talk or didn't respond: Tony Alt, John Barclay, David Batts, Mike Brearley, Derek Brewer, David Brooks Wilson, Isabelle Duncan, Robert Ebdon, Angus Fraser, Mike Gatting, Simon Gibb, David Faber, Ian Hawksworth, Mike Hussey, Margaret Joseph, Guy Lavender, Colin Maber, Guy Macauley, Sir John Major, Charles Martin, Charlie Naughten, Alasdair Nicholls, Nigel Peters, Nick Pocock, Jamie Ritblat, Jon Robinson, John Stephenson, Simon Williams, Anthony Wreford.

Far more accommodating were *Wisden* editor Lawrence Booth, who provided valuable advice, while Michelle and Chloe Martin, Daniel Singh, Helen McGreal and Hannah Beer were all extremely helpful during the research, writing and production of the book.

My wife Sue and children Emma, Nicola and Richard were constantly encouraging and very forgiving of me having my nose to the grindstone for the best part of two years when there were grandfather duties to attend.

Bibliography

Books

Pavilions of Splendour: An Architectural History of Lord's edited by Duff Hart-Davis, Methuen, 2004.

Conflicts in Cricket by Jack Bailey, Kingswood, 1989.

Gubby Allen: Man of Cricket by E. W. Swanton, Hutchinson, 1985.

Lord's 1787–1945 by Sir Pelham Warner, Harrap, 1946

The Vision for Lord's by Herzog & de Meuron, 2009.

My Life and Times at MCC by Keith Bradshaw (unpublished).

CMJ: A Cricketing Life by Christopher Martin-Jenkins, Simon & Schuster, 2012.

Members' Independent Online Pavilion

MCC 'At Home with Cricket' email series

www.lordsredevelopment.co.uk

Documents

Minutes of meetings of MCC committee, development committee, finance committee, negotiating group.

Minutes of meetings/letters/email exchanges between MCC and RLP/RA representatives.

Notes of meetings between RLP/RA representatives

MCC Letters/emails sent by MCC Reform Action Group

MCC Newsletters

MCC Annual Reports, Accounts and SGM literature

Lord's Cricket Ground Proposal (RLP, 2006)

David Morley Plan: Delivering the World-Leading 'Home of Cricket' (2017)

MCC 'Development Review Report' (2017)

MCC 'Focused on the Future Report' (2018)

'Updated Masterplan for the Redevelopment of Lords' (2019)

Timeline

1787 MCC is founded and first Lord's ground opens at Dorset Fields.

1811 MCC start playing at second Lord's ground at Brick and Great Fields.

1813 The current Lord's ground becomes MCC's home.

1825 William Ward buys out Thomas Lord.

1835 James Dark purchases the Lord's lease.

1858 Isaac Moses buys the Lord's freehold at auction.

1864 MCC buy the Lord's lease from Dark.

1866 MCC purchase the Lord's freehold from Robert Marsden.

1880 MCC buy James Dark's house.

1887 Henderson's Nursery is acquired by MCC.

1891 MCC is granted the freehold of the Clergy Orphan School, in return for the Nursery End strip of land to build railway tunnels.

1929 Lord's estate is at its height, with the ownership of all 14 properties around the ground's perimeter.

1940–45 Air raids during the Second World War damage a number of MCC-owned houses.

1951 A bomb site on Grove End Road becomes a Lord's car park.

1954 Seven new houses are built on Grove End Road, before being sold on 60-year leases in the late 1950s.

1965 A corner plot on Grove End Road is sold for a residential development named Century Court.

1966 Great Central Railway is closed. One Nursery End tunnel remains in use for commuter trains, and the other two became redundant.

1967 The Leasehold Reform Act allows a number of the owners of MCC houses to purchase the freeholds.

1978 Six houses on Elm Tree Road are sold to a development company.

1982 The rest of the Elm Tree Road houses are sold off.

1988 The Nursery Pavilion is constructed. MCC's lease to a depth of 18 inches on the Nursery End strip is renewed until 2137.

1989 MCC buy 4 Grove End Road from the estate of Gubby Allen.

1998 Johnny Sandelson presents his Wellington Road development proposals to MCC.

1999

March: Railtrack start negotiating to sell the head lease on the Nursery End strip to MCC.

December: Charles Rifkind buys lease at auction for £2.35 million.

2000

January: Rifkind meets Roger Knight in Cape Town.

December: Rifkind buys development rights for tunnels from Railtrack.

2003

April: MCC seek development partner and Rifkind is invited to apply.

May: Estates committee hears presentations from British Land, Development Securities, Grosvenor Estates and Rifkind Levy Partnership.

November: Grosvenor Estates is chosen as MCC's development partner.

2004

April: Grosvenor put forward a residential scheme on St John's Wood Road.

October: MCC main committee rejects Grosvenor plans.

2005

March: Estates committee commissions HOK to draw up new development scheme.

July: Development Securities propose deal, with RLP backing.

August: Estates committee rejects Development Securities plan.

2006

February: Rifkind starts purchasing houses on Grove End Road.

October: Keith Bradshaw takes over from Roger Knight as MCC chief executive. Estates chairman Maurice de Rohan dies.

December: MCC committee meets Rifkind at his Tea House office.

2007

February: Masterplan working party under Sir Michael Jenkins is set up to review HOK proposals and RLP plans.

May: MCC committee decide to enter development negotiations with RLP.

June: Rifkind introduces Investec to MCC, and the bank sponsor the media centre.

September: MCC property adviser Stephen Hubbard suggests a 75/25 land value split .

2008

February: Masterplan architect selection panel is established.

April: Alistair Parker replaces Stephen Hubbard as MCC property adviser.

July: Herzog & de Meuron are chosen as architects for the Masterplan.

October: MCC committee approve a budget of £1.4m for the Vision for Lord's.

November: Masterplan working party is renamed the development committee, with Robert Griffiths elected chairman.

December: A letter from Bradshaw to Rifkind confirms agreement in principle for joint venture.

2009

April: MCC committee increase the budget of the Vision for Lord's.

May: Meetings with Westminster Council planning department and London Mayor Boris Johnson.

August: Roadshows exhibit Vision for Lord's models.

October: Oliver Stocken becomes MCC committee chairman.

Griffiths selects an 11-strong development committee, including Sir John Major.

December: The first meeting of the development committee.

2010

January: RLP voice concern over two pre-conditions of joint agreement.

February: MCC committee approve the removal of pre-conditions.

April: Rifkind offers to sell land interests to MCC.

October: Almacantar, Capital & Counties and Native Land are shortlisted as development partners.

November: Capital & Counties and Native Land submit non-compliant bids

December: The development committee recommend Almacantar's bid.

2011

January: Griffiths complains about Almacantar delay and calls for chairman Stocken and treasurer Dowley to stand down.

February: Trustees' report supports Stocken and Dowley and development committee is disbanded.

Almacantar are appointed as development partners.

March: Masterplan working party is set up to replace development committee.

August: Keith Bradshaw resigns.

September: Savills report says residential development on leasehold land is high-risk.

October: Masterplan working party is closed down.

November: MCC committee dissolve Almacantar partnership.

December: Sir John Major resigns from main committee.

2012

February: MCC committee turn down a revised Almacantar offer.

March: Major says he resigned over the way in which decisions were made.

April: Almacantar claim £400,598.20 over broken contract.

May: Derek Brewer takes over as chief executive.

July: Ground working party select Populous to develop the MCC Masterplan.

2013

May: MCC announce a 20-year Masterplan redevelopment.

October: Members vote 6,191 to 1,556 at an SGM not to proceed with an independent inquiry into the handling of the Vision for Lord's.

December: MCC agree a £125,000 settlement with Almacantar.

2014

April: Architect David Morley presents latest RLP development plan to MCC committee.

May: Announcement made at AGM not to consider Morley Plan or any other alternative until 2019. MCC pay £8.5m for 6 Grove End Road.

2015

January: Stocken stars four candidates for four vacancies on the MCC committee.

May: AGM resolution passed for a development review run by MCC.

June: Mark Williams dies of cancer, aged 70.

October: Gerald Corbett succeeds Stocken as MCC committee chairman.

2016

June: Rifkind is guest of Corbett in chairman's box at Lord's Test.

December: Morley and Rifkind make a presentation to members of MCC's principal committees.

2017

March: MCC write a letter to Rifkind claiming that the Morley Plan brochure is misleading.

May: The new Warner Stand opens.

Tony Alt makes 'I don't want flats' speech at annual dinner.

June: Development review is sent to members.

July: MCC committee recommend their Masterplan to members.

September: SGM vote overwhelmingly supports the MCC Masterplan.

2018

January: WilkinsonEyre are appointed to design new Compton and Edrich Stands.

April: Rifkind launches a plan to sell parcels of his Lord's leasehold land via blockchain technology.

August: Tunnel sales mothballed, due to its use of technology that is not yet globally regulated.

2019

May: Members approve plans for the new Compton and Edrich stands at AGM.

September: Work starts on the Compton and Edrich stands.

2020

April: Rifkind proposes the development of a health and sports clinic at the Nursery End - rejected by MCC Committee.

June: Virtual AGM passes resolution to sell life memberships, in order to raise £15 million needed for Compton and Edrich Stands due to the coronavirus pandemic.

October: MCC raise £26 million through the sale of 339 life memberships.

2021

May: New Compton and Edrich stands are completed.

A Note on the Author

CHARLES SALE WORKED AS A sports journalist for 40 years. Between 2001 and 2018 he wrote a column for the *Daily Mail* that held the main sporting bodies, including MCC, to account.

The Covers Are Off is his second book on cricket. The first, *Korty*, told the story of Essex bowler Charles Kortright, the fastest of his day during the Golden Age of cricket.

Sale's claim to cricketing fame is what is reportedly a world record for the slowest innings of all time – 1 not out, in 2 hours 32 minutes – to salvage a draw for Repton School against Malvern College in 1974.